With Service in Mind

Concepts and Models
for Service-Learning
in **Psychology**

Robert G. Bringle and Donna K. Duffy, volume editors

Edward Zlotkowski, series editor

A PUBLICATION OF THE

AMERICAN ASSOCIATION
FOR HIGHER EDUCATION

AMERICAN
PSYCHOLOGICAL
ASSOCIATION

With Service in Mind: Concepts and Models for Service-Learning in Psychology
(AAHE's Series on Service-Learning in the Disciplines)
Robert G. Bringle and Donna K. Duffy, *volume editors*
Edward Zlotkowski, *series editor*

Opinions expressed in this publication are those of the contributors and do not necessarily represent those of the American Association for Higher Education or its members.

About This Publication
This volume is one of eighteen in AAHE's Series on Service-Learning in the Disciplines to be released during 1997-1999. Additional copies of this publication, or others in the series from other disciplines, can be ordered using the form provided on the last page or by contacting:

AMERICAN ASSOCIATION FOR HIGHER EDUCATION
One Dupont Circle, Suite 360
Washington, DC 20036-1110
ph 202/293-6440 x11, fax 202/293-0073
www.aahe.org
This Psychology volume only can also be ordered from:
APA BOOK ORDER DEPARTMENT
750 First Street, NE
Washington, DC 20002-4242
toll free 1-800/374-2721, fax 202/336-5502
email: order@apa.org

ISBN 1-56377-010-5
ISBN (18 vol. set) 1-56377-005-9

Contents

Appendix

About This Series

by Edward Zlotkowski

The following volume, *With Service in Mind*, represents the sixth in a series of monographs on service-learning and the academic disciplines. Ever since the early 1990s, educators interested in reconnecting higher education not only with neighboring communities but also with the American tradition of education for service have recognized the critical importance of winning faculty support for this work. Faculty, however, tend to define themselves and their responsibilities largely in terms of the academic disciplines/interdisciplinary areas in which they have been trained. Hence, the logic of the present series.

The idea for this series first surfaced approximately four years ago at a meeting convened by Campus Compact to explore the feasibility of developing a national network of service-learning educators. At that meeting, it quickly became clear that some of those assembled saw the primary value of such a network in its ability to provide concrete resources to faculty working in or wishing to explore service-learning. Out of that meeting there developed, under the auspices of Campus Compact, a new national group of educators called the Invisible College, and it was within the Invisible College that the monograph project was first conceived. Indeed, a review of both the editors and contributors responsible for many of the volumes in this series would reveal significant representation by faculty associated with the Invisible College.

If Campus Compact helped supply the initial financial backing and impulse for the Invisible College and for this series, it was the American Association for Higher Education (AAHE) that made completion of the project feasible. Thanks to its reputation for innovative work, AAHE was not only able to obtain the funding needed to support the project up through actual publication, it was also able to assist in attracting many of the teacher-scholars who participated as writers and editors.

Three individuals in particular deserve to be singled out for their contributions. Sandra Enos, former Campus Compact project director for Integrating Service and Academic Study, was shepherd to the Invisible College project. John Wallace, professor of philosophy at the University of Minnesota, was the driving force behind the creation of the Invisible College. Without his vision and faith in the possibility of such an undertaking, assembling the human resources needed for this series would have been very difficult. Third, AAHE's endorsement — and all that followed in its wake — was due largely to then AAHE vice president Lou Albert. Lou's enthusiasm for the monograph project and his determination to see it adequately supported have been critical to its success. It is to Sandra, John, and Lou that the monograph series as a whole must be dedicated.

Another individual to whom the series owes a special note of thanks is Teresa Antonucci, who, as AAHE project assistant, has helped facilitate much of the communication that has allowed the project to move forward.

The Rationale Behind the Series

A few words should be said at this point about the makeup of both the general series and the individual volumes. At first glance, psychology may seem like a natural choice of disciplines with which to link service-learning. However, "natural fit" has not in fact played a determinant role in helping decide which disciplines/interdisciplinary areas the series should include. Far more important have been considerations related to the overall range of disciplines represented. Since experience has shown that there is probably no disciplinary area — from architecture to zoology — where service-learning cannot be fruitfully employed to strengthen students' abilities to become active learners as well as responsible citizens, a primary goal in putting the series together has been to demonstrate this fact. Thus, some rather natural choices for inclusion — disciplines such as anthropology, geography, and religious studies — have been passed over in favor of other, sometimes less obvious selections from the business disciplines and natural sciences as well as several important interdisciplinary areas. Should the present series of volumes prove useful and well received, we can then consider filling in the many gaps we have left this first time around.

If a concern for variety has helped shape the series as a whole, a concern for legitimacy has been central to the design of the individual volumes. To this end, each volume has been both written by and aimed primarily at academics working in a particular disciplinary/interdisciplinary area. Many individual volumes have, in fact, been produced with the encouragement and active support of relevant discipline-specific national societies. For this volume on psychology, in fact, we owe thanks to the American Psychological Association.

Furthermore, each volume has been designed to include its own appropriate theoretical, pedagogical, and bibliographical material. Especially with regard to theoretical and bibliographical material, this design has resulted in considerable variation both in emphasis and in level of discourse. Thus, for example, a volume such as Accounting necessarily contains more introductory and less bibliographical material than does Composition — simply because there has been less written on and there is less familiarity with service-learning in accounting. However, no volume is meant to provide a detailed introduction to service-learning *as a generic concept*. For material of this nature, the reader is referred to such texts as Kendall's *Combining Service and Learning: A Resource Book for Community and Public Service* (NSIEE, 1990) and Jacoby's *Service-Learning in Higher Education* (Jossey-Bass, 1996).

I would like to conclude with a note of special thanks to Robert Bringle and Donna Duffy, the coeditors of this Psychology volume. Not only have they demonstrated great skill and resourcefulness in putting it together, they have also maintained throughout the entire process a flexibility and patience I have much appreciated. I would also like to acknowledge the generous assistance of Irwin Altman of the University of Utah, who provided valuable feedback on the manuscript.

June 1998

Introduction

Collaborating With the Community:
Psychology and Service-Learning

by Donna K. Duffy and Robert G. Bringle

The work of understanding human behavior and how the mind operates is inextricably linked to our social context. As Sarason has noted, the philosophical roots of psychology reflect this tenet, although it is sometimes more tacit than explicit: "Dewey saw clearly what psychology is still blind to: the substance of psychology cannot be independent of the social order. It is not that it *should not* be independent but that it *cannot* be" (1982: 236). As such, the nature of psychology incorporates and must acknowledge the values and assumptions that shape and guide its practice within the social context. Prilleltensky (1997) challenges psychologists to actively confront this issue:

> The problems associated with value inarticulateness, moral indecision, and narrow codes of ethics can be addressed by expecting psychologists to meet two minimal criteria. The first criterion requires that psychologists articulate their personal and collective vision of the good life and the good society. That is, they should make clear the values, models, and ideals they wish for individuals and for societies. . . . The second criterion is that psychologists should formulate ways of translating these visions into action. . . . The objective is to generate dialogue about the different conceptions of the good society and how to get there. (518)

Examining and communicating these criteria is a significant challenge for a discipline that manifests 49 American Psychological Association (APA) divisions, each with a unique perspective on how psychology contributes to human welfare as a science and a profession. However, academic psychologists and practitioners need to engage in dialogue that centers on how psychologists can use their knowledge in a more socially responsive manner to collaborate with their communities (Altman 1996). Psychologists involved in research, education, or practice who follow Prilleltensky's advice and articulate values and assumptions that guide their work are more likely to find commonalties.

Communicating within the discipline about these issues is essential (Slife and Williams 1997). Portraying psychology to external constituencies is equally important. Whether it is done in the popular media, the classroom, or the professional office, presenting an accurate and coherent view of the discipline is challenging. Psychologists who teach in institutions of higher education play a particularly important role because introductory psychology is one of the most popular courses in the undergraduate curriculum and psychology is the most frequent major in the arts and sciences. Communicating the nature of psychology to students is challenging not only because of the nature of the discipline but also because of the increasing diversity among the students who study psychology. The full-time student at a residential college is no longer the typical undergraduate. Reich (1996) points out that today's students follow various paths, including taking time off after high school and taking courses sporadically at local colleges while they work.

> By the time these students decide to complete their college degree — whether as full- or part-time students — they likely have completed an associate degree at the local community college; have accumulated course credits from more than one institution; and comprise a student population that is not only more diverse in experience, background, and age but more divergent in knowledge of and approach to psychology. (45)

In framing the educational task of communicating to students the nature of the science of human behavior, psychologists must define the role of psychology within a changing society and find ways to integrate psychological education from high school through graduate school.

Brewer (1997) reviewed significant conferences and reports on undergraduate psychology from 1951 to the present and concludes that the "Principles for Quality Undergraduate Psychology Programs" (McGovern and Reich 1996) developed from the St. Mary's Conference in 1991 is the "closest APA has come to providing specific direction about undergraduate programs in psychology" (Brewer 1997: 439). Although the principles represent different facets of psychology education, the section on common curricular elements is particularly relevant:

> Faculty determine the essential elements of a curriculum to achieve the goals they identify. Common elements of the curriculum include
> a. multiple opportunities for students to be active and collaborative learners
> b. research projects to help students learn the science of psychology
> c. fieldwork, practica, and community service experiences to help students learn the applications of psychology
> d. an emphasis on learning across the curriculum about ethical issues and values
> e. multiple courses and research methods which heighten students' understanding of diversity in behavior. (McGovern and Reich 1996: 255)

Thus, psychology is a discipline searching for (1) coherence within the tension of basic and applied traditions, (2) a better understanding of the values that can give meaning and relevance to the application of its knowledge base, and (3) effective ways to educate a significant number of undergraduate students. Within this context, it is understandable that psychology educators are attracted to a pedagogy such as service-learning that engages students and faculty in their communities in educationally meaningful ways. For as "a course-based, credit-bearing educational experience," service-learning allows students to "(a) participate in an organized service activity that meets identified community needs and (b) reflect on the service activity in such a way as to gain further understanding of course content, a broader appreciation of the discipline, and an enhanced sense of civic responsibility" (Bringle and Hatcher 1995: 112).

As a form of experiential education, service-learning shares similarities with internships, field education, practica, and voluntary service. Furco (1996) places these forms of education on a continuum. At one end of the continuum are internships and practica, with their primary focus on the students' career development. At the other end are volunteer activities, in which the emphasis is on civic involvement and the services provided to recipients. Furco locates service-learning in the middle of the continuum, and states that it is unique in its "intention to equally benefit the provider and the recipient of the service as well as to ensure equal focus on both the service being provided and the learning that is occurring" (1996: 5).

Thus, in high-quality service-learning courses, no one is exploited and reciprocity exists so that the service providers (i.e., students) and service recipients each give and receive. Furthermore, students do not receive academic credit for community service. Engaging in community service is necessary, but not sufficient; academic credit is contingent upon the learning that occurs as a result of the community service activities. Engaging students in their communities through service allows them to examine critical issues related to motivation, learning, relationships, and development. By providing students with community service opportunities that are integrated with academic studies, students are faced with what Dewey refers to as "forked-road situations" in which challenging circumstances result in new learning and understanding of the course content. The connections between the service activities and course content are facilitated through regularly engaging students in structured reflection activities as part of the course (Hatcher and Bringle 1997). Service-learning, then, provides a means for psychologists to be directly involved with changes in society and creates an opportunity for students to see the illustration and application of psychological concepts. In addition, agency personnel become important resources through which solutions to perplexing problems are explored.

By collaborating with communities in the educational process, psychologists and students are also presented with an opportunity to reflect on their values and assumptions (Hatcher and Bringle 1997). In doing so, service-learning integrates the cognitive with the affective domain, theory with practice, and knowledge with context. Altman (1996) contends that such socially responsive knowledge, a domain that has not been emphasized recently in higher education, should be an integral part of the undergraduate curriculum, along with foundational knowledge (content and cross-disciplinary knowledge) and professional knowledge (practitioner skills and content). According to Altman, socially responsible knowledge has three goals that service-learning helps achieve: "first, to educate students in the problems of society; second, [to] have them experience and understand firsthand social issues in their community; and third, and most important, [to] give students the experiences and skills to act on social problems" (Altman 1996: 375-376). Thus, unlike practica and internships, service-learning contains specific learning objectives focused on civic involvement and social responsibility, and students not only learn through service but also learn to serve.

Because service-learning creates an excellent environment for better learning the content of psychology courses by engaging students in active, relevant, collaborative learning — attributes that are known to maximize learning (Pascarella and Terenzini 1991) — it is not surprising that according to a 1995 survey of 221 colleges by the National Service-Learning Research Project, 52 percent of psychology departments had added service-learning components to their courses (Murray 1997). This volume itself reflects the growing interest among psychology educators in service-learning from the perspectives of research, practice, and teaching. The expertise of many areas in psychology is relevant to the implementation of service-learning because service-learning "combines a strong social purpose with acknowledgment of the significance of personal and intellectual growth in participants" (Giles, Honnet, and Migliore 1991: 7).

This book begins with six articles that address how psychological theory, research, and practice bear on collaborating with communities, interpreting changes in students, and using psychological techniques to understand and act on social problems. The remaining articles demonstrate how service-learning can be effectively integrated into a variety of psychology courses so that student learning is enhanced in breadth and depth. Woven through all of the chapters are the five values that Prilleltensky (1997) identifies as most salient for how psychologists can foster the good life: compassion, self-determination, human diversity, collaboration and democratic participation, and distributive justice.

How Psychological Research Can Facilitate Effective Ways of Collaborating With Communities

The ideas of one of psychology's founders, John Dewey, form the theoretical basis for understanding how students learn from experiences in the community (Giles and Eyler 1994), while Kolb's research on experiential learning (1984) provides a frequently cited model in the practice of service-learning. These two examples illustrate how effectively psychological theory and research can be employed to provide support and strategies for the growing field of service-learning. As psychologists discuss the values and assumptions that guide their practice and frame the ideals they wish to promote for individuals and societies, more questions will require systematic and objective inquiry.

Answering Basic Questions

What motivates people to serve others? How can helping situations be structured to provide the most benefit for students, agencies, and recipients? How and why are students changed when they participate in service-learning courses? Does psychological research suggest approaches for creating more caring communities? These questions or variations of them are often heard in discussions about service-learning. There are no simple answers to such questions, but the first three chapters in this volume provide thoughtful explorations of critical issues and possible ways to begin to frame solutions.

In reviewing literature dealing with altruism and prosocial behavior, Kitzrow examines some of the psychological research that suggests approaches for creating more caring communities. She begins by providing a historical overview of early work in the study of altruism and helping. An important milestone for psychological research occurred in 1964 in New York City with the fatal stabbing of Kitty Genovese. Not one of the 38 bystanders who witnessed the murder intervened to help, not even to call the police. This event raised many questions within society and among psychologists about why people failed to help and about the lack of caring and compassion in communities.

Kitzrow presents cognitive, moral, and social-development theories dealing with prosocial behaviors and supports the multimotivational views of Clary, Snyder, and Stukas (the second essay) in citing research showing that individuals providing help to others experience positive benefits for themselves. In a study of some 1,700 helpers, Luks (1988) found that participants experienced an improved sense of well-being, increased energy and strength, greater self-worth, and decreased aches and pains.

A central topic raised in all three of these chapters concerns whether people's motivation for helping others is based on selfish or unselfish motives. Although many theorists support the view that help is either altruistically or egoistically motivated, Clary, Snyder, and Stukas recommend a functional approach, stating that people are motivated both by concern for others and by concern for the self. They suggest that prosocial attitudes and behaviors serve six functions: understanding ("to learn, to gain a greater understanding of people, to practice skills and abilities"), career ("to enhance one's job and career prospects, to gain experience and contacts"), values ("to act on important values such as humanitarian values, altruistic concerns, or desires to contribute to society"), social ("to fit into important reference groups, to gain social approval/avoid social disapproval"), protective ("to reduce feelings of guilt, to resolve or escape from one's own personal problems"), and enhancement ("to enhance self-worth, self-confidence, and expand one's social network") [see pp. 37-38]. Using these six functions, Clary and his colleagues developed a Volunteer Functions Inventory (VFI) to assess volunteers' motivations. Research with the VFI shows that the values function is the most important motivation of volunteers, followed by the enhancement and understanding functions, suggesting that motivation to serve others involves both selfish and unselfish motives.

Given these findings, Clary, Snyder, and Stukas raise questions that reflect Prilleltensky's (1997) criteria for defining and working toward the good society and how to get there. Clary and his colleagues ask whether it is good to strive for a society where self-interest is secondary to the interests of others in need. They argue against such a society for three reasons. First, unselfish motives alone are more likely to lead to burnout in the helper; second, recipients of help are more apt to establish a reciprocal relationship with a helper having mixed motives; and third, more prosocial behavior is probable if the society has an ideal allowing for a mixture of self and selfless motivations rather than the more unrealistic ideal of pure altruism.

Clary, Snyder, and Stukas suggest specific ways to translate their vision of the good society into action. They state that prosocial values are established most effectively following action and suggest that students become engaged in prosocial action based on motivations and functions important to them. Faculty introducing service-learning to a class might be more successful in engaging a wider range of students if they addressed and honored all six functions served by prosocial behaviors. Clary and his colleagues argue against mandatory service because the requirement may impede the internalization of prosocial attitudes and values and may prevent the development of a long-term commitment to act on these values.

In chapter three, Bringle and Velo consider in greater detail the social and situational factors that influence helping by analyzing how observers make attributions about misery in others. They cite critical findings from attribution theory that have direct implications for service-learning settings. Based on the "fundamental attribution error" (Ross 1977), students engaged in service-learning may tend to identify problems in others as due to internal rather than external causes. According to the "actor-observer bias," students may see the causes of their own behaviors as less stable and more external, whereas they view the causes of behaviors in others as more fixed and internal (Jones and Nisbett 1972). Because of these attribution biases, students' explanations of recipients' circumstances may be quite different from the explanations provided by recipients themselves. Furthermore, explanations by students about why they are helping can deviate from explanations by their professors, recipients, and agency personnel.

Bringle and Velo cite the importance of understanding recipients' explanations for why they need help, how they feel about receiving help, and how they perceive those who are providing help. Students venturing to service-learning sites are more likely to be successful if they reflect on the needs of those being helped ahead of time and realize that recipients may have many different feelings and responses to receiving help. By applying basic findings from attribution theory to preservice activities, faculty can begin to structure helping situations in ways that will provide maximum benefits for students, agencies, and recipients.

Interpreting Changes in Students

What *are* the benefits for students who participate in service-learning? Brandenberger examines theories of cognitive development, psychosocial development, and moral development to show their relationship to the assumptions and processes of service-learning. He demonstrates how the work of Piaget, Erikson, Kohlberg, and others supports service-based pedagogies, especially the focus on active and collaborative learning, concern for values and ethics, and understanding of diversity. Brandenberger cites the work of Parks (1986) that considers how young adults seek meaning from their experiences. Parks maintains that the emphasis on objectivity and neutrality prevalent in the dominant academic paradigm may not help students as they try to integrate experience and reflection into a meaningful worldview. She states that higher education needs to enlarge students' experiences through active participation and elaborates:

> Further, as students and their teachers experience the discernment of truth as indissolubly linked with act and its consequences, the dichotomies between method and morality, theory and practice, knowledge and context, self and society, private and public — dichotomies that plague both higher education and society as a whole — are transcended, and the best impulses of the searching mind are honored. (Parks 1986: 143-144)[also see pp. 76-77]

Brandenberger states that through service-learning, students can learn "that context matters, that stereotypes may not reflect reality, that multiple viewpoints have merit, that social problems have complex etiologies, and that solutions come from dialogue and cooperation" [see p. 77]; such lessons can have a critical influence on students' epistemological assumptions, resulting in growth in intellectual and ethical development.

In summarizing his overview of developmental theories, Brandenberger discusses several concrete implications for practice and research in service-learning. He urges practitioners to attend to internal factors within students as well as to external factors in the service-learning setting, to understand how students' developmental levels may influence their interpretations of service experiences, and to align with other educational initiatives such as collaborative learning and critical thinking. He recommends that researchers examine how service experiences influence students' epistemological assumptions over time, as well as their motivation for learning about social conditions.

Eyler, Root, and Giles, in the following chapter, also provide insight into these topics, as they explore differences in the ways novice and experienced service-learning students solve community problems. Eyler and her colleagues cite similarities in how cognitive scientists and service-learning professors view effective instruction. Both support the value of confronting problems in complex contexts, the importance of reflecting on experiences in structured ways, and the need for multiple opportunities to apply knowledge. Eyler, Root, and Giles suggest that research on differentiating the cognitive processes of expert and novice problem solvers may provide another way in which cognitive psychology can inform the practice of service-learning. Using the expert-novice research as a guide, they interviewed novice and expert service-learning students to assess how the two groups analyzed causes and solutions for a social problem related to their community service. Results indicated that expert students defined problems in more elaborate and coherent ways, cited the interaction of social processes rather than individual mental states as sources of problems, proposed multifaceted solutions to problems, and provided sophisticated approaches for how to become personally involved in solving a community problem. This research begins to answer the question raised by Brandenberger regarding how students' epistemological assumptions change over time; it also demonstrates how service-learning can enhance the socially responsive knowledge recommended by Altman (1996).

Using Psychological Techniques to Act on Social Problems

Although research in the areas of social, developmental, and cognitive psychology can help to answer fundamental questions about service-learning, work in more applied areas such as clinical, community, and counseling psychology can provide guidance for practitioners in dealing with the human relationships involved in service-learning settings. Students engaged in service-learning must, like clinicians, establish rapport with their clients, define a plan of action for the client's concerns, and obtain closure at the end of the relationship. A student's skill or lack of skill in dealing with any aspect of this relationship cycle will influence the success of the service-learning endeavor.

In his essay concluding Part 1, Leeds uses the concept of "helping alliance" to frame these relationship issues. He adapts the work of Bordin (1979) and defines a helping alliance as the working relationship between a person seeking change and a change agent with agreed-upon goals, tasks, and bonds. "Goals" vary in their specificity and time frame, "tasks" represent the roles each participant will take on, and "bonds" refers to the nature of the relationship between the participants. Leeds suggests that the goals-tasks-bonds triad of the helping alliance can provide a practical approach for discussing the complexity of relationships in service-learning settings.

Students in Leeds's service-learning classes develop scenarios that represent relationship dilemmas typical in community agencies, and then they role play the scenarios in training sessions for audiences new to service-learning. Students encourage the audience to use the goals-tasks-bonds formula in analyzing relationships and to understand appropriate and inappropriate ways for handling difficult situations. Pellitteri (1996) used the goals-tasks-bonds framework to interview tutors regarding their relationship to those being tutored. He found that being a friend was the key role tutors sought to establish with their students. Pellitteri states that a friend relationship representing the bond aspect of the helping alliance may be in conflict with the goals and tasks required in an academic program such as tutoring. As Leeds points out, relationships often have many, sometimes contradictory components; an approach such as the goals-tasks-bonds framework provides a strategy for analyzing the complexity in a more objective and systematic manner.

Leeds recommends exploring the concept of friendship that students envision as part of the bond in service-learning relationships. He suggests that students may want a positive emotional connection to those being tutored, but the relationship (due to differences in age, class, status, and other dimensions) may be more like that of an older sibling rather than a friend. He cites research on friendship (Garrett 1989) showing cross-class friendships to be rather rare, and raises the question of exactly what undergraduates mean when they say they want to be someone's "friend." Similar to Bringle and Velo's suggestion that it is critical to understand how students' attributions about helping influence their perceptions of service,

Leeds recommends that it is important to know how students classify the type of relationship formed with recipients of help. Research on friendship as well as work in the area of emotional intelligence (Goleman 1995) may be useful in outlining effective ways to maximize effective interpersonal relationships in a community service setting.

How Service Experiences in the Community Can Enhance the Ways Students Learn in Their Courses

Providing Multiple Opportunities for Students to Be Active and Collaborative Learners

Professors are besieged by waves of educational initiatives that claim to provide the "answer" to dealing with the demands of today's changing classrooms. How does service-learning fit among these initiatives? What can the addition of service-learning provide for a professor teaching the standard introductory psychology course? In the first chapter of Part 2, we ourselves present the case of Professor McKenna, who ponders the value of adding a service-learning component to her class. Through McKenna's musings and reflections, we integrate research from a number of perspectives to show the relationship of service-learning to other higher education initiatives and to provide support for the effectiveness of service-learning as a pedagogy.

Relationships between individuals are central to service-learning, but it is also important to consider relationships with the broader community. As work by Kretzmann and McKnight (1993) indicates, examining a community's needs and problems is less conducive to fostering productive relationships than focusing on a community's capacities and assets. In the next chapter, Werner's holistic perspective on service-learning emphasizes that service projects should be seen as part of the total community system and should provide opportunities for enhancing both individual and social identities. Werner's essay provides a clear example of how psychological research can facilitate collaboration with communities *and* how service experiences in the community can enhance the ways students learn in their courses. She advocates service projects that empower rather than undermine recipients, and cites research suggesting that the most effective community programs are those that *expect* participation and contributions by the recipients (Zimmerman and Perkins 1985). In accord with Prilleltensky's recommendation that psychologists clearly articulate the values and assumptions that guide their practice, Werner delineates her goals for and philosophy of service-learning. Although she believes that teaching social responsibility is the job of higher education, she opposes requiring service in her classes. Werner supports elective service because she does not want to impose her values on others, she believes required service is not really service, and she agrees with motivational research that shows that requiring a behavior decreases intrinsic motivation for the behavior.

In Werner's view, service projects should focus on a defined community need, be manageable for the time constraints of a course, and leave mechanisms in place to maintain projects once students leave. For example, students in Werner's environmental psychology course not only establish recycling centers in communities but also devise ways to provide ongoing support for these centers. Students are more likely to feel empowered if they can achieve success and can feel that their work will have long-term consequences. In contrast, students involved in ill-defined, overly ambitious projects may become discouraged and generate negative rather than positive impacts in a community. Werner supports community involvement in all phases of service-learning projects and suggests that having students create papers and presentations for community agencies results in more engaged and authentic learning.

Using the course Emotional and Behavioral Disorders of Childhood and Adolescence, Osborne, Weadick, and Penticuff describe in their article the process of incorporating service-learning into an advanced psychology course, from writing the objectives through designing assignments to assessing the impact of service-learning on students. They list specific questions for faculty to consider based on Howard's (1993) ten principles for effective service-learning programs. Because of the worthwhile ways in which students apply theories and findings from a course to individuals at their service sites, Osborne and his colleagues illustrate how service-learning activities enhance a professor's ability to teach the content of the course. They recommend using multiple ways of assessing student reactions including collaborative groups and exit cards at the end of each class session. They describe many concrete examples of reflection activities that could be adapted to other courses and settings.

As he describes next, Johnson's Human Relations course also provides multiple opportunities for students to be active and collaborative learners. In addition to completing a minimum of 30 hours of community service, students select chapters to be covered in the course and take responsibility for presenting the material they select. The first five weeks of the course focus on conceptual and textual information, but after the fifth week, one class each week is devoted to structured dialogue sessions in which students reflect on their service experiences in small groups using approaches such as journal reading, story telling, or specific questions from chapters. Grading in the course is based on two take-home analytical papers, journals, group presentations, and participation in reflective dialogue sessions.

To assess how effectively service and reflection experiences contributed to learning concepts in the course, Johnson designed a survey that separated course content into nine major conceptual areas. Students were instructed to check off areas in which their understanding and skill had been enhanced by the service and reflection experience. Results indicated that the service experience was successful in increasing understanding in all nine areas, with high scores for "effective communication" (96.1%) and for "achieving independence and interdependence" and "perceiving others" (92.2% each). Johnson observes that through these new pedagogies, he has changed his teaching style "from disseminator to facilitator" [see p. 149]. Although he initially was uncomfortable with giving up some control in the classroom, he has been gratified to see his students taking responsibility and using effective strategies for learning.

Learning About Applications of Psychology

Professors who use service-learning do so for a variety of reasons. Elias and Gambone introduced service-learning as a one-credit adjunct to the two courses Community Psychology and Atypical Child Development as a way for students to gain firsthand experience with children in high-risk, urban environments. About one third of students in the two courses have participated in the one-credit service-learning option each semester. These students are placed at one of nine urban Head Start centers, and they share their experiences with class members who are not participating.

Elias and Gambone stress the use of "five C's" (compassion, communication, connection, comprehension, closure) in all levels of their program, but especially in supervision. In their essay, they provide specific strategies for following the five C's, as well as ideas for evaluating students with a multidimensional format. According to Elias and Gambone, their course design engenders a sense of citizenship, increases enthusiasm in the entire class, provides personal rewards from working with an underserved population, promotes knowledge of child development, and fosters an understanding of the complexity of social problems while promoting a sense of commitment and optimism.

In teaching a course on action research, Nigro and Wortham were also concerned about giving students a better understanding of the complexity of social problems. They recognized that action research and service-learning share many similarities: Both involve acting in a setting, reflecting on what has happened, and modifying the practice. And both require more collaboration with experts and less direction from professors. As they describe in their essay, combining service-learning and action research provided an opportunity for students to gain firsthand experience using empirical methods in a real-world setting and developing partnerships with local practitioner-researchers.

Prior to their course, Nigro and Wortham met with local teachers and service providers to organize research projects that could be completed within the time constraints of the five-week term. Students selected projects on the first day of class and collaborated with staff at schools or agencies to devise an action plan. In one project, students surveyed elementary and secondary schools in the county and conducted focus groups to identify violent incidents and violence prevention strategies used in the schools. Using the survey data, the partner agency applied for funding and received money to support a pilot program in violence prevention. These results exemplify Werner's ideas that service projects should empower recipients and enhance both individual and social identities.

Understanding Diversity in Behavior

Nigro and Wortham's course on action research and service-learning supports the APA curriculum mandate to provide research methods for increasing students' understanding of diversity in behavior; the three chapters by GreyWolf, by Fluharty and Kassaie, and by Carlebach and Singer highlight how service-learning is an effective pedagogy for increasing students' comprehension of differences.

GreyWolf describes how she set goals, reflected on results, and modified activities in her Cross-Cultural Psychology course over a period of three years. She notes that studying cross-cultural psychology requires understanding the limitations and culture-bound nature of the discipline and points out that although most psychologists have been trained in Western theories and methods, the majority of the world is not white and may not value Western perspectives (Segall et al. 1990). At her homogeneous campus, GreyWolf engaged students in problem solving with people from other cultures. Her students worked in teams of four to assist refugees in activities that would help them adapt to their new environment. Students reflected on these experiences through use of a class journal, papers, and group discussions. In the class journal, students used pseudonyms to make entries that involved reacting to class presentations and responding to other student entries. GreyWolf reports that the anonymity of the journal allowed students to confront ethnocentrism and unclear thinking in each other, while the service teams engendered more cooperation and support among class members. Assisting refugees allowed students to meet the course goal of problem solving with people from other cultures. The reflection activities helped them move beyond the experience to question their own assumptions and to integrate lessons from cross-cultural psychology.

In describing the Developmental Disabilities Immersion Program (DDIP) at UCLA, Fluharty and Kassaie reflect on the use of service-learning as a pedagogy from the program's inception in 1976 to the present. DDIP is a two-quarter full-time program in which students work with children and adults with disabilities, take courses, and conduct research. The service activities are designed to develop civic values and responsibilities, as well as to help students decide on a career in the field of developmental disabilities. Fluharty and Kassaie explain that most of their students begin by "wanting to help those with disabilities" [see p. 181]. Through working directly with individuals with disabilities at service sites, students have the opportunity to make more informed choices about their future career paths. Although DDIP has evolved over the past 20 years, the service-learning component has remained a standard part of the program. Fluharty and Kassaie claim that due to deinstitutionalization, there are pressing needs for more human resources to assist those with developmental disabilities. They suggest that student service can help to meet these needs and they recommend various ways that components of DDIP can be adapted to other institutions.

As they describe in their essay, Carlebach and Singer help students understand diversity issues through an interdisciplinary course that applies service-learning, psychology, and theater to the problem of prejudice. Using three learning modes that theater and psychology have in common (empirical exploration of human actions, empathic understanding of the other, and experiential techniques), Carlebach and Singer formulated a course drawing on theory and research in psychology and on theory and practice in theater. Student groups used techniques developed by Augusto Boal to create tableaus of oppression and selected images of oppression that deeply affected them as a group. In the service component of the course, students shared the techniques learned in the course with a group of individuals in the community. One group of students presented an oppression workshop at a residential alcohol and drug rehabilitation facility; a second group prepared a gender-stereotyping workshop at a middle school; and a third group organized prejudice awareness exercises at a camp for juvenile offenders.

Students stated that they found the service-learning experience empowering because it enabled them to participate in a process to confront problems such as racism and bias rather than to feel overwhelmed by them. Many students reported that following work in the community they returned to their course readings to gain greater perspective and understanding of the experience. Although Carlebach and Singer recognize the limitations inherent in having students participate in a short-term involvement with communities, they note that some of the techniques introduced by students have been incorporated into future programming at the community sites.

Implications of Collaborating With the Community

Psychologists study the science of human behavior and mental processes through many different lenses. The lenses of the theoretician, the researcher, the clinician, and the professor illuminate different aspects of a complex picture. Because of these diverse viewpoints, the divisions within psychology can become separate communities isolated from each other.

Although the authors of essays in this volume use different approaches to research issues in service-learning or to incorporate service-learning into courses, they share the belief that collaborating with communities is a worthwhile enterprise for students and faculty. Coye (1997) broadens this belief and states that strong connections with communities will be an essential component in higher education in the future:

> The change is most evident in the number of campuses that have opened their gates to encourage greater connection with the local community. Today, the number of students and faculty involved in community service has reached astonishing levels; some people estimate that the proportion of students volunteering for community work is as high as two-thirds, while 78 percent of faculty in the 1995 Higher Education Research Institute (HERI) survey had performed community service or volunteer work in the previous two years. (26)

The increased involvement of students and faculty in the community requires more reflection on how to make the collaboration effective. Mintz and Hesser (1996) suggest that "as the practice of service-learning continues to evolve, so must practice continue to translate into principles" (39). They present the metaphor of the kaleidoscope and suggest that principles for service-learning be assessed through the lenses of collaboration, reciprocity, and diversity. It is our hope that readers of this volume will appreciate how the image of the kaleidoscope "constantly reminds all partners that the relationships among academy, students, and community are shifting, unpredictable, and delicate, requiring regular and ongoing communication" (40).

References

Altman, I. (1996). "Higher Education and Psychology in the Millennium." *American Psychologist* 51: 371-378.

Bordin, E.S. (1979). "The Generalizability of the Psychoanalytic Concept of the Working Alliance." *Psychotherapy: Theory, Research and Practice* 16: 252-259.

Brewer, C.L. (1997). "Undergraduate Education in Psychology: Will the Mermaids Sing?" *American Psychologist* 52: 434-441.

Bringle, R.G., and J.A. Hatcher. (Fall 1995). "A Service-Learning Curriculum for Faculty." *Michigan Journal of Community Service Learning* 2: 112-122.

Coye, D. (May/June 1997). "Ernest Boyer and the New American College: Connecting the 'Disconnects.'" *Change* 29(3): 20-29.

Furco, A. (1996). "Service-Learning: A Balanced Approach to Experiential Education." In *Expanding Boundaries: Serving and Learning,* edited by the Corporation for National Service, pp. 2-6. Columbia, MD: Cooperative Education Association.

Garrett, S. (1989). "Friendship and the Social Order." In *Dialectics of Friendship,* edited by R. Porter and S. Tomaselli, pp. 130-142. London: Routledge.

Giles, D.E., Jr., and J. Eyler. (Fall 1994). "The Theoretical Roots of Service-Learning in John Dewey: Toward a Theory of Service-Learning." *Michigan Journal of Community Service Learning* 1: 77-85.

Giles, D.E., E.P. Honnet, and S. Migliore. (1991). *Research Agenda for Combining Service and Learning in the 1990s.* Raleigh, NC: National Society for Experiential Education.

Goleman, D. (1995). *Emotional Intelligence.* New York: Bantam.

Hatcher, J.A., and R.G. Bringle. (1997). "Reflections: Bridging the Gap Between Service and Learning." *Journal of College Teaching* 45: 153-158.

Howard, J. (1993). "Community Service in the Curriculum." In *Praxis I: A Faculty Casebook on Community Service Learning,* edited by J. Howard, pp. 3-12. Ann Arbor, MI: OCSL Press.

Jones, E., and R. Nisbett. (1972). "The Actor and the Observer: Divergent Perceptions of the Causes of Behavior." In *Attribution, Perceiving the Causes of Behavior,* edited by E. Jones et al., pp. 79-94. Morristown, NJ: General Learning Press.

Kolb, D. (1984). *Experiential Learning: Experience as a Source of Learning and Development.* Englewood Cliffs, NJ: Prentice-Hall.

Kretzmann, J.P., and J.L. McKnight. (1993). *Building Communities From the Inside Out: A Path Toward Finding and Mobilizing a Community's Assets.* Evanston, IL: Center for Urban Affairs and Policy Research, Northwestern University.

Luks, A. (1988). "Helper's High." *Psychology Today* 10: 39-42.

McGovern, T.V., and J.N. Reich. (1996). "A Comment on the *Quality Principles.*" *American Psychologist* 51: 252-255.

Mintz, S.D., and G.W. Hesser. (1996). "Principles of Good Practice in Service-Learning." In *Service-Learning in Higher Education,* edited by B. Jacoby and Associates, pp. 26-52. San Francisco: Jossey-Bass.

Murray, B. (February 1997). "Service Learning Growing More Popular." *APA Monitor,* 44.

Parks, S. (1986). *The Critical Years: The Young Adult Search for a Faith to Live By.* San Francisco: Harper & Row.

Pascarella, E.T., and P.T. Terenzini. (1991). *How College Affects Students: Findings and Insights From Twenty Years of Research.* San Francisco: Jossey-Bass.

Pellitteri, J. (1996). "The Working Alliance and the Tutor-Student Relationship." Unpublished candidacy paper, Department of Applied Psychology, New York University.

Prilleltensky, I. (1997). "Values, Assumptions, and Practices: Assessing the Moral Implications of Psychological Discourse and Action." *American Psychologist* 52: 517-535.

Reich, J. (March 1996). "Keeping Up With Students on the Move." *APA Monitor*, 45.

Ross, L. (1977). "The Intuitive Psychologist and His Shortcomings: Distortions in the Attribution Process." In *Advances in Experimental Social Psychology*, Vol. 10, edited by L. Berkowitz, pp. 174-221. New York: Academic Press.

Sarason, S.B. (1982). *Psychology and Social Action: Selected Papers.* New York: Praeger.

Segall, M.H., P.R. Dasen, J.W. Berry, and Y.H. Poortinga. (1990). *Human Behavior in Global Perspective.* Needham Heights, MA: Allyn & Bacon.

Slife, B.D., and R.N. Williams, eds. (1997). "Toward a Theoretical Psychology." *American Psychologist* 52: 117-129.

Zimmerman, M.A., and D.D. Perkins, eds. (1985). *American Journal of Community Psychology* (Special Issue: Empowerment Theory): 23(5).

An Overview of Current Psychological Theory and Research on Altruism and Prosocial Behavior

by Martha A. Kitzrow

Many people are concerned about the loss of a sense of caring and community, characterized by a willingness to help others. Given the multitude of current social problems, it is more critical than ever to find effective methods for helping young people develop into caring and responsible citizens who are willing and able to help others and make a positive contribution for the public good. Service-learning programs provide structured opportunities for college students to make a difference by participating in meaningful service in conjunction with related academic coursework. The purpose of this chapter is to review major psychological research on altruism and prosocial behavior and explore how this information can be used to validate and enhance service-learning programs.

The Altruism Controversy: A Historical Overview

A heated controversy about whether human beings are fundamentally selfish or fundamentally altruistic has been waged by philosophers, religious scholars, and most recently by social scientists and psychologists. Generally the debate falls into three categories. The first (and perhaps predominant) view is that human beings are fundamentally selfish (egoistic) and non-altruistic. Machiavelli argued that human beings are universally self-serving:

> For it may be said of men in general that they are ungrateful, voluble, dissemblers, anxious to avoid danger and covetous of gain. For love being held by a chain of obligation, which men being selfish, is broken whenever it serves their purpose. (Machiavelli 1950: 61)

A second view, articulated by the British philosopher John Locke (1632-1704), proposes that human beings are inherently neither selfish nor altruistic but are capable of behaving either way. Behavior is the result of learning and experience. The mind may be described as "white paper, void of all characters, without any ideas. How comes it to be furnished? . . . from *experience*" (Locke 1939: 248).

Yet a third view is represented by humanistic philosophers such as David Hume (1711-1776), who argued that human beings are fundamentally altruistic: "We must renounce the theory which accounts for every moral sentiment by the principle of self-love" (Hume 1900: 438). "It cannot be disputed . . . that there is some benevolence infused in our bosom, some spark of our friendship for human kind" (469).

Altruism has also been a source of controversy within psychology. Each of the three major theoretical orientations within psychology (i.e., psychoanalysis, behaviorism, and humanistic psychology) has taken a different position on altruism. Freud (1994) stated that "Men are not gentle, friendly creatures" (40). On the one hand, they are driven by aggression (Thanatos), and on the other hand by the pursuit of pleasure (Eros), "which draws up the programme of life's purpose" (10). On the question of altruism, Freud conceded that individuals may experience competing egoistic and altruistic impulses, but stated that "the main accent falls on the egoistic trend" (66). Freud attributed altruistic behavior to guilt and anxiety imposed by the superego, the powerful inner voice of morality, which sublimates and redirects sexual or aggressive drives into socially acceptable channels (67).

The second influential force in psychology was behaviorism. Behavioral theorists, such as John Watson and B.F. Skinner, shared the views of Locke that individuals are comparable to a blank slate. They are innately neither selfish nor altruistic but rather they learn specific behaviors based on experience and conditioning. According to Skinner, "the good person is one who has been conditioned to behave that way, and the good society would be one based on behavioral engineering — the scientific control of behavior through methods of positive reinforcement" (in Cohen 1977: 283).

Humanistic psychology, which holds a positive view of human nature, has been the strongest advocate for altruism. According to Carl Rogers (1957),

> Man . . . is basically a trustworthy member of the human species, whose deepest characteristics tend toward development, differentiation, cooperative relationships; . . . whose total character is such as to tend to preserve and enhance himself and his species, and perhaps to move it toward further evolution. (200-202)

Another humanistic psychologist, Abraham Maslow, best known for developing the "hierarchy of needs" (1970), proposed that self-actualization and altruism are closely related. Self-actualized individuals develop "being values," which include a strong sense of goodness and justice, and "they are, without one single exception, involved in a cause outside their own skin, in something outside of themselves" (1971: 43). He was convinced that the self-actualized, or "Good Person," was necessary "to make the Good Society" (1971: 19).

Altruism and Prosocial Behavior Defined

The word *altruism* itself originated with the French philosopher Auguste Comte (1798-1857). Comte, who is regarded as the founder of modern sociology and social psychology, wrote about the development of "sympathetic" human instincts — i.e., empathy, compassion, and altruism toward others. Comte believed that the purpose of an advanced society was to foster the development of such instincts.

According to the strict definitions of altruism that prevailed during much of this century, true altruism could only exist if the action was completely selfless, did not benefit the actor in any way, and required some kind of self-sacrifice. Given this restrictive definition, it is not surprising that altruism in its purest form was seldom, if ever, found to exist. Contemporary definitions are less restrictive and define altruism simply as "a motivational state with the ultimate goal of increasing another's welfare" (Batson 1991b: 6). In general, altruistic behavior must benefit another person and must be performed voluntarily and intentionally, without expecting any external reward (Bar-Tal and Raviv 1982). Behaviors such as sharing, empathy, and cooperation, that benefit others and improve social relationships, are known as "prosocial" (rather than "*anti*social") behaviors (Radke-Yarrow, Zahn-Waxler, and Chapman 1983).

An Overview of Theory and Research on Altruism and Prosocial Behavior

Sociobiological Theories

Sociobiological theories propose that human beings have an innate biological and social capacity for altruism. Biological mechanisms facilitate the development of empathy, attachment, and altruism. For instance, the structure of the brain permits human beings to respond to emotional stimuli, including the distress of others, thus establishing the foundation for basic empathy (MacLean 1973). Furthermore, the capacity for emotional communication that forms "the basis of all social behaviors, including empathic emotions and altruism" is genetically based (Buck and Ginsburg 1990: 163).

Sex hormones and hormones secreted during pregnancy also appear to facilitate the development of altruism by sensitizing females to respond in a nurturing and altruistic manner to the cry of an infant in distress. In contrast, female adults who were exposed to greater levels of the male sex hormone testosterone during a critical phase of their fetal development were found to be less sensitive to infants (Money and Erhardt 1972).

Perhaps the most compelling sociobiological theory is that altruism has evolved because it is beneficial for the welfare of the species. The theory of group selection states that groups with altruistic members are more likely to survive and less likely to become extinct (Wynne-Edwards 1962). The theory of kin selection or relatedness further states that individuals are more likely to engage in altruistic or self-sacrificing behavior that will benefit others to whom they are biologically related and with whom they share a high proportion of genes (Hamilton 1975). Another argument for the sociobiological basis of altruism is reciprocal altruism, which states that individuals who perform altruistic acts for nonrelatives also benefit and ultimately increase their chances for survival because they may receive assistance in return (Trivers 1971).

These sociobiological mechanisms create the potential for an "altruistic gene" that can be passed on within a relatively isolated group (Morgan 1985). Twin studies have also provided some evidence that altruism may be inherited. Rushton et al. (1986) conducted a study of 1,400 adult twins on three measures: altruism, empathy, and nurturance. For each measure, more than 50 percent of the variance could be explained by genetic effects: altruism (56%), empathy (68%), and nurturance (72%).

Although sociobiological research has demonstrated that biologically based mechanisms for the development of empathy, attachment, and altruism may exist, the mechanisms do not guarantee the development of altruism. Rather, "they only permit or facilitate the learning of certain forms of behavior" (Hill 1984: 23). As Jonas Salk put it, "I think that goodness and nobility are genetically inscribed, but they need to be evoked . . . they must be taught actively" (1984: 9).

Cognitive, Social, and Moral Developmental Theories

From the perspective of social learning and developmental theories, altruism and prosocial behavior are primarily learned behaviors, which evolve in a series of developmental stages (Bar-Tal, Sharabany, and Raviv 1981; Hoffman 1981; Kohlberg 1976; Krebs and Van Hesteren 1994; Staub 1979). Furthermore, the ability to experience empathy for another is fundamental to the development of altruism. According to the empathy-altruism hypothesis (Batson 1991a), emotion evokes empathy, which in turn evokes altruism. The hypothesis further predicts that the greater an individual's capacity for empathy and the stronger the empathic emotion, the stronger the altruistic motivation will be.

Piaget (1972) was among the first developmental theorists to realize that children must first achieve a level of cognitive development that permits them to experience others as separate from self and take another person's perspective before they are truly able to experience empathy. Later, Hoffman (1981) developed a model that describes the cognitive development of empathy. Newborns and infants display a primitive form of "global empathy" and respond to distress in others by experiencing distress themselves (49). However, because infants are unable to differentiate between *self* and *other,* they cannot determine whether the distress is occurring to them or to someone else. Toddlers achieve "egocentric empathy" (49) when they are able to distinguish the self from others and to become aware that another person, and not the self, is experiencing distress. They are still likely to experience confusion between self and others and tend to comfort another in distress by giving the other person something that they find comforting, such as a favorite blanket or teddy bear.

As cognitive maturity progresses, children develop the capacity for role taking (e.g., imagining how they would feel in another child's place), and thus are able to experience "empathy for another's feelings" (Hoffman 1981: 50). Older children also develop the capacity to feel "empathy for another's general plight" (50) that transcends the immediate situation. The final stage in the "cognitive transformation of empathy" (48) is "sympathetic distress" (51), "a feeling of compassion . . . along with a conscious desire to help because they feel sorry for him or her and not just to relieve their own empathic distress" (51).

Moral reasoning is also strongly associated with the development of altruism and prosocial behavior. Piaget (1972) found that younger children in the heterogamous stage generally obey rules of social conduct because they believe that rules are absolute and that disobedience may result in punishment. Thus, their behavior is based on external factors rather than on internalized moral values. In contrast, older children who have achieved the autonomous stage of moral development understand that rules are not absolute and that they are capable of making independent moral decisions.

Kohlberg (1984) expanded on Piaget's ideas and developed a three-stage model of moral development based on external and internal locus of control: In the preconventional stage, individuals are motivated to engage in moral behavior by a fear of punishment or to gain personal rewards. During the conventional stage, individuals are motivated by conformity to social norms and adherence to law and order. It is only in the postconventional stage that behavior is motivated by individual principles and conscience.

Based on extensive research with children, Bar-Tal, Sharabany, and Raviv (1981) proposed that altruism and prosocial behavior develops in six stages. Later stages of development are characterized by a decrease in external motivation and an increase in internal motivation. In stage one (compliance), children help because they have been asked or ordered to do so and they are motivated by concrete rewards or punishment. In stage two, helping is still motivated by compliance with authority so as to gain approval or avoid punishment; however, concrete rewards are no longer necessary. By stage three (internal initiative), children are beginning to help based more on internal motivation but can still be motivated by concrete rewards. As children enter stage four (normative behavior), their helping behavior is motivated primarily by conformity to social norms and nonconcrete rewards (approval). With increasing maturity, children in stage five (generalized reciprocity) help others based on internalized principles of mutual social exchange. Finally, in stage six (altruistic behavior), a mature form of altruism emerges in which helping behavior is based on the desire to benefit another person without expectations of any external reward.

Eisenberg et al. (1984) also developed a sequential model of social and moral development in which children move from a hedonistic, self-focused orientation to an internalized, altruistic orientation. Ultimately, children are able to relate to others based on internalized moral values and a sense of individual responsibility and are motivated by a genuine desire to help another person. Empirical research with children has confirmed that age is positively correlated with both the quality and the quantity of helping behavior (Bar-Tal and Raviv 1982; Green and Schneider 1974).

Krebs and Van Hesteren (1994) reviewed existing developmental theories and proposed an integrative model that emphasizes that "the primary source of altruism is cognitive structure" (148) and that altruism develops in a stage-like sequence along a continuum, "ranging from behaviors exclusively directed toward the maximum enhancement of the self to behaviors exclusively directed toward the maximum enhancement of others" (104). They also concluded that "later developing forms of altruism are more altruistic than earlier developing forms" (103) and that individuals generally become more altruistic as they mature.

Other Factors Related to the Development of Altruism

Cultural Differences

Anthropologists have found that societies vary considerably in the extent to which they promote and practice altruistic behavior based on the values, beliefs, and customs that are unique to a particular culture and religion. Margaret Mead (1937) differentiated between cultures that are competitive and those that are cooperative. In cooperative cultures, such as the Arapesh of New Guinea, social rules encourage interdependence and altruistic behavior. Similarly, the anthropologist Ruth Benedict (1970) identified "high synergy" and "low synergy" cultures. In high synergy cultures, cultural values and institutions encourage citizens to act for the benefit of others rather than at their expense. Thus, "the social institutions are set up to transcend the polarity between selfishness and unselfishness, between self-interest and altruism. . . . The society with high synergy is one in which virtue pays" (Maslow 1971: 202).

Individual Differences

Research also has been conducted to determine whether some individuals are more altruistic than others and to determine whether specific personality traits are associated with altruism. In general, individuals who demonstrate high self-esteem, self-efficacy, an internal locus of control, a low need for approval, and a high degree of moral development are more likely to engage in prosocial behavior (Aranoff and Wilson 1984; Piliavin et al. 1981; Rushton 1981; Staub 1979). Altruistic individuals demonstrate a stronger "prosocial orientation" than others (Staub 1979), as measured by higher scores on the Social Responsibility Scale (Berkowitz and Lutterman 1968) and the Ascription of Responsibility Scale (Schwartz 1968).

Oliner and Oliner (1988) and Rushton (1981) both conducted research to determine whether an altruistic personality type exists. Rushton argued that the foundation for the altruistic personality is to be found in the individual's capacity for empathy and his/her internalized norms of social responsibility, equity, and reciprocity. He also found that personal efficacy, self-esteem, and dispositional empathy (the ability to take another's perspective) were associated with altruism and prosocial behavior.

Oliner and Oliner conducted interviews with 231 individuals who rescued Jews during World War II and compared them with 126 nonrescuers. They determined that rescuers shared certain personal qualities related to "extensivity" — i.e., involvement with and commitment to others, empathy, and caring combined with a strong sense of social responsibility, justice, and equality. In comparison, nonrescuers held a more "constrictive" worldview — i.e., "more centered on themselves and their own needs . . . less conscious of others and less concerned with them" (186).

Situational and Social Factors

Situational and social factors can also influence an individual's decision about whether to help another in distress. Research on situational factors was catalyzed by the stabbing of a young woman, Kitty Genovese, in 1964. Although 38 persons witnessed the event, no one intervened to help her, not even by calling the police. Following the Kitty Genovese murder, Latane and Darley (1968) conducted extensive research to determine why bystanders sometimes fail to intervene in emergencies. They found that the failure to help others in emergencies was based not on a lack of empathy or altruism but rather on social and situational factors such as group size and social influence. The larger the group, the less likely it is that a witness will intervene, because the presence of others available to help leads to a diffusion of individual responsibility. Furthermore, the tendency to be influenced by the responses of others (e.g., inactivity) may lead to a wait-and-see attitude and also inhibit helping. Bystanders may also decide not to intervene if they decide that the personal cost of responding is too high (Piliavin and Piliavin 1972).

Bystanders are more likely to help victims if the bystanders determine that the victims do not have control over the circumstances causing the distress. However, if bystanders believe that the victims have some control over their problem (they are perceived as somehow causing their own problem or failing to help themselves), bystanders are less likely to lend assistance (Ickes and Kidd 1976).

Practices Correlated With the Development of Altruism and Prosocial Behavior

Research has identified certain practices that are correlated with promoting the development of altruism. Four social processes are associated with creating caring relationships:

> (1) bonding: *forming positive connections and a sense of communion with others;* (2) empathizing: *understanding others' feelings and emotions, sometimes even feeling what they feel;* (3) learning caring norms: *acquiring rules and values; and* (4) practicing care and assuming personal responsibility: *participating in activities and developing a sense of personal obligation for doing so. (Oliner and Oliner 1995: 6-7)*

Parents, care givers, and teachers all have a critical role to play in helping children form bonds, learn empathy, and establish caring norms and values and in promoting prosocial behavior toward others. An emotionally secure, nurturing relationship between parents and children provides the foundation for empathy and altruism to develop (Staub 1971a). Poor parent-child relationships and lack of appropriate training and modeling from parents, care givers, and teachers can have a negative impact on the development of empathy, altruism, and prosocial behavior.

Specific child-rearing techniques, including modeling, experiential learning, role taking, induction, attributions, and reinforcement, can promote and enhance the development of altruism and prosocial behavior. Modeling, which allows children to observe prosocial behavior, is especially effective when combined with direct training on how to be helpful through role playing (Rushton 1981). There is also evidence that children can learn to increase prosocial behavior by watching television shows that model cooperation, helping, and generosity (Collins and Getz 1976; Friedrich-Cofer et al. 1979).

Staub (1971a, 1971b, 1979) determined that children learn how to behave in a prosocial manner through hands-on participation (experiential learning) and that schools can play an important role in promoting the development of empathy and prosocial behavior by providing opportunities for such experiential learning. Staub found that when children participated in helping others in an experimental setting, they continued to demonstrate increases in that behavior at a later point in time (1979). Other factors, such as whether the child is reinforced for the behavior, are also important in determining subsequent behavior.

Induction, explaining to a child how both caring and noncaring behavior affects others, is another effective method for teaching empathy (Staub 1971b; Bar-Tal and Raviv 1982). Children also learn to be empathetic through role taking, imagining events from another's perspective.

Attribution, labeling a child's helping behavior as "caring" or "unselfish," also has been associated with increases in prosocial behavior (Grusec et al. 1978; Staub 1979). Presumably, children who are told that they are caring and helpful will begin to see themselves that way and behave accordingly. However, several studies have indicated that attributions may be effective for children older than age 7 but not younger children (Grusec and Redler 1980; Livesley and Bromley 1973; Peevers and Secord 1973) due to differences in cognitive maturity.

When children demonstrate empathy and behave in a prosocial manner, it is important for adults to provide *reinforcement* for the desired behavior. Rewards may be in the form of verbal praise, nonverbal approval (smiling, hugs), or tangible objects (Bar-Tal and Raviv 1982). Reinforcement and rewards may be equally important for older, college-age students as well. Fitch (1987) found that college students performed community service based on both egoistic and altruistic motivations.

The Benefits of Helping

Altruism involves acting to increase the welfare of others (Batson 1994). However, increasingly, the helping relationship is being regarded as reciprocal rather than "unidirectional" (Midlarsky 1991: 249). In a reciprocal relationship, the individual giving help may benefit as much as the person receiving help. Midlarsky has defined helping as a form of coping behavior that can result in positive outcomes for the helper. She argues that the motivation to help others leads to helping behavior, which in turn leads to a sense of well-being for the helper, and that the relationship between helping and well-being is "mutually reinforcing" (249). The positive outcomes of helping may include providing a distraction from one's own troubles, an enhanced personal sense of meaning and value, increased feelings of mastery and competence, improved self-esteem, better social integration and an increased sense of community, and a more positive mood and sense of well-being (240).

Research on the relationship between personal mood and helping behavior supports Midlarsky's theory. According to the "negative state relief model" (Cialdini, Darby, and Vincent 1973), individuals may be motivated to help others in order to relieve their own distress or negative mood. Positive mood has been correlated with consistent increases in empathy and prosocial behavior (Clark and Teasdale 1985; Kidd and Berkowitz 1976; Rosenhan, Underwood, and Moore 1974).

Another study confirmed that volunteers benefit from helping others. Participants in a recent study of more than 1,700 volunteers reported that they experienced positive physical and emotional changes (i.e., a kind of "helper's high"), including an overall sense of well-being and calmness, increased energy and strength, greater self-worth, and decreased aches and pains (Luks 1988: 42). This study suggests that helping others may be an effective means of decreasing stress and improving overall health and well-being.

Implications for Service-Learning

Psychological research on altruism and prosocial behavior can be used to validate and enhance service-learning programs. Research has confirmed that altruism is primarily a learned behavior and that learning may occur in a variety of ways. This means that to a large extent altruism can be taught, and it underscores the important role that teachers and educational institutions can play in helping young people develop their capacity for caring and altruism. Research also has validated that experiential learning is an effective method for promoting the development of prosocial behavior.

Teachers can apply the information about effective methods for promoting the development of empathy, altruism, and prosocial behavior in the classroom. For instance, they can incorporate the four processes (bonding, empathizing, establishing caring norms, and practicing care) that have been identified as the basis for caring relationships (Oliner and Oliner 1995) into the classroom. They can facilitate the process of bonding by establishing caring relationships with their students and by encouraging students to make positive connections with each other. The caring teacher communicates respect and interest, and takes the time to listen, assist, and interact with students.

There are several effective techniques for promoting the development of empathy. As discussed earlier, mature empathy occurs when individuals are able to distinguish others as separate from themselves (Hoffman 1981). Therefore, self-awareness and self-knowledge are important prerequisites for the development of mature empathy. Individuals who know themselves are less likely to confuse their own needs with the needs of others and are more capable of forming caring relationships with others (Oliner and Oliner 1995). It is important for teachers to set aside sufficient time and develop structured exercises that encourage students to identify and articulate who they are and what they think and feel. Reflection is critical because "the service experience alone does not insure that either significant learning or effective experience will occur" (Honnet and Poulsen 1989: 3).

For instance, before students select a site for their service, they should be encouraged to reflect and write about themselves. Some suggested reflection questions follow: Why are they interested in helping? What experiences or people or values have been influential in the development of their interest in helping? What interests and skills can they bring to community service? What kind of work do they feel they would be best suited for and why? What apprehensions do they have about helping others? What positive benefits do they expect to gain?

During the service experience, teachers should encourage students to continue the process of self-awareness and reflection by asking them to keep a journal and to verbally share their experiences with other students in the class. At the end of their service experience, it is valuable to ask students to reflect and write about what they learned about themselves and about the process of helping others, as well as about any future plans for service.

Because "practicing care requires social competence" (Oliner and Oliner 1995: 80), service-learning programs may also wish to prepare students for helping by including basic training in communication skills, especially listening and conflict-resolution skills. Listening is essential because

> The more deeply we listen, the more we attune ourselves to the roots of suffering and the means to help alleviate it. It is through listening that wisdom, skill, and opportunity find form in an act that truly helps. But more than all these, the very act of listening can dissolve distance between us and others as well. (Dass and Gorman 1985: 112)

Teachers also may incorporate role playing into the curriculum to teach students how to take another's perspective. Both students and teachers can develop scenarios and may choose to use costumes or props to enhance realism. Other techniques that can be used to teach and encourage the development of altruism include induction (i.e., facilitating discussions about how caring and noncaring behavior affects others) and attribution (i.e., recognizing and verbally labeling a student's prosocial behavior).

Teachers are also instrumental in helping students establish caring norms through values clarification exercises and discussions of moral dilemmas. Discussions also could explore cultural values, norms, and social influences that either encourage or discourage students from helping others.

Modeling (i.e., having students observe others engaged in helping) is another effective means of preparing students for service. Ideally, service-learning programs should identify students, faculty, and administrators to serve as role models and to talk with students about the importance of service and their own experiences with helping. Establishing a peer mentor program also may provide opportunities for new students to shadow and observe those who are already engaged in a service project.

As noted earlier, reinforcement is important in encouraging and maintaining altruistic behavior. Because individuals will respond to different kinds of reinforcement, different kinds of rewards should be offered and tailored to the individual. In addition to academic credit, service-learning programs need to develop a variety of methods for recognizing and rewarding students who help others. In fact, "understanding what student responds to what reward may be the key to increasing the quantity and quality of involvement in community service" (Fitch 1987: 430).

Furthermore, research on motivations for volunteering suggests that individuals serve for a variety of egoistic and altruistic reasons (Clary, Snyder, and Stukas 1998; Fitch 1987; Winniford, Carpenter, and Grider 1997). Therefore, recruiting and marketing strategies should recognize and appeal to both dimensions. Some students may be more likely to serve when publicity emphasizes the positive benefits (e.g., self-esteem, social needs, self-actualization, tangible benefits such as academic credit) they can expect to gain through service, whereas other students may respond to a more straightforward appeal to help others and contribute to the community (Winniford, Carpenter, and Grider 1997). Elsewhere in this volume, Clary, Snyder, and Stukas [see p. 35ff] suggest that not only is it more realistic to expect that individuals will serve based on mixed motives (i.e., concern for self and others) but it is preferable to establish a reciprocal relationship in which the needs of both the individual helping and the individual being helped are served. Finally, it is important to note that service-learning programs can themselves provide an opportunity to conduct research on motivation and effective reinforcement and reward strategies.

References

Aranoff, J., and J. Wilson. (1984). *Personality in the Social Process.* Hillsdale, NJ: Lawrence Erlbaum Associates.

Bar-Tal, D., and A. Raviv. (1982). "A Cognitive-Learning Model of Helping Behavior: Possible Implications and Applications." In *The Development of Prosocial Behavior,* edited by N. Eisenberg, pp. 199-217. New York: Academic Press.

Bar-Tal, D., R. Sharabany, and A. Raviv. (1981). "Cognitive Basis for the Development of Altruistic Behavior." In *Cooperation and Helping Behavior: Theories and Research,* edited by V. Derlega and J. Grzelak, pp. 377-396. New York: Academic Press.

Batson, C.D. (1991a). "Empathic Joy and the Empathy-Altruism Hypothesis." *Journal of Personality and Social Psychology* 61: 413-427.

——— . (1991b). *The Altruism Question: Toward a Social-Psychological Answer.* Hillsdale, NJ: Lawrence Erlbaum Associates.

——— . (1994). "Why Act for the Public Good? Four Answers." *Personality and Social Psychology Bulletin* 20: 603-610.

Benedict, R. (1970). "Synergy: Patterns of the Good Culture." *American Anthropologist* 72: 320-333.

Berkowitz, L., and K. Lutterman. (1968). "The Traditionally Socially Responsible Personality." *Public Opinion Quarterly* 32: 169-185.

Buck, R., and B. Ginsburg. (1990). "Spontaneous Communication and Altruism." In *Review of Personality and Social Psychology: Vol. 12. Prosocial Behavior,* edited by M. Clark, pp. 149-175. Newbury Park, CA: Sage.

Cialdini, R., B. Darby, and J. Vincent. (1973). "Transgression and Altruism: A Case for Hedonism." *Journal of Experimental Social Psychology* 9: 502-516.

Clark, D., and A. Teasdale. (1985). "Constraints on the Effects of Mood on Memory." *Journal of Personality and Social Psychology* 48: 1595-1608.

Clary, E.G., M. Snyder, and A. Stukas. (1998). "Service-Learning and Psychology: Lessons From the Psychology of Volunteers' Motivations." In *With Service in Mind: Concepts and Models for Service-Learning in Psychology,* edited by R.G. Bringle and D.K. Duffy, pp. 35-50. AAHE's Series on Service-Learning in the Disciplines. Washington, DC: American Association for Higher Education.

Cohen, D. (1977). *Psychologists on Psychology: Modern Innovators Talk About Their Work.* New York: Taplinger.

Collins, W., and S. Getz. (1976). "Children's Social Responses Following Modeled Reactions to Provocation: Prosocial Effects of a Television Drama." *Journal of Personality* 44: 488-500.

Dass, R., and P. Gorman. (1985). *How Can I Help? Stories and Reflections on Service.* New York: Alfred A. Knopf.

Eisenberg, N., J. Pasternack, E. Cameron, and K. Tyron. (1984). "The Relations of Quantity and Mode of Prosocial Behavior to Moral Cognitions and Social Style." *Child Development* 55: 1479-1485.

Fitch, R.T. (1987). "Characteristics and Motivations of College Students Volunteering for Community Service." *Journal of College Student Personnel* 28: 424-431.

Friedrich-Cofer, L., A. Huston-Stein, D. Kipnis, E. Susman, and A. Clewett. (1979). "Environmental Enhancement of Prosocial Television Content: Effects on Interpersonal Behavior, Imaginative Play, and Self-Regulation in a Natural Setting." *Developmental Psychology* 15: 636-647.

Freud, S. (1994). *Civilization and Its Discontents*. 1930. Reprint, New York: Dover.

Green, F., and F. Schneider. (1974). "Age Differences in the Behavior of Boys on Three Measures of Altruism." *Child Development* 45: 248-251.

Grusec, J., L. Kuczynski, J. Rushton, and Z. Simutis. (1978). "Modeling, Direct Instruction, and Attributions: Effect on Altruism." *Developmental Psychology* 14: 51-57.

Grusec, J., and E. Redler. (1980). "Attribution, Reinforcement, and Altruism." *Developmental Psychology* 16: 525-534.

Hamilton, W. (1975). "Innate Social Aptitudes in Man: An Approach From Evolutionary Genetics. In *Biosocial Anthropology*, edited by R. Fox, pp. 238-264. London: Malaby Press.

Hill, J. (1984). "Human Altruism and Socialcultural Fitness." *Journal of Social Biological Structure* 7: 17-35.

Hoffman, M. (1981). "The Development of Empathy." In *Altruism and Helping Behavior: Social, Personality and Developmental Perspectives*, edited by J.P. Rushton and R.M. Sorrentino, pp. 41-63. Hillsdale, NJ: Lawrence Erlbaum Associates.

Honnet, E., and S. Poulsen, eds. (1989). "Principles of Good Practice in Combining Service and Learning." *Wingspread Special Report*. Racine, WI: The Johnson Foundation.

Hume, D. (1900). *Essays Literary, Moral and Political*. 1740. Reprint, London and New York: George Routledge & Sons.

Ickes, W., and R. Kidd. (1976). "An Attributional Analysis of Helping Behavior." In *New Directions in Attribution Research: Vol. 1*, edited by J. Harvey, W. Ickes, and R. Kidd, pp. 311-334. Hillsdale, NJ: Lawrence Erlbaum Associates.

Kidd, R., and L. Berkowitz. (1976). "Dissonance, Self-Concept, and Helpfulness." *Journal of Personality and Social Psychology* 33: 613-622.

Kohlberg, L. (1976). "Moral Stages and Moralization: The Cognitive-Developmental Approach." In *Moral Development and Behavior: Theory, Research and Social Issues*, edited by T. Liken, pp. 31-53. New York: Holt, Rhinehart & Winston.

———. (1984). *Essays on Moral Development: Vol. 2. The Psychology of Moral Development*. San Francisco: Harper & Row.

Krebs, D., and F. Van Hesteren. (1994). "The Development of Altruism: Toward an Integrative Model." *Developmental Review* 14: 103-158.

Latane, B., and J. Darley. (1968). "Group Inhibition of Bystander Intervention in Emergencies." *Journal of Personality and Social Psychology* 10: 215-221.

Livesley, W., and D. Bromley. (1973). *Person Perception in Childhood and Adolescence*. London: Wiley.

Locke, J. (1939). "An Essay Concerning Human Understanding." In *The English Philosophers From Bacon to Mill*, edited by E. Burtt, pp. 238-402. 1690. Reprint, New York: Modern Library.

Luks, A. (1988). "Helper's High." *Psychology Today* 10: 39-42.

Maslow, A. (1970). *Motivation and Personality*. New York: Harper & Row.

———. (1971). *The Farther Reaches of Human Nature*. New York: Viking.

Machiavelli, N. (1950). *The Prince and His Discourses*. New York: Random House. (Original work published 1591)

MacLean, P. (1973). *A Triune Concept of the Brain and Behavior*. Toronto, Canada: University of Toronto Press.

Mead, M. (1937). *Cooperation and Competition Among Primitive Peoples*. Boston: Beacon.

Midlarsky, E. (1991). "Helping as Coping." In *Review of Personality and Social Psychology: Vol. 12. Prosocial Behavior*, edited by M. Clark, pp. 238-264. Newbury Park, CA: Sage.

Money, J., and A. Erhardt. (1972). *Man and Woman, Boy and Girl: The Differentiation and Dimorphism of Gender Identity From Conception to Maturity*. Baltimore: Johns Hopkins University Press.

Morgan, C. (1985). "Natural Selection for Altruism in Selected Populations." *Ethnological Sociobiology* 6: 211-218.

Oliner, S., and P. Oliner. (1988). *The Altruistic Personality: Rescuers of Jews in Nazi Europe*. New York: Free Press.

———. (1995). *Toward a Caring Society: Ideas Into Action*. Westport, CT: Praeger.

Peevers, B., and C. Secord. (1973). "Developmental Changes in Attributions of Descriptive Concepts to Persons." *Journal of Personality and Social Psychology* 27: 120-128.

Piaget. J. (1972). *The Moral Judgment of the Child*. 1932. Reprint, London: Routledge and Kegan Paul.

Piliavin, J., J. Dovidio, S. Gaertner, and R. Clark. (1981). *Emergency Intervention*. New York: Academic Press.

Piliavin, J., and I. Piliavin. (1972). "Effect of Blood on Reactions to a Victim." *Journal of Personality and Social Psychology* 23: 353-361.

Radke-Yarrow, M., C. Zahn-Waxler, and M. Chapman. (1983). "Children's Prosocial Dispositions and Behavior." In *Handbook of Child Psychology: Vol. 4. Socialization, Personality and Social Development*, edited by P. Mussen (series) and E. Hetherington (volume), pp. 469-545. New York: Wiley.

Rogers, C. (1957). "A Note on the Nature of Man." *Journal of Counseling Psychology* 4: 199-203.

Rosenhan, D., B. Underwood, and B. Moore. (1974). "Affect Moderates Self-Gratification and Altruism." *Journal of Personality and Social Psychology* 30: 546-552.

Rushton, J. (1981). "Television as a Socializer." In *Altruism and Helping Behavior: Social, Personality and Developmental Perspectives,* edited by J. Rushton and R.M. Sorrentino, pp. 91-107. Hillsdale, NJ: Lawrence Erlbaum Associates.

Rushton, R., D. Fulker, M. Neale, D. Nias, and H. Eysenck. (1986). "Altruism and Aggression: The Heritability of Individual Differences." *Journal of Personality and Social Psychology* 50: 1192-1198.

Salk, J. (November 4, 1984). "Courage, Love, Forgiveness." *Parade Magazine,* 9-10.

Schwartz, S. (1968). "Words, Deeds, and the Perception of Consequences and Responsibility in Action Situations." *Journal of Personality and Social Psychology* 10: 232-242.

Staub, E. (1971a). "A Child in Distress: The Influence of Nurturance and Modeling on Children's Attempts to Help." *Developmental Psychology* 5: 124-132.

———. (1971b). "The Use of Role Playing and Induction in Children's Learning of Helping and Sharing Behavior." *Child Development* 42: 805-817.

———. (1979). "Positive Social Behavior and Morality." In *Positive Social Behavior and Morality: Socialization and Development.* Vol. 2. New York: Academic Press.

Trivers, R. (1971). "The Evolution of Reciprocal Altruism." *Quarterly Review of Biology* 46: 35-57.

Winniford, J., D.S. Carpenter, and C. Grider. (1997). "Motivations of College Student Volunteers: A Review." *NASPA Journal* 34: 134-146.

Wynne-Edwards, V. (1962). *Animal Dispersion in Relation to Social Behavior.* Edinburgh: Oliver & Boyd.

Service-Learning and Psychology: Lessons From the Psychology of Volunteers' Motivations

by E. Gil Clary, Mark Snyder, and Arthur Stukas

A critical task facing all societies is the transmission of important values, goals, and attitudes to successive generations. These values, goals, and attitudes are often regarded as essential to the group, providing order within the group and ensuring its long-term survival. Attitudes and values of a prosocial nature may be particularly valuable in achieving these ends. Prosocial attitudes and values underlie actions such as contributing to the betterment of the community and providing assistance to the less fortunate members of a society; such attitudes and values also promote inclinations toward humanitarian concern, community service, altruism, charitable giving, and voluntarism.

Societies, then, are faced with the task of promoting prosocial attitudes, values, and behaviors among their members, and developing these attitudes, values, and behaviors among successive generations. To ensure transmission, however, it is clear that the task is not simply to induce *compliance* by establishing mechanisms such as rewards for conformity and punishments for nonconformity, because such compliance leads people to adhere to standards only when under surveillance. Nor would it be sufficient to induce *identification*, by convincing individuals to act appropriately in order to have satisfying relationships with another person or group of people that is liked or respected. Instead, the best strategy for society's goal of value transmission may be to induce the *internalization* of prosocial attitudes and values. In other words, societies need individual members to adopt these socially important values, goals, and attitudes as their own, with the result that individuals will act in accord with these standards even in the absence of explicit rewards, punishments, or desirable relationships (for further discussion of compliance, identification, and internalization, see Kelman 1958).

Correspondence concerning this essay should be addressed to E. Gil Clary, Department of Psychology, College of St. Catherine, St. Paul, MN 55105; or Mark Snyder, Department of Psychology, University of Minnesota, Minneapolis, MN 55455. Our research has been supported by grants from the Gannett Foundation and the Aspen Institute's Nonprofit Sector Research Fund to E. Gil Clary and Mark Snyder, and grants from the National Science Foundation and the National Institute of Mental Health to Mark Snyder.

The internalization of socially important attitudes and values is especially critical to the socialization of young people. Educational settings are often one venue for the introduction and advancement of society's central attitudes, values, and behaviors (for example, lessons in civic responsibility are common). Service-learning programs have been specifically designed to promote prosocial values and attitudes in an educational context (among other goals). In service-learning, students perform service to and in the community and do so within the context of an academic course. From the standpoint of "learning" in service-learning, the experiences of students participating in service-learning programs emphasize the educational importance of combining action with reflection: Students are asked both to engage in prosocial behaviors and to deliberate the merit and implications of those actions for themselves and for society as a whole. With respect to the "service" in service-learning, such programs stress that service to the community is not performed as charity but, rather, conducted in a spirit of reciprocity — students and service recipients both give and receive (Keith 1994; Kendall 1991).

With this description as a backdrop, it should be clear that service-learning activities have much in common with the phenomenon of voluntarism, in which individuals offer assistance to others on an unpaid basis. An understanding of voluntarism, then, promises to shed some light on the processes involved in service-learning experiences, some of the positive outcomes that may result, and some of the difficulties that may arise. In this chapter, we will discuss our program of research on voluntarism, focusing on the motivational dynamics underlying participation in volunteer service, and we will consider some of the implications of our research for service-learning experiences and programs.

Our examination of these issues is guided by two overall considerations drawn from our framework for understanding the motivations of volunteers. First, we will argue that it is critical that prosocial values and attitudes, which tend to emphasize the concerns and needs of others, are also linked to people's own self-interests and individual concerns. Our conceptualization of volunteers' motivation, thus, is compatible with, and indeed fleshes out, the service-learning notion that community service is a reciprocal arrangement that is beneficial for both the helper and recipient. Second, we will assert that prosocial values are most effectively established at the "back-end" (i.e., following action) rather than at the "front-end" (i.e., prior to action) of the transmission process; this is in keeping with the service-learning principle of action-reflection. Thus, our perspective should be directly applicable to classroom settings as it offers a conceptual map for students to reflect on and understand their own motivations and behaviors relevant to community service.

Motivations Underlying Community Service

Before considering questions about the development of prosocial values, attitudes, and actions, we turn first to the issue of the form that these values should take. Should society instill a principled approach to prosocial action or a more pragmatic one? In other words, should those engaged in the socialization of others stress that prosocial behavior that conforms to society's desires is wholly motivated by the goal of assisting others? Or should they emphasize that performing the prosocial behavior is most important and that the motivations underlying the behavior are merely secondary? In a nutshell, should a society such as our own strive to instill "pure altruism" in its young people or not? Within psychology, this question is part of the egoism versus altruism debate, an argument that centers on whether caring for, and helpfulness toward, others is based on a *selfless desire to assist others* or a *selfish desire to help oneself via assisting others* (Kohn 1990). For our purposes, there are two fundamental issues that deserve critical examination: (1) identifying the motivations that actually do underlie prosocial values and attitudes, and determining whether these ever take the form of pure altruism (assisting others out of concern for others and without regard for the self); and (2) determining whether pure altruism is a worthwhile goal for a society to pursue.

Does Pure Altruism Exist?

In the psychological literature on helping (see Batson 1987) and in the literature on volunteers' motivations (see Van Til 1988), the debate over the selflessness versus selfishness of a help giver's motives has been a hotly contested one. In these literatures, one can find theorists arguing for one extreme or the other; that is, either for the position that for some people and in some conditions help is altruistically motivated, or for the position that for all people regardless of circumstances help is egoistically motivated. Our reading of the literatures, as well as our own research, suggests an intermediate position that integrates features of both of these claims; we hold that people are motivated both by concern for others and by concern for the self.

According to our "functional" approach to volunteers' motivations (Clary and Snyder 1991, 1993; Clary, Snyder, and Ridge 1992), prosocial attitudes and actions can serve six psychological and social motivations or functions. Through participation, a volunteer may seek to satisfy an *understanding function* (to learn, to gain a greater understanding of people, to practice skills and abilities), a *career function* (to enhance one's job and career prospects, to gain experience and contacts), a *values function* (to act on important values such as humanitarian values, altruistic concerns, or desires to contribute to society), a *social function* (to fit into important reference groups, to gain social approval/avoid social disapproval), a *protective function* (to reduce feelings of guilt, to resolve or escape from one's own personal problems), and/or an *enhancement function* (to enhance self-worth, self-confidence, and expand one's social network). Moreover, the functional approach is multi-motivational, in that an individual volunteer can seek to satisfy more than one function, and that in any given group different volunteers may be motivated by different sets of functions.

Given this multimotivational conceptualization, pure altruism is unlikely in that people can and do combine the values function (the most altruistic-like function) with other functions (which tend to involve concerns important to the self; see results reported by Clary, Snyder, and Stukas 1996). In addition, even the values function itself seems to incorporate other-concern and self-concern elements. That is, the values function includes both holding values related to caring and concern for others and the need to express and affirm the self as the kind of person who holds such values. Furthermore, those functions that appear to center on benefits to the self may also contain elements of concern for others. As an illustration, those motivated to volunteer by the social function may do so not only to fit into important reference groups but also out of a genuine respect for friends or family members with prosocial leanings.

Is there, however, empirical support for the proposition that prosocial activists actually possess both self- and other-oriented motivations? To address this question, and other questions about the motivations of people involved in community service activities, we have developed an inventory to measure volunteers' motivations. The Volunteer Functions Inventory, or VFI, consists of 30 motivations for volunteering, with each of the six functions identified above assessed by five items. In our research, we have found considerable evidence for the reliability and validity of the VFI: The scales of the VFI are internally consistent and temporally stable; factor analyses of responses to the VFI produced the predicted six factor solutions, with items loading on appropriate scales; examination of the VFI in a persuasion context indicated that the scales of the VFI possess predictive validity; discriminant validity was demonstrated by comparing the scales of the VFI against conceptually similar measures; and, in an actual volunteering context, satisfaction with the volunteer experience was associated with volunteers receiving feedback indicating that their own important motivational needs and goals (as measured by the VFI) were being met (Clary, Snyder, Ridge, Copeland et al. in press).

Based on our research with the VFI, the values function emerges as the most strongly endorsed motivation of volunteers, followed by the enhancement and understanding functions. In other words, our research with the VFI indicates the presence of both concern for the other and concern for the self in the motivations of volunteers. The research of other investigators has produced consistent results, although using different conceptualizations, different measures, and different items. Anderson and Moore's (1978) survey of volunteers' motivations found respondents reporting both self- and other-oriented motivations; Pearce (1983) observed that volunteer employees, relative to paid employees, possessed greater levels of both service and social motivations; and Callero, Howard, and Piliavin (1987) found that for some veteran blood donors, the altruistic role of blood donor merged with the self (i.e., the values of helping others and the need to identify oneself as one who expresses those values). Thus, it appears that the motivations of individual volunteers do combine other-oriented motivations with self-oriented motivations. Add to this the strong contention that individual motivational components themselves incorporate both self- and other-oriented features, and it seems that "pure altruism" is an altogether unlikely phenomenon.

Is Pure Altruism a Worthwhile Goal?

These considerations suggest that, in volunteer activity, community service, and the activities that occur as part of service-learning, pure altruism may be rare (that is, it is more generally the case that people engage in these activities with a mixture of self-oriented and other-oriented motivations). Even so, the question remains of whether this form of prosocial values, goals, and attitudes is a goal that we, as a society, should strive to create. Should we, therefore, attempt to instill in our young people a motivational state where the interests of needy others take precedence over their own interests? Several considerations argue *against* this socialization goal.

A first concern arises as we reflect on the phenomenon of *burnout,* a condition sometimes found in helping professionals whereby helpers lose the ability to care about clients they once deeply cared about (Maslach 1978). According to Brickman (1987), burnout can be traced to people coming to feel that their actions are not meaningful and/or to believe that their actions cannot be effective in helping their clients. This latter aspect suggests that the "pure altruist" may be especially vulnerable, given that the task facing the helper involves a long and arduous process, with the problem often appearing to be insolvable. A mixture of self- and other-concern motives, however, may reduce the likelihood of burnout in that effectiveness can involve satisfying the client or satisfying one's own needs. That is, attempts to satisfy two (or more) motives increase the probability that at least one set of needs, at any point in time, will actually be met; one's motivational eggs, in other words, are placed in multiple baskets.

A second concern becomes evident when one takes the perspective of the recipient of help. As many have suspected, and research has confirmed, receiving help is a mixed blessing — recipients can achieve their goals with the help, but may also be left feeling somewhat helpless, relatively power-less, and generally inferior to the helper (Nadler and Fisher 1986). Even if recipients may not feel much gratitude toward helpers with ulterior (i.e., selfish) motives or whose help is not intentional, how do recipients feel about altruistic helpers? If such helpers are acting intentionally and helping out of concern for the needy other, recipients may feel indebted and may desire to repay the kindness. However, such circumstances create an inequitable relationship, and recipients may not know how to go about repaying helpers who are striving to be selfless in their helping. This kind of relationship may leave recipients with the feeling of an open-ended obliga-tion and a sense of powerlessness. From this perspective, then, the "mixed-motive" helper (one with both self-concern and other-concern motives for helping) may be preferred in that each party's benefits and costs are explic-it and the relationship can maintain a more equal footing, at least relative to that between a recipient and a purely egoistic or purely altruistic helper. Thus, the interaction between a mixed-motive helper and a recipient has considerable potential to involve a reciprocal relationship, and may there-fore take on some of the features typically found in helping among families and friends; in other words, closer and more lasting psychological connec-tions (see Hatfield and Sprecher 1983).

As a final point, let us consider the observations of Alexis de Tocqueville. In his advocacy of the doctrine of "self-interest properly understood," where individual citizens seek to combine their own interests with those of other citizens, Tocqueville speculates:

> If the doctrine of self-interest properly understood ever came to dominate all thought about morality, no doubt extraordinary virtues would be rarer. But I think that gross depravity would also be less common. Such teaching may stop some men from rising far above the common level of humanity, but many of those who fall below this standard grasp it and are restrained by it. Some individuals it lowers, but mankind it raises. (1969: 527)

Thus, to apply Tocqueville's doctrine to helping behavior, if society begins to socialize individuals to hold prosocial values and attitudes based on a mix-ture of motivations, some of which focus on themselves and some of which focus on others, then "pure altruism" will certainly become much rarer. However, those who might never have engaged in prosocial behavior, because "pure altruism" was upheld as the ideal (surely, a difficult ideal to reach given the evidence), and because they had not considered the possi-bility that they might combine their own self-interests with the interests of others, would now be enlightened. In other words, the rates of prosocial behavior should certainly go up if the doctrine of self-interest properly understood were in place, since the number of pure altruists who would be lost is far outweighed by the number of mixed-motive helpers who would be gained.

To summarize, our reading of the literature is that pure altruism, if it exists at all, is rare, and, more important, that pure altruism should not be the educational goal. Nor, we hasten to add, is the desired goal one of pure egoism (Tocqueville also wrote eloquently about the dangers of extreme individualism). Rather, we argue that the ideal for a society is one where there is a mixture of concern for self with concern for others; in the language of the functional approach, people combine the values functions with the understanding and/or enhancement functions, for example. Finally, let us note that this theme runs through discussions of service-learning, as evidenced by the emphasis on reciprocity and the goal that service-learning programs should stress that the student both serves and is served and the service recipient, in turn, is being served while serving (Keith 1994).

To return to our earlier discussion of burnout, we noted that this condition can be traced to caring people coming to believe that their helping behaviors are no longer effective. As mentioned earlier, a possible solution is helping helpers to see that multiple goals (both self-interested and other-interested) are being met by their prosocial action and that focusing on a different goal may help to stem any disillusionment they might feel about their effectiveness. But also recall that burnout has been tied to people coming to feel that their actions are not meaningful. We submit that values such as humanitarian concern, community service, and helping the less fortunate provide an important framework of meaning within which one's helpful actions are embedded (see also Jeavons 1993). Thus, just as the "pure altruist" may be susceptible to burnout, so, too, may be the "pure egoist." Having self-interested motivations alone is not the answer; instead, motivations of self-concern and other-concern each contributes its own advantages and serves to protect against the disadvantages of the other.

The Transmission of Prosocial Values and Attitudes

As we have argued above, prosocial attitudes and values are an important part of the process leading to prosocial action. The question then arises, what is the most effective way of transmitting these prosocial attitudes and values to younger generations? Our interest here is in exploring *when* values are best brought into the educational process in an explicit way. Generally speaking, the tendency is often to begin the transmission process with a focus on values, so that one strives to instill the values and then expects value-related actions to follow. But is this approach to values transmission actually the most effective? Research from several sources suggests that the answer may be no.

In a pair of studies, Clary, Snyder, Copeland, and French (1994) created different types of print advertisements promoting involvement in volunteer work. The advertisements took one of four approaches: (1) emphasized abstract reasons for volunteering (e.g., "people have a duty to help those in need, it's the humanitarian thing to do"), (2) emphasized concrete reasons for volunteering (e.g., "I could make a lot of new friends through a volunteer organization"), (3) counter-argued abstract reasons for not performing volunteer work (e.g., "volunteering is really someone else's responsibility" countered by "if everybody says that, nothing is going to get done"), or (4) counter-argued concrete reasons for not performing volunteer work (e.g., "I don't have the time" countered by "maybe I could rearrange my schedule to fit it in"). The key finding here concerns the first advertisement, the one that reminded people of their values about volunteering. In two separate studies, one using a sample composed largely of nonvolunteers and the other a sample recruited from an organization already using volunteers, that advertisement emphasizing values was judged to be the least effective; this held whether we asked for overall evaluations or for a more specific judgment of the ads' effectiveness in attracting new volunteers. The only circumstance in which there was some acceptance of the values ad was when we asked the sample of volunteers about each advertisement's effectiveness in retaining current volunteers: Here, the values advertisement was judged comparable to advertisements two and four, although one, two, and four all received lower ratings than advertisement three. Thus, these findings suggest that values such as humanitarian concern may play a less important role in the early stages of the volunteer process (i.e., recruitment) than in the later stages (i.e., retention).

A similar interpretation comes from Independent Sector's (1992) survey of Americans' patterns of giving and volunteering, in which a representative sample of American adults were queried about many aspects of their involvement in the nonprofit sector. Our analyzes of these responses, which included representative items from the VFI, revealed a tendency for nonvolunteers' motivations to cluster together and volunteers' motivations to spread out (Clary, Snyder, and Stukas 1996). That is, when reporting on the importance of the six motivations assessed by the VFI, the range of importance given to the motivations was greater for respondents reporting volunteer experience in the previous year, even though both groups reported that the values function was most important. This finding suggests that the process of volunteer action leads to a strong and clear values component, one that is distinct from other motivations for performing volunteer work. That is not to say that originally one's motivations are an amorphous mass, but rather that action serves to clarify and solidify the various psychological functions for performing volunteer work. We should note, however, that this hypothesis awaits further empirical confirmation, which can best come from an investigation in which a group of (previous) nonvolunteers are followed through the volunteer process to determine whether their values do indeed become more distinct through action.

Although these studies clearly speak to values related to voluntarism, community service, and service-learning activities, research from several other domains also argues for allowing attitudes and values to emerge from action. Much of this work comes from the social psychological literature concerning the conditions under which people are most likely to act on their attitudes. One line of research reports that people whose attitudes and values are formed on the basis of direct experience with the attitude/value domain are more likely to engage in behaviors consistent with the attitudes than those whose attitudes and values are traced to indirect experience, such as messages from others (Fazio and Zanna 1981). In addition, research on self-perception processes has also shown that people engaged in a particular type of action will come to see themselves as that type of person; for example, people induced to act helpfully come to see themselves as helpful people (e.g., Bem 1972; DeJong 1979). Thus, such research suggests that attitudes and values that come from action will be more likely to guide future action.

In sum, our research on voluntarism, as well as research on the relations between attitudes and actions, argues that prosocial attitudes and values are a critically important part of the creation of a prosocial society, but it may be more effective to include values later rather than earlier in the values transmission process. We believe that values transmission might be more fruitfully viewed as a *two-stage* process. In the first stage, involvement in volunteer work and community service is promoted by linking this action to the satisfaction of the individual's psychological functions and motivations. The second stage, however, is devoted to framing one's actions, which are now current actions, in the context of a broader, more abstract values system. This two-stage process, then, has much in common with the action-reflection model found in the service-learning literature: Students are encouraged to perceive their actions (in this case, service to individuals and the community) as a reflection of the kind of people they are (that is, as activists working for the "common good").

Creating a Prosocial and Activist Generation

Up to this point, our argument has been that the desired outcome of the internalization process is an individual whose prosocial attitudes, values, and behaviors are based on a mixture of concern for self and concern for others. Furthermore, we have argued that this outcome can most effectively be achieved if the process begins with promoting actions via appeals to self-interest, and then later embedding the actions within a framework of values. In this section, we wish to look more closely at the process of creating prosocial generations through the processes of socialization. An examination of these processes can inform our thinking about service-learning programs both as being mechanisms of socialization themselves and as providing opportunities for action related to already internalized values and attitudes.

From both the social psychological and developmental psychological literatures, many investigations have revealed that prosocial behaviors can be influenced by the presence of prosocial models. For example, people are more likely to donate money to sidewalk Salvation Army solicitors if they first observe a model making a donation (Bryan and Test 1972). More importantly for our purposes here, prosocial actions and values have been linked to these processes occurring within the family. And, as we see in the following discussion of three naturalistic studies, the influence of modeling helpfulness combines with a warm, nurturant relationship between model and recipient, in this case the parent and child.

In a retrospective study of participants in the civil rights movement, Rosenhan (1970) found that "fully committed" activists (who participated in the movement full-time for at least one year) reported that their parents had modeled helpfulness and established warm, nurturant relationships with them. On the other hand, the "partially committed" activists (who participated in one or two marches) reported negative relationships with parents who preached but did not practice helpfulness. These results were recently replicated in Clary and Miller's (1986) prospective study of crisis-counseling volunteers: Volunteers who reported a socialization experience of nurturant parental models of helpfulness were more likely to complete the expected length of service, while volunteers who reported an experience of more negative relationships with parents who did not model helpfulness were more likely to terminate their participation early. Finally, Oliner and Oliner's (1988) comparison of rescuers of Jews in Nazi-occupied Europe with nonrescuers also found modeling and identification processes to be important influences in the background of rescuers.

The findings of these studies are consistent with conceptual analyzes of the socialization process and with the results of many laboratory investigations. Specifically, one important way for the internalization of prosocial attitudes and values to occur is to provide children with nurturant relationships with parents and other care givers who model helpfulness. This socialization experience appears to have multiple effects, with children developing an intrinsic motivation to behave helpfully (in the language of the functional approach, the "values function"), empathic orientation to others in distress, and standards for action. Moreover, it seems highly unlikely that these parents (nurturant models) simply present a helpful episode in the same way as a television program does; rather the parents invite and expect their children to be active receivers of their message. That is, parents discuss the message with their children and most probably encourage their children to act helpfully. In fact, several of Rosenhan's fully committed activists recalled participating in helpful activities with their parents. Thus, consistent with our overall theme, the development and internalization of prosocial attitudes and values seem to be grounded in action.

Although this discussion has focused on the values transmission process when children are the target, research suggests that the same mechanism can also result in prosocial attitudes and values in adults. For example, Piliavin and her colleagues' studies of blood donors have observed two subgroups among "rookie" donors. One group of first-time donors appears to come to this activity with intrinsic motivation in hand, whereas the second group appears to be more extrinsically motivated. With repeated donations, there is a tendency for helpfulness-related values to gain in strength (the intrinsic group seems to be further along in this regard), and finally, for some donors, continued donations result in a "role-person" merger whereby the blood donor role becomes a central part of one's self (Callero, Howard, and Piliavin 1987; Piliavin, Evans, and Callero 1984).

To summarize, then, effective transmission of values, by which we mean here that prosocial attitudes and actions are internalized and provide the basis for later action, often appears to follow a course from extrinsic pressures to act helpfully (such as guidance from parents, teachers, and other adults) to intrinsic pressures to behave helpfully (see also Brickman 1987). Moreover, it seems to us that it is critical that the entire process be grounded in action. In other words, it is unlikely that simply being exhorted to feel and act in a prosocial manner will produce the desired result; rather, one must have direct behavioral experience in community service. Finally, it also appears that this goal of internalization of prosocial attitudes and values will be more likely to occur if people, and especially young people, are encouraged to explicitly link these actions to a values framework (i.e., they come to perceive community activism as an integral part of their selves).

Implications for Service-Learning Programs

In considering the process by which successive generations internalize values related to providing service to the community, two major points deserve emphasis. First, we have argued that these values and standards should combine concerns about the interests of other people with concerns about one's own interests; the mixture of self-interest and other-interest seems to be both more realistic and more effective than the alternatives of pure altruism and pure egoism. Second, we have proposed that the internalization of this state within individuals may best be accomplished by first encouraging prosocial action and then embedding the action within a framework of prosocial attitudes and values. These themes have clear implications for service-learning programs. We will consider two issues here: The first centers on the mandatory nature of many service-learning activities; the second involves the question of what is the most appropriate and effective relationship between helpers and recipients.

Mandatory Community Service

In discussions of service-learning programs and activities, it is important to consider that students are often *required* to offer service to the community. The question then arises as to the effects of this requirement, and in the context of our previous discussions, the question concerns the effect that mandatory service has on the internalization of community service values and attitudes. Although requiring students to participate in service activities may have some merit, we do have some concerns, based on our reading of relevant psychological theory and research, about this approach. Our first concern centers on those young people who have, through their socialization experiences, internalized prosocial attitudes and values. Research from several different domains has found an *undermining effect*: If someone with an intrinsic desire to perform some action has that action placed under external control, then the result is often a decrease in intrinsic interest (e.g., Thomas, Batson, and Coke 1981). To illustrate, people who are motivated by their values to help others may well become less motivated if they are exposed to external pressures to behave helpfully; in other words, they become convinced that their helpful behavior no longer comes from within but from without, and thus are less willing to help in the absence of external pressures.

And what about those who have not internalized prosocial attitudes and values? Although a mandatory program is quite likely to provoke action among those who would otherwise not act, it is doubtful that the action alone would necessarily result in internalized prosocial values. As we noted earlier, young people would probably benefit from receiving assistance with the task of framing their actions within a system of prosocial values (this is not to say that people cannot do so alone, but it seems risky to leave this to chance); or perhaps to put it more succinctly, programs should couple action with reflection. To illustrate this point with the functional perspective on volunteers' motivations, service-learning helpers might be encouraged to view their work as providing the opportunity to express values that are important to their selves, as well as offering opportunities to fulfill current needs and goals.

Mandatory programs, then, present some very real concerns with respect to the goals of, first, the internalization of prosocial attitudes and values and, second, the creation of citizens who will then act on these prosocial values over the course of their lifetimes (see also Switzer et al. 1995). From our perspective, a safer course may be one that brings people into prosocial action on the basis of the motivations and the functions important to the individual. For example, the student with an already developed values function should be involved on this basis, whereas the student with a more personal focus (e.g., career concerns) should be involved on that basis. Continuing our example, over the course of participation, both students should be encouraged to link their actions to other motivations, with the values person finding ways in which other, more personal needs are met and the career person finding that this work is also connected to important values. Multiply motivated prosocial actors will be beneficial both to themselves and to society.

The Experience of Receiving Aid

As we have already seen, research that has been devoted to people's reactions to receiving help from others has found that receiving help is a mixed blessing. With respect to the benefits of helping, the assistance of others can result in recipients having needs met that might otherwise go unmet. In terms of costs, receiving help can lower recipients' self-esteem (i.e., needing others' assistance suggests that one is incapable and/or incompetent), place recipients in a position of being relatively powerless, and may even create long-term dependency and helplessness.

Research on the experiences of the target or recipient of others' assistance, then, has illuminated this important aspect of the helping process. It should be pointed out that research on recipients' reactions to aid has, by and large, focused on helping that occurs in brief helping encounters. This is not to suggest that these reactions would not also occur in the long-term helping that occurs in voluntarism, service-learning activities, and other forms of community service, but rather to note that the benefits and costs to the recipient may well be greatly increased in these settings. That is, many of the problems addressed in community service settings are long-standing problems facing the least-advantaged members of a society (e.g., the many manifestations of poverty — hunger, homelessness, illiteracy, illness). Thus, in these kinds of settings, the needs of potential recipients are greatest and more accompanied by the dangers of helplessness and dependency.

Although much remains to be learned about the experiences and reactions of people who are receiving long-term aid, in the meantime we believe that a case can be made in favor of the "mixed-motive" helper. A long-term relationship between this kind of helper and a recipient should certainly be able to provide the same level of direct assistance as would any other kind of helper and would, at the same time, reduce the likelihood of the negative effects of receiving help. It seems to us that mixed-motive helpers, and especially helpers who are explicit about their own self-interests, would be better able to establish a relationship marked by the giving and receiving of both parties. That is, the obligations would be clear, the recipient would have the opportunity to reciprocate, and the result would be a relationship in which the power would be distributed more equitably; in effect, each party is both helper and recipient. Moreover, recipients should be less likely to have their self-esteem threatened, and should even have the opportunity to have experiences that will boost self-esteem. All in all, we expect that the mixed-motive helper may be better able to establish effective helping relationships with people in need. In doing so, both helper and recipient gain, which stands in contrast to the altruistic framework whereby one party sacrifices for the benefit of the other. Moreover, the mixed-motive helper seems more likely to create a relationship in which there is a psychological connection between the two people and one marked by closeness rather than distance.

In closing, let us note that the concerns we have been discussing are precisely ones that have been recognized by those involved in service-learning activities and programs. In service-learning, there is an emphasis on *reciprocity*, and a deemphasis on *charity* (see Keith 1994; Kendall 1991). Thus, according to Kendall, "[a] good service-learning program helps participants see their questions in the larger context of issues of social justice and social policy — rather than in the context of charity" (19). Similarly, service-learning programs have focused on the principle of action-reflection, suggesting that these larger issues and values involved are introduced after the activities have begun. In this way, internalization can best be conceived and the transmission of vital prosocial values, attitudes, and behaviors to successive generations successfully accomplished.

References

Anderson, J., and L. Moore. (1978). "The Motivation to Volunteer." *Journal of Voluntary Action Research* 7: 51-60.

Batson, C.D. (1987). "Prosocial Motivation: Is It Ever Truly Altruistic?" In *Advances in Experimental Social Psychology, Vol. 20*, edited by L. Berkowitz, pp. 65-122. New York: Academic Press.

Bem, D. (1972). "Self-Perception Theory." In *Advances in Experimental Social Psychology*, Vol. 6, edited by L. Berkowitz, pp. 1-62. New York: Academic Press.

Brickman, P. (1987). *Commitment, Conflict, and Caring*. Englewood Cliffs, NJ: Prentice-Hall.

Bryan, J., and M. Test. (1972). "Models and Helping: Naturalistic Studies in Aiding Behavior." *Journal of Personality and Social Psychology* 6: 400-407.

Callero, P., J. Howard, and J. Piliavin. (1987). "Helping Behavior as Role Behavior: Disclosing Social Structure and History in the Analysis of Prosocial Action." *Social Psychology Quarterly* 50: 247-256.

Clary, E., and J. Miller. (1986). "Socialization and Situational Influences on Sustained Altruism." *Child Development* 57: 1358-1369.

Clary, E., and M. Snyder. (1991). "A Functional Analysis of Altruism and Prosocial Behavior: The Case of Volunteerism." In *Review of Personality and Social Behavior: Vol. 12. Prosocial Behavior*, edited by M. Clark, pp. 119-148. Newbury Park, CA: Sage.

————. (1993). "Persuasive Communications Strategies for Recruiting Volunteers." In *Governing, Leading, and Managing Nonprofit Organizations*, edited by D. Young, R. Hollister, and V. Hodgkinson, pp. 121-137. San Francisco: Jossey-Bass.

————, J. Copeland, and S. French. (1994). "Promoting Volunteerism With Persuasive Messages: An Empirical Examination." *Nonprofit and Voluntary Sector Quarterly* 23: 265-280.

Clary, E., M. Snyder, and R. Ridge. (1992). "Volunteers' Motivations: A Functional Strategy for the Recruitment, Placement, and Retention of Volunteers." *Nonprofit Management and Leadership* 2: 333-350.

Clary, E., M. Snyder, and A. Stukas. (1996). "Volunteers' Motivations: Findings From a National Survey." *Nonprofit and Voluntary Sector Quarterly* 25: 485-505.

Clary, E., M. Snyder, R. Ridge, J. Copeland, A. Stukas, J. Haugen, and P. Meine. (In press). "Understanding and Assessing the Motivations of Volunteers: A Functional Approach." *Journal of Personality and Social Psychology*.

DeJong, W. (1979). "An Examination of Self-Perception Mediation of the Foot-in-the-Door Effect." *Journal of Personality and Social Psychology* 37: 221-239.

Fazio, R., and M. Zanna. (1981). "Direct Experience and Attitude-Behavior Consistency." In *Advances in Experimental Social Psychology*, Vol. 14, edited by L. Berkowitz, pp. 162-202. New York: Academic Press.

Hatfield, E., and S. Sprecher. (1983). "Equity Theory and Recipient Reactions to Aid." In *New Directions in Helping*, Vol. 1, edited by J. Fisher, A. Nadler, and B. DePaulo, pp. 113-141. New York: Academic Press.

Independent Sector. (1992). *Giving and Volunteering in the United States: Findings From a National Survey, 1992*. Washington, DC: Author.

Jeavons, T. (1993). "The Role of Values: Management in Religious Organizations." In *Governing, Leading, and Managing Nonprofit Organizations*, edited by D. Young, R. Hollister, and V. Hodgkinson, pp. 52-76. San Francisco: Jossey-Bass.

Keith, N.Z. (1994). "Introduction: School-Based Community Service: Answers and Some Questions." *Journal of Adolescence* 17: 311-320.

Kelman, H. (1958). "Compliance, Identification, and Internalization: Three Processes of Attitude Change." *Journal of Conflict Resolution* 2: 51-60.

Kendall, J.C. (1991). "Combining Service and Learning: An Introduction for Cooperative Education Professionals." *Journal of Cooperative Education* 27: 9-26.

Kohn, A. (1990). *The Brighter Side of Human Nature: Altruism and Empathy in Everyday Life.* New York: Basic Books.

Maslach, C. (1978). "The Client Role in Staff Burnout." *Journal of Social Issues* 34: 111-124.

Nadler, A., and J. Fisher. (1986). "The Role of Threat to Self-Esteem and Perceived Control in Recipient Reaction to Help: Theory Development and Empirical Validation." In *Advances in Experimental Social Psychology,* Vol. 19, edited by L. Berkowitz, pp. 81-122. New York: Academic Press.

Oliner, S., and P. Oliner. (1988). *The Altruistic Personality: Rescuers of Jews in Nazi Europe.* New York: Free Press.

Pearce, J. (1983). "Job Attitude and Motivation Differences Between Volunteers and Employees From Comparable Organizations." *Journal of Applied Psychology* 68: 646-652.

Piliavin, J., J. Evans, and P. Callero. (1984). "Learning to 'Give to Unnamed Strangers': The Process of Commitment to Regular Blood Donation." In *Development and Maintenance of Prosocial Behavior: International Perspectives on Positive Morality,* edited by E. Staub, D. Bar-Tal, J. Karylowski, and J. Reykowski, pp. 471-492. New York: Plenum.

Rosenhan, D. (1970). "The Natural Socialization of Altruistic Autonomy." In *Altruism and Helping Behavior,* edited by J. Macauley and L. Berkowitz, pp. 251-268. New York: Academic Press.

Switzer, G., R. Simmons, M. Dew, J. Regalski, and C. Wang. (1995). "The Effect of a School-Based Helper Program on Adolescent Self-Image, Attitudes, and Behavior." *Journal of Early Adolescence* 15: 429-455.

Thomas, G., C. Batson, and J. Coke. (1981). "Do Good Samaritans Discourage Helpfulness? Self-Perceived Altruism After Exposure to Highly Helpful Others." *Journal of Personality and Social Psychology* 40: 194-200.

Tocqueville, A., de. (1969). *Democracy in America,* Vol. 2, 1840. Translated by G. Lawrence and edited by J. Mayer. New York: Doubleday, Anchor Books.

Van Til, J. (1988). *Mapping the Third Sector: Voluntarism in a Changing Social Economy.* New York, Foundation Center.

Attributions About Misery:
A Social Psychological Analysis

by Robert G. Bringle and Pamela M. Velo

During much of the history of civilization, explanations for an individual's or community's suffering centered on religious explanations. Sickness, famine, floods, and earthquakes were "acts of God" that represented just punishments directed toward those who sinned. Secular explanations are now offered for such plights. A psychological analysis of secular explanations for events that produce suffering and misery involves attribution theory, an established area of research within social psychology that describes and analyzes how individuals answer "why?" questions about events in their personal lives and social worlds.

The theories and research on the cognitive interpretations of social events, including events that have caused misery, provide a rich source of knowledge that can be useful to educators engaging students in helping situations. Attribution theory offers interesting commentary on those who view misery, those who attempt to intervene, those who experience misery, and those who are recipients of attempts by others to reduce their suffering.

Attribution Theory

People are compelled to engage in making attributions. Attributions include causal inferences people make in an attempt to explain the behaviors of themselves, the behavior of others, and the events that occur in the world. These attributions provide the basis for people to believe that they can explain and understand an event and the connection the event has to other events in their social world. The belief that there is a causal relationship between events is fundamental, so fundamental that it is easy to miss. Being able to posit causal relationships between events avoids confronting an "Alice in Wonderland" world in which events have no connection to one another and nothing seems to follow understandable rules. People need and want to believe that there is a relationship between how they live their lives today and what happens to them tomorrow. These causal inferences are important because they not only provide a basis for explaining, predicting, and controlling the social environment but also help people change their behavior and improve their outcomes. For instance, teaching children to explain their successes and failures as outcomes directly related to the effort expended caused them to work harder, thereby increasing their chances for future success (Dweck 1975).

Attributions are rather well established for the mundane, routine occurrences in everyday life. Deliberate, effortful attributional processes become more likely when (1) an event is out of the ordinary, (2) people are personally affected by the event, (3) the event or behavior of others is unexpected, or (4) people are unsure of the motives behind someone's behavior (Weiten 1995). Thus, students in service-learning courses who are placed in unfamiliar service settings and who are interacting with persons with unfamiliar circumstances are prone to engage in a flourish of attributional processes about the persons with whom they work, those they serve, and others (e.g., family) who are associated with those circumstances.

According to attribution theory, people engaged in the inferential process will make attributions about events and behavior that can be organized along four key dimensions: locus of causality, stability, controllability, and globality (Weiner 1979). There are also biases in the inferential process for some of these dimensions, and it is important that service-learning educators understand how these biases influence the conclusions reached by students who observe misery.

Locus of Causality

Locus of causality refers to whether the attributed cause is internal to the victim (e.g., abilities, dispositions, health, traits, feelings, preferences) or is external to the victim (e.g., financial resources, task difficulty, physical environment, luck, situational demands). However, internal and external attributions do not have equiprobablility of being used by an observer. The *fundamental attribution error* (Ross 1977) notes that observers are biased toward identifying internal or dispositional causes, rather than external reasons or situational causes. Thus, students are predisposed toward blaming the victim for his or her plight. This is not to say that internal causes will be used exclusively; they may emerge mixed with situational factors. For example, students confronted with unemployment may acknowledge how economic conditions contributed to a factory closing (an external attribution). But those students may also consider the degree to which the workers are or are not motivated to search for work (an internal attribution) as a factor in understanding their continued unemployment.

Stability

Stability refers to the perceived permanency of the inferred cause. For instance, a student's success or failure on an examination may be a result of intelligence (internal, stable), mood (internal, unstable), particular difficulty of the task (external, stable), or luck (external, unstable). Both stability and locus of causality are influenced by whether the person making the attribution is the one engaged in the behavior (the "actor") or is an observer. Termed the *actor-observer bias*, the tendency exists for actors to see the causes of their own circumstances, outcomes, or behavior as less stable and more external than do observers about the actor's circumstances. On the other hand, observers are inclined to make more stable, internal attributions about other people than do actors about themselves (Jones and Nisbett 1972). This difference represents an important effect when students are engaged in helping others. For example, it implies that the student's attributions about the causes of the victim's plight may be different from the victim's explanation. It also suggests that the student's explanation for the efficacy of the assistance may be different from the instructor's or the victim's attribution about the student's behavior and its consequences.

Controllability

Controllability refers to the degree to which an event is perceived to be malleable or changeable. Controllability may covary with the internal/external or stable/unstable dimensions or be independent of them. For instance, students may attribute poverty to lack of effort and motivation (an internal, unstable, yet controllable cause) or low intelligence (an internal, stable, yet uncontrollable cause). Furthermore, students may differ as to whether those in poverty can increase their motivation on their own (i.e., under their control) or whether intervention from others is required (i.e., under someone else's control).

The *illusion of control* refers to the tendency of people to overestimate their ability to control events in their lives and to underestimate the importance of uncontrollable factors (Langer 1975). Thus, victims may blame themselves for their misery, thinking that there must have been something that they could have done to prevent the incident. Again, this may be done against a backdrop that acknowledges the role of other causes. For example, victims of a tornado may understand the capriciousness of the weather but still believe that they could have done more to prevent the deaths of loved ones or the government could have done more to warn them.

Globality

Globality refers to how far-reaching or specific the scope of the attribution is. Failure on a job may be explained by not having a particular skill for that specific task (i.e., specific) or by general incompetence (i.e., global). For example, observers and victims may disagree on the globality of attributions made about the plight of poverty, and this dimension may covary with the other dimensions.

The Observer's Attributions About Misery

Although secular and sacred explanations for misery are both available, even when secular causes are salient there are still moral connotations. When the cause of misery is ascribed to the natural world rather than the supernatural world, and to external causes beyond a person's control (e.g., a sickness), the plight inherits morally benign connotations and is construed as being a *misfortune*. Being born with a birth defect is a misfortune. In contrast, acts or conditions that cause misery and that are attributable to controllable acts by human agents are labeled *injustices* and carry connotations of being moral and social transgressions (Shklar 1990). Civilian casualties of children during war are an injustice, particularly when they reflect free choice (i.e., under the perpetrator's control). The distinction between a misfortune and an injustice is not always readily apparent. For example, to what degree is famine a misfortune (e.g., weather) or an injustice (e.g., due to political factors, government policies, deforestation)?

As previously mentioned, the attributions by observers of misery, such as students, are biased toward blaming the victim by making internal attributions and, therefore, viewing the suffering as brought on by the victim's own volition or deficiencies. To attribute the misery to the victim's behavior is a relatively safe attribution for the observer, because it implies that the observer can avoid a similar fate. Alternatively, observers may label the victim's plight a misfortune. This tendency among observers is particularly likely when they feel that they could be held responsible for the misery. For example, governments are inclined to explain floods as acts of nature rather than as deficiencies in flood control programs. Both victims and observers like to blame others (e.g., government) and turn misfortunes into injustices. The blaming provides a causal agent and heightens the perception of control in the future (e.g., the government can do more in the future to warn, to prevent, to abate, to repair).

The interpretation of misery as an injustice, then, is most likely when the cause is attributable to external agents who have caused the suffering through acts of omission or commission. The attribution of responsibility hinges on the presumption that the external agent freely engaged in a choice of action. When the attributions are internal to those agents, stable across time, unchangeable, and global, the agents are viewed as being repugnant and morally corrupt. Such attributions are more likely to be made by the victims and interested parties than by disinterested parties and those who potentially could be blamed for the suffering.

Unfortunately, the observer's bias toward making internal attributions about victims can foster indifference to the plight of the victims. Even though observers may initially feel compassion for a victim, if in their attempt to explain the victim's situation, observers are unable to take the perspective of the victim, then they may conclude that the victim is responsible for her or his suffering. We will return to the role of empathy for the victim when examining the motives of helpers.

According to Weiner (1993), the key dimension in shaping the observer's attributions about misery is controllability. For example, reaction toward an AIDS victim is influenced by knowing whether the disease resulted from a blood transfusion or promiscuous sexual behavior. The perception of high controllability heightens attributions of responsibility, and assigning responsibility for events over which the victim is perceived to have had control (e.g., sexual choices) results in more negative affective responses toward the victim (e.g., anger, disgust), less sympathy, less helping, and increased aggression. Conversely, attributing lack of control on the part of the victim (e.g., blood transfusion) evokes attributions of misfortune and more sympathy, tolerance, acceptance, and subsequent helping.

Americans may be particularly susceptible to making attributions about misery that accentuate internality, controllability, and personal responsibility. *Individualism* is an American ideology reflected in "making it on your own" and "pulling oneself up by one's bootstraps." Such phrases reflect a tendency toward expecting others to help themselves and an intolerance for those who are capable of doing but don't. This is in contrast to members of collectivistic cultures, who emphasize interdependence and situational influences and who make more external attributions (Weisz, Rothbaum, and Blackburn 1984).

Although observers are inclined to use internal or dispositional attributions to explain the victim's suffering, being offered plausible situational factors outside the victim's control can lead observers to make external attributions and increase the likelihood of helping. For instance, classroom discussions that focus on the economic and social forces that contribute to poverty can result in students making fewer internal attributions about these victims and allow students to see external forces (e.g., political, systemic) as plausible causes for the poverty.

Positive attributions by helpers are more likely when educators are able to communicate specific causal information about the recipient that is not stigmatizing to the recipient. Referring back to attributional biases, if the helper perceives the condition as being due to an external cause outside the control of the recipient, then the helper will make a more positive, empathetic, and receptive response and will more readily offer help. For instance, Weiner (1991) found physical problems (e.g., medical, genetic) were perceived to be outside the control of the individual and prompted offers of help. However, mental problems (e.g., behavioral) were considered to be internally controlled by the recipient and they elicited less help giving. Discussions of controllability and internal/external causative factors prior to the helping situation can result in more positive attributions by the helper and an increase in future help offered.

Although making external causal attributions about victims may help convince the observer that a victim deserves help, these attributions may not be sufficient to transform an observer into a helper. What motivates the observer to help someone in need?

Motives to Help

Although there are several theoretical perspectives from which social psychologists have analyzed motives to help (Krebs and Miller 1985; Latane and Darley 1970; Rushton and Teachman 1978), the dominant positions in the discussion have focused on the degree to which motives are distilled to (1) an altruistic motive, the goal of which is the desire to alleviate the suffering of a victim, versus (2) an egoistic motive, the goal of which is the helper's self-interest and self-enhancement.

Empathy-Altruism Hypothesis

Although self-oriented, egoistic explanations for helping are pervasive, there is evidence that some helping is done for primarily altruistic reasons (Coke, Batson, and McDavis 1978; Dovidio, Schroeder, and Allen 1990; Krebs and Miller 1985). Batson defines altruism as a "motivational state with the ultimate goal of increasing another's welfare" (1991: 6). The empathy-altruism hypothesis contends that the perception of another's need may result in feelings of empathy. Batson (1991) believes that empathy is an other-oriented vicarious emotion that is different from the personal distress that is experienced by an observer whose behavior is self-oriented. Furthermore, he proposes that the more empathy an observer feels for a person in need, the more motivated the observer will be to act in an altruistic fashion to reduce the need of the victim of misery. Upon reducing the need of the victim, the helper may indeed feel rewarded in some way. However, the primary goal of the helping act is to alleviate the suffering of the other, and rewards to the self are incidental (Batson 1991; Krebs 1975; Toi and Batson 1982).

Empathetic feelings are a result of two factors: (1) the ability to take another's perspective, and (2) a perspective-taking set, that is, a set to imagine how the person in need is affected by his or her situation (Batson 1991: 84). According to Batson, perspective-taking sets may be brought about by experiences that may have occurred in the perceiver's background that are similar to the situation of the victim, close attachment to the person in need, similarity to the person in need, or formal instruction. Each of these factors presents an appropriate target for service-learning educators. For example, instruction in perspective taking and subsequent encouraging of students to take the perspective of a needy other have been found to increase the incidence of helping (Mussen and Eisenberg-Berg 1977). Educators can structure reflection activities so that students can explore their empathetic responses and some of the factors that result in empathy.

Egoism Hypothesis

Proponents of the egoism hypothesis (Cialdini, Darby, and Vincent 1973; Cialdini and Kendrick 1976) propose that helping is done with the ultimate goal of increasing one's own welfare. Motives of self-interest may include gaining a reward, avoiding punishment, or escaping the personal distress caused by perceiving another's need. Cialdini contends that witnessing another's misery causes people to respond with one of three vicarious, uncomfortable emotional responses: (1) reflexive distress, an intense aversive arousal, relieved by helping another; (2) normative distress, which occurs when we fail to uphold the social norm of helping; and (3) sadness. This final response is most similar to empathy but is a temporary, affective state that has a cost-benefit orientation wherein helping will only take place if helping is the most rewarding and least costly option. In all three cases, the primary goal is alleviating the observer's personal distress, not the victim's distress.

According to the egoism hypothesis, socialization plays a primary role in shaping observers' reactions to viewing misery, their assumptions about what is expected and appropriate, their expectations about what might be gained or lost, and, therefore, whether or not they help. Three classes of self-oriented helping motives are identified. In the first, *empathy-specific reward*, it is argued that people learn through socialization that helping can lead to praise, honor, and pride. Therefore, helping produces mood enhancement specifically related to the helping situation. Critics of the egoism hypothesis argue that if this were indeed the case, then feedback on the likelihood of success should moderate helping. That is, if there is a low likelihood of feedback on the success that the helping had in alleviating the suffering, then egoistically oriented helpers would be less likely to help than when there is a high likelihood of feedback on success. However, contrary to the egoism position, but consistent with the empathy-altruism position, high-empathetic persons helped the same regardless of the level of feedback on the likelihood of success (Batson 1991).

In the second class of motives, *empathy-specific punishment*, potential helpers learn, as a result of socialization, that not helping a victim can lead to ridicule, shame, and guilt. Thus, helping is motivated by the desire to avoid these social sanctions. Although this may occur, if it were always the case, then helping would occur only when persons anticipate a negative social consequence (e.g., shame) for not helping. In addition, however, supporters of the egoism hypothesis propose that even for those persons who are not influenced by social evaluations, self-administered punishments and negative self-evaluations can motivate them to help.

A third class of self-oriented helping is *aversive arousal reduction*, in which observers of misery experience a vicarious emotional response of personal distress, which motivates the observer to help the needy person in order to relieve the observer's empathetic or vicarious distress. Studies testing this hypothesis have altered the ease of escape from an aversive situation to determine whether help would still be forthcoming under the easy-escape conditions. The presumption is that if escape is easy and the motive is to relieve the observer's suffering, then the observer will be more likely to escape than to help (which would also reduce the observer's ill feelings, but with more effort). This effect differs from the empathy-specific punishment effect because the aversive arousal that is experienced is actually a vicarious emotional response resulting from the observer's perception of another's need, whereas in the empathy-specific punishment model, the helping is performed only because the helper *anticipates* shame, guilt, or ridicule for not helping and is motivated to avoid it. Research studies examining this effect have yielded mixed results (Batson et al. 1991; Schroeder et al. 1987).

Because egoism has been a popular theoretical perspective, researchers supporting the empathy-altruism hypothesis have had the burden of proving that not all helping is egoistic. Their research does demonstrate that altruistically motivated helping, for which self-gain is not the ultimate goal, is possible (Batson 1991). However, the research supporting the altruistic motive as being distinct from the egoistic motive does not show any of the following: (1) that helping is more often altruistic than selfish, (2) that helping is always altruistic, or (3) that altruistic helping does not have secondary egoistic gains.

Functional Approach

Although the egoism-altruism controversy continues, Clary and Snyder (1991; this volume) have developed a functional approach to motivation that integrates these two theories. Clary and Snyder (1991) suggest that although these functions (values, social-adjustive, ego-defensive, knowledge, career, enhancement) may not represent a complete array of possible functions served by volunteer helping, they encompass many of the major functions found by previous researchers. Additionally, this functional approach incorporates the altruistic/egoistic perspectives of volunteer motivation, and examines the complexity of volunteer motivation in a realistic manner by considering the multiplicity of personal and social motivations.

An understanding of volunteer motives has been found to increase the incidence of volunteering and also to sustain volunteers (Clary, Snyder, and Ridge 1992). Instructors of service-learning classes may also wish to address this set of functional motives as a way of enabling students to explore their own feelings about their motives to help. However, Batson (1991) notes that such reflection may result in a transformation of motives from altruistic, idealistic ones to more functional, pragmatic, and exchange-oriented motives. Batson et al. (1987) found that (1) simply asking people to reflect on their motives reduced the perception of altruistic motives, and (2) this reduction was greatest for those who placed a high value on honest self-knowledge.

Attributions by Recipient About Help Received

There may be instances in which aid is offered to those who do not perceive that they are in need. In addition, some may recognize a need, but not seek help because they assume that the problem may abate on its own or that they can solve the problem. Finally, there are those who seek help. Understanding how the recipient decides whether and when help is needed, and how the recipient reacts to help that is offered, are important issues in determining whether or not a positive helping experience occurs for both helper and recipient.

When potential helpers decide to become involved in helping situations, they often are perplexed by the reactions of help recipients. Helpers expect that their help will be graciously received and acknowledged. However, this may not be the case. A lack of understanding about why recipients of help sometimes react with hostility and resentment, instead of the expected warmth and gratitude, can negatively affect helpers' behavior in that situation and their future motivation and behavior in other situations. In addition, just as observers use attributions to understand misery, recipients of help use attributions to understand whether or not they need help, why they need help, and why others are offering to help.

Seeking Help

Before recipients can even react to the helping behavior, they must make a decision about whether or not the problem at hand can be alleviated by outside help, and then decide whether help should be sought. Although some conditions are universally recognized as serious enough to require outside support or assistance (e.g., serious injury), many other conditions are ambiguous, and there can be wide variability among individuals as to whether or not a problem is perceived as requiring help from others. Differences in experiences, knowledge, socioeconomic status, gender, ethnicity, and cultural and group norms all influence the decision-making process to seek help. For instance, regardless of ethnicity or social class, women seek more help than do men (McMullen and Gross 1983). Because individualistic norms of self-sufficiency and independence are traditionally masculine traits, and it has traditionally been more culturally acceptable for females to appear dependent or in need of help, it is not surprising that many females feel more comfortable in seeking and receiving help than do males.

Attributions by the Victim About the Need for Help

Once a problem has been identified and deemed serious enough to require outside help, the aid recipient needs to explain why help is needed. This is an attributional task. That is, are external forces, such as economic conditions, responsible for the present situation? Or, are internal or dispositional forces, such as incompetence or inadequacy, responsible?

A person in need is more likely to seek help if the problem or condition can be attributed to external forces (Fisher, Nadler, and Whitcher-Alagna 1982). Tessler and Schwartz (1972) found that when subjects were told that consensus was high on a problem (i.e., 90% of the other subjects also needed assistance on the task), an external attribution was made and more subjects sought help. Conversely, there are threats to the victim's self-esteem when dispositional (internal) attributions are made about the causes of the condition. When those in need of help perceive their need to be an indicator of incompetence or of their inability to be self-reliant, this threatens their self-esteem. This threat is especially salient if the inadequacy is thought to be related to characteristics of the individual that are central to the person's self-concept and identity. Self-esteem is less likely to be threatened if the recipient can be persuaded that seeking help is not an admission of failure (Tessler and Schwartz 1972).

Interestingly, it was found that recipients were more likely to seek help when it was offered than when they were required to request assistance (Gross, Wallston, and Piliavin 1979). Persons who requested help reported more anxiety and negative self-ratings than persons who were offered help. These researchers suggest that asking for help prompts an internal attribution, and this negative experience decreases help seeking, whereas the offer of help is less threatening and may result in increased acceptance of aid and more favorable impressions of the helper.

Receiving help can be perceived by recipients as being supportive: Recipients receive direct benefits as well as the care and concern of the helper and confirmation that the social environment is responsive to their needs. But helpers often do not understand that help can also be threatening to the recipient. The asymmetrical, inferior-superior nature of the relationship between helper and recipient, the heightened saliency of the recipient's inadequacy or incompetence to engage in self-help, and the recipient's embarrassment or humiliation may all assault the recipient's self-esteem. This, in turn, may cause resentment of the helper, decrease the quality of the aid, and prevent the recipient from seeking aid in the future (Nadler, Fisher, and Streufert 1976).

Thus, there are two scenarios: Receiving help can be affirming or threatening. Interestingly, each of these can have positive and negative outcomes. The affirming, rewarding, and supporting message that is carried with help can enhance the person's well-being and sense of security with the social network. On the other hand, it can create and foster dependency on others, because seeking help is found to be rewarding and leads to lower levels of subsequent self-help.

A similar pattern emerges when receiving help is perceived as threatening to an individual's sense of self-worth. Threatened individuals may find being recipients of assistance repugnant, and this can lead to increased levels of self-help (e.g., "I'm too proud to accept welfare"). However, the examples of welfare and foreign aid demonstrate that this is not always the case. Research suggests that there are circumstances under which receiving help is self-deprecating, but individuals continue to seek and accept it. Why?

Nadler and Fisher (1986) note that when self-efficacy and perceived control are high and receiving help is aversive, self-help will increase. However, when perceived self-efficacy and control are low and stable, then recipients will continue to accept help. However, under these circumstances the recipients will be predisposed to derogate the help and the helper.

The degree of threat that is implied when receiving assistance is influenced by additional factors. For example, it has been found that recipients prefer help from strangers rather than friends when the nature of the need for help reflects on issues central to their self-esteem. However, when the need is peripheral to their self-concept, they prefer help from friends rather than strangers (Nadler and Fisher 1986).

Attributions by the Victim About the Helper

Once recipients have decided to ask for or accept help, they are likely to make inferences about those who help them. The theory of *correspondent inference* (Jones and Davis 1965) suggests that the helper's intent will probably not be inferred if the helping is situationally constrained. That is, if the helping action is part of a job description (e.g., firefighter, police officer, nurse) or is a socially desirable action, the recipient will not be able to make attributions that the helper's motivations or dispositions are altruistic, empathetic, or caring. This is the case unless the helper displays extraordinary behavior "above and beyond the call of duty." If, however, recipients perceive that the help was spontaneously offered and not a result of coercion or duty, and if the helper had to make some type of inordinate effort in order to help, then the helper will be judged to be more altruistic and, thus, viewed more positively (Greenberg and Frisch 1972).

Educators need to sensitize students to the possibility that their help may not be warmly received. It may also help students to understand the dynamics of these effects. If helpers are perceived as helping of their own volition and not as a function of their role or as part of an obligation (e.g., the service-learning course is an elective), or if the helper is perceived to be demonstrating a true concern for the recipients' welfare or is incurring some type of cost as a result of helping, then the aid will be perceived as being supportive and the recipient is more likely to make positive attributions about the helper. These conditions may also bolster the recipient's self-esteem by making the recipient feel important and worthy of help.

There are other ways in which the feelings and assumptions of helpers and recipients diverge. Recipients report feeling better when they are able to express negative feelings, but helpers prefer that recipients express positive or neutral feelings because the helpers think that it will be counterproductive and depressing to focus on negative feelings (Cohn 1983). Recipients who blame themselves by making behavior-based attributions (e.g., "I shouldn't have walked down that dark alley") cope better because they believe that they can change their behavior and prevent similar situations in the future. In contrast, helpers believe that the recipients cope better if they blame others. An additional difference in helper/recipient perception is that, once engaged in receiving helping, recipients may feel that they need this help for a longer period of time than helpers believe that the victims need aid.

Reactance and Equity Theories

Although help that is offered is less threatening than help that must be requested, and voluntary, cost-incurring help is more easily accepted and appreciated, reactance theory posits that these conditions contribute to a sense of loss of freedom for the recipient of aid (Brehm 1966). Recipients need to be able to choose the conditions of help in order to minimize loss of freedom and reduce feelings of obligation. Reactance theory also suggests that when the help is voluntary and costly to the helper, it engenders an even greater feeling of obligation that is difficult to remove. Help that is conditional, that is, help that comes with "strings attached," is particularly uncomfortable for the recipient, as are types of help that are not appropriate for the circumstances (Fisher, Nadler, and Whitcher-Alagna 1983). Under obligating conditions, recipients may react by attempting to reciprocate or, if that is not possible, by derogating the aid or the helper.

Equity theory suggests yet another explanation for why recipients resist help and have unfavorable opinions of the helper and the help. Equity theorists posit that recipients are likely to feel a sense of unfulfilled obligation if they accept aid because they are receiving high benefits at low costs, whereas the helper is providing assistance at high costs but with low returns. These perceived inequities may inhibit help seeking, inhibit help acceptance, and promote dislike of helpers (Greenberg and Westcott 1983). Traditional help organizations that offer help in a charitable or altruistic manner allow the recipient little or no opportunity for reciprocity. This anticipated obligation is often enough to keep many individuals from accepting needed help. Or, it may make them resentful. In contrast, organizations that charge nominal amounts for goods or services attenuate this problem.

New Ways of Providing Aid

Structuring a positive helping situation can be a perplexing challenge for educators. The differing perceptions of and attributions by recipients necessitate thoughtful and careful planning on the part of educators to ensure that the needs of all parties are successfully met. New paradigms of helping may offer solutions to these and other helping dilemmas. Self-help groups, peer helping, and help situations that are structured to maximize recipient control are examples of providing assistance that will be acceptable alternatives to traditional helping situations.

Self-help and peer helping groups are predicated on the theory that people who have a common problem or experience will be more adept at offering insight, compassion, knowledge, and coping skills than a helper who has only learned about the problem indirectly. Medvene's (1991) definition of self-help groups includes the following elements: (1) homogeneity of members' problem type, (2) ability of members to be help seekers as well as help providers, (3) lay members or professionals as leaders working with the consent of the group, (4) voluntary member participation, and (e) little or no fee.

In these groups with experientially similar others, the helper is in a position to benefit and gain support in the helping relationship while, at the same time, providing assistance to others. This reciprocity is especially important in abating feelings of inequity. Additionally, in the structure of these groups, the recipient who has been a group member for some time becomes an adviser to newer members, and therefore, self-esteem is enhanced by the move to helper position. Help groups structured in this manner also address the dilemma raised by reactance theory, because participation in the group is by choice and the sense of freedom is not lost by the recipient. Finally, Riessman (1990) points out that in self-help groups such as Alcoholics Anonymous, or in peer tutoring situations in the schools, by converting the recipient into the helper, help resources are expanded and more people will be able to receive assistance.

Within the traditional help structure, comprehensive and complete care can be overwhelming to recipients and diminish their sense of having control over their lives, making them feel helpless. This type of help may also serve to retard the acquisition of new skills necessary for future coping, as well as contribute to feelings of inferiority and incompetence (Coates, Renzaglia, and Embree 1983). These feelings of incompetence may be further compounded by confusion about who is responsible for the helping outcomes. That is, if the outcome is positive, the recipient may attribute it to the efforts of the helper, and the recipient's feelings of inferiority will be magnified. Recipients then become more helpless, because they believe that they cannot solve their own problems.

Allowing recipients to exercise control over the type and amount of help received significantly enhances their sense of well-being. This was the case for institutionalized elderly patients who were allowed to control the duration and frequency of college student visits (Midlarsky 1991). If the recipient is encouraged to actively participate in the helping process, loss of control and subsequent helplessness are less likely to occur. Saxe and Dougherty (1983) suggest structuring the help in such a way that promotes self-help in the future.

Conclusion

An attributional analysis of helping situations provides an important tool from which educators can enhance student understanding of the complexity of cognitive interpretations associated with helping and their implications for feelings and behaviors on the part of students, agency personnel, and recipients. The attributional analysis of helping highlights several dilemmas of helping. For example: Why do people help? Why is the help not appreciated by recipients? Is it better to help, which may reduce perceived self-efficacy of the person being helped, or to encourage self-help? Why do victims acknowledge external causes to their suffering, yet still blame themselves, which seems to be counterproductive? Attribution theory provides a means through which educators can design better service-based curricula and students can gain new insights into the nature of their experiences in helping situations and an enhanced understanding of psychological factors that play a role in their reactions and the reactions of others.

References

Batson, C.D. (1991). *The Altruism Question.* Hillsdale, NJ: Lawrence Erlbaum Associates.

————— , J. Batson, J. Slingsby, K. Harrell, H. Peekna, and R. Todd. (1991). "Empathetic Joy and the Empathy-Altruism Hypothesis." *Journal of Personality and Social Psychology* 61: 413-426.

Batson, C.D., J. Fultz, P.A. Schoenrade, and A. Paduano. (1987). "Critical Self-Reflection and Self-Perceived Altruism: When Self-Reward Fails." *Journal of Personality and Social Psychology* 53: 594-602.

Brehm, J. (1966). *A Theory of Psychological Reactance.* New York: Academic Press.

Cialdini, R., K. Darby, and J. Vincent. (1973). "Transgression and Altruism: A Case for Hedonism." *Journal of Experimental Social Psychology* 9: 502-516.

Cialdini, R., and D. Kendrick. (1976). "Altruism as Hedonism: A Social Development Perspective on the Relationship of Negative Mood State and Helping." *Journal of Personality and Social Psychology* 34: 907-914.

Clary, G., and M. Snyder. (1991). "A Functional Analysis of Altruism and Prosocial Behavior." In *Review of Personality and Social Behavior: Vol 12. Prosocial Behavior,* edited by M.S. Clark, pp. 119-148. Newbury Park, CA: Sage.

————— , and R. Ridge. (1992). "Volunteer's Motivation: A Functional Strategy for the Recruitment, Placement, and Retention of Volunteers." *Non-Profit Management and Leadership* 2: 333-350.

Coates, D., G. Renzaglia, and M. Embree. (1983). "When Helping Backfires: Help and Helplessness." In *New Directions in Helping,* Vol. 1, edited by B. Depaulo, A. Nadler, and J. Fisher, pp. 253-276. New York: Academic Press.

Cohn, E. (1983). "Effects of Victims' and Helpers' Attributions for Problem and Solution on Reactions to Receiving Help." In *New Directions in Helping,* Vol. 3, edited by B. Depaulo, A. Nadler, and J. Fisher, pp. 46-68. New York: Academic Press.

Coke, J., C. Batson, and K. McDavis. (1978). "Empathetic Mediation of Helping: A Two-Stage Model." *Journal of Personality and Social Psychology* 36: 752-766.

Dovidio, J., D. Schroeder, and J. Allen. (1990). "Specificity of Empathy-Induced Helping: Evidence for Altruistic Motivation." *Journal of Personality and Social Psychology* 59: 249-260.

Dweck, D. (1975). "The Role of Attributions and Expectations in the Alleviation of Learned Helplessness." *Journal of Personality and Social Psychology* 31: 674-685.

Fisher, J., A. Nadler, and S. Whitcher-Alagna. (1982). "Recipient Reactions to Aid." *Psychological Bulletin* 91: 27-54.

————— . (1983). "Four Conceptualizations of Reactions to Aid." In *New Directions in Helping,* Vol. 1, edited by B. Depaulo, A. Nadler, and J. Fisher, pp. 51-80. New York: Academic Press.

Greenberg, M., and D. Frisch. (1972). "Effect of Intentionality on Willingness to Reciprocate a Favor." *Journal of Experimental Psychology* 8: 99-111.

Greenberg, M., and D. Westcott. (1983). "Indebtedness as a Mediator of Reactions to Aid." In *New Directions in Helping,* Vol. 1, edited by B. Depaulo, A. Nadler, and J. Fisher, pp. 86-110. New York: Academic Press.

Gross, A., B. Wallston, and I. Piliavin. (1979). "Reactance, Attribution, Equity, and the Help Recipient." *Journal of Applied Social Psychology* 9: 297-313.

Jones, E., and K.E. Davis. (1965). "From Acts to Dispositions: The Attribution Process in Person Perception." In *Advances in Experimental Social Psychology, Vol. 2,* edited by L. Berkowitz, pp. 219-266. New York: Academic Press.

Jones, E., and R. Nisbett. (1972). "The Actor and the Observer: Divergent Perceptions of the Causes of Behavior." In *Attribution, Perceiving the Causes of Behavior,* edited by E. Jones et al., pp. 79-94. Morristown, NJ: General Learning Press.

Krebs, D. (1975). "Empathy and Altruism." *Journal of Personality and Social Psychology* 32: 1134-1146.

———, and D. Miller. (1985). "Altruism and Aggression." In *Handbook of Social Psychology, Vol. 2,* edited by G. Lindzey and E. Aronson, pp. 1-71. 3rd Ed. New York: Random House.

Langer, E. (1975). "The Illusion of Control." *Journal of Personality and Social Psychology* 32: 311-328.

Latane, B., and J. Darley. (1970). *The Unresponsive Bystander: Why Doesn't He Help?* New York: Appleton-Century Crofts.

McMullen, P., and A. Gross. (1983). "Sex-Differences, Sex-Roles, and Health-Related Help-Seeking." In *New Directions in Helping, Vol. 2,* edited by B. Depaulo, A. Nadler, and J. Fisher, pp. 233-256. New York: Academic Press.

Medvene, L. (1991). "Self-Help Groups, Peer-Helping, and Social Comparison." In *Review of Personality and Social Psychology: Vol. 12. Prosocial Behavior,* edited by M.S. Clark. Newbury Park, CA: Sage.

Midlarsky, E. (1991). "Helping as Coping." In *Review of Personality and Social Psychology: Vol. 12. Prosocial Behavior,* edited by M.S. Clark, pp. 238-264. Newbury Park, CA: Sage.

Mussen, P., and N. Eisenberg-Berg. (1977). *Roots of Caring, Sharing and Helping.* San Francisco: Freeman.

Nadler, A., and J.D. Fisher. (1986). "The Role of Threat to Self-Esteem and Perceived Control in Recipient Reaction to Help: Theory Development and Empirical Validation." In *Advances in Experimental Social Psychology, Vol. 19,* edited by L. Berkowitz, pp. 81-122. New York: Academic Press.

———, and S. Streufert. (1976). "When Helping Hurts: The Effect of Donor-Recipient Similarity and Recipient Self-Esteem on Reactions to Aid." *Journal of Personality* 44: 392-409.

Riessman, F. (1990). "Restructuring Help: A Human Services Paradigm for the 1990s." *American Journal of Community Psychology* 18: 221-230.

Ross, L. (1977). "The Intuitive Psychologist and His Shortcomings: Distortions in the Attribution Process. "In *Advances in Experimental Social Psychology, Vol. 10,* edited by L. Berkowitz, pp. 174-221. New York: Academic Press.

Rushton, J., and G. Teachman. (1978). "The Effects of Positive Reinforcement, Attributions, and Punishment on Model-Induced Altruism in Children." *Personality and Social Psychology Bulletin* 4: 322-325.

Saxe, L., and D. Dougherty. (1983). "Escalators, Ladders, and Safety Nets: Experiments in Providing Aid to People in Need." In *New Directions in Helping, Vol. 3,* edited by B. Depaulo, A. Nadler, and J. Fisher, pp. 294-324. New York: Academic Press.

Schroeder, D., J. Dovidio, M. Sibicky, L. Mathews, and J. Allen. (1987). "Empathetic Concern and Helping Behavior: Egoism or Altruism?" *Journal of Experimental Social Psychology* 24: 333-353.

Shklar, J.N. (1990). *The Faces of Injustice.* New Haven, CT: Yale University Press.

Tessler, R., and S. Schwartz. (1972). "Help-Seeking, Self-Esteem, and Achievement Motivation: An Attributional Analysis." *Journal of Personality and Social Psychology* 21: 318-326.

Toi, M., and C. Batson. (1982). "More Evidence That Empathy Is a Source of Altruistic Motivation." *Journal of Personality and Social Psychology* 43: 281-292.

Weiner, B. (1979). "A Theory of Motivation for Some Classroom Experiences." *Journal of Educational Psychology* 71: 3-25.

———— . (1991). "Metaphors in Motivation and Attribution." *American Psychologist* 46: 921-930.

———— . (1993). "On Sin Versus Sickness: A Theory of Perceived Responsibility and Social Motivation." *American Psychologist* 48: 957-965.

Weiten, W. (1995). *Themes and Variations.* 3rd ed. Pacific Grove, CA: Brooks/Cole.

Weisz, J., F. Rothbaum, and T. Blackburn. (1984). "Standing Out and Standing In: The Psychology of Control in America and Japan." *American Psychologist* 39: 955-969.

Developmental Psychology and Service-Learning: A Theoretical Framework

by Jay W. Brandenberger

The rhetoric is strong: Service-learning has the potential to enhance knowledge, facilitate self-understanding, and promote active engagement with community concerns. In making such claims, those who advocate service-learning may draw upon intuition, their own learning histories, stories of individuals changed by service involvements, or democratic cultural traditions. Direct research in this arena is limited, though recent initiatives are encouraging (see Giles, Honnet, and Migliore 1991). Much of the research to date, however, is atheoretical in nature, often involving descriptive analyses of outcome measures in the attitude domain (Yates and Youniss 1996a). Less common have been attempts to examine underlying developmental processes that may frame the constraints and potentials of service-learning.

The challenge that remains, and that will be addressed in this chapter, is an overall examination of developmental theory in relation to the assumptions and conditions of service-learning. Such a theoretical analysis has the potential to contribute (1) an understanding of the developmental challenges and processes most actively engaged during service-learning experiences, and the potential impact of these for growth; (2) an awareness of interrelated developmental factors that explain how service-learning works (or does not work) in particular contexts; and (3) insights for practice and future research. The challenge is to employ and develop theory that can explain the complexity of individual development in relation to complex social concerns inherent to service-learning involvements. This review will focus on overlapping developmental domains that have the most direct relevance to service-learning, including cognitive development, psychosocial development (and identity formation), and moral development. Throughout, I will examine how individuals make meaning and develop understanding of their own ways of knowing as they encounter the challenges of youth and young adulthood. My intention is to put forth not a singular theoretical position but a map of relevant theory and resources.

From Practice to Theory and Back

Increased acceptance and support for service-learning during the current decade has brought a reciprocal call for research, usually to document expected outcomes. Practitioners convinced of the merit of service-learning are increasingly seeking means to assess participant differences or attitude change. A limited number of theoretical works, mostly from a philosophical perspective, have attempted to integrate developments in the field (see Liu 1995).

In an effort to organize and direct research activity, Giles, Honnet, and Migliore (1991) proposed an agenda that calls for examination of both institutional and individual factors, including "the relationship of service-learning activities to individual and moral development" (7). While an interdisciplinary focus with respect to such questions is important, psychology offers unique insights into developmental processes.

Many claims made with respect to service-learning are developmental in nature, and student participants served by most program initiatives (based in high schools and colleges) are facing key developmental challenges inherent to adolescence and early adulthood. This review begins in developmental theory and is framed by these questions: What do we know about human development that is applicable to service-learning? What resources are available to build a developmental theory of service-learning?

Any attempt to ground service-learning in psychological theory does well to begin with the work of John Dewey (who, in addition to his philosophical focus, taught psychology and served as president of the American Psychological Association). Dewey's focus on the relation between experience and learning and his clarity with respect to the social purposes of education provide a strong foundation for service-learning theory (see Giles and Eyler 1994). Kolb (1984) integrated Dewey's thought with that of current psychologists in his analysis of experiential learning. And Delve, Mintz, and Stewart (1990) integrate various psychological perspectives to outline a basic model of service-learning. Each of these early theorists in this arena draws from the seminal work of Jean Piaget.

Cognitive Development: Jean Piaget

Piaget's work spans decades and volumes (see Gruber and Voneche 1995). Although he may be known best for his delineation of stages of cognitive development — undergraduate psychology students can often label the stages without understanding their epistemological implications — Piaget focused his research on the overall nature of learning from a structural, genetic view. He took seriously the epistemological questions of philosophy, applying the lens of psychology to examine how humans develop in ability to know. Piaget (1970) noted that "all epistemologists refer to psychological factors in their analyses, but for the most part their references to psychology are speculative and are not based on psychological research" (7). One could make a similar critique of service-learning, that practitioners often speculate about psychological processes and growth. As we examine the potential of service-learning as alternative means of knowing, Piaget's work is highly relevant.

Piaget's conception of intelligence parallels the assumptions basic to service-learning. For him, intelligence is an *activity*, a process of learning through interaction with the environment. Learning is not a passive result of etchings on a tableau rasa that has a predetermined capacity. Learning and cognitive development result from the continual interaction of the growing individual with the environment. According to Piaget,

> The essential aspect of thought is its operative and not its figurative aspect. . . . Human knowledge is essentially active. To know is to assimilate reality into systems of transformations. To know is to transform reality in order to understand how a certain state is brought about. (1970: 15)

Thus, Piaget defines *constructivism*, that individuals must construct their own ideas and principles of reality, "must make and remake the basic concepts and logical thought forms that constitute . . . intelligence" (Gruber and Voneche 1995: xxxix). Note, too, that Piaget makes a clear distinction between discovering and inventing reality. We do not simply discover what is out there; we construct or invent our understandings in relation to preexisting cognitive structures and expectations (Gruber and Voneche 1995).

After relatively slow acceptance in the United States, where a behavioral orientation dominated, Piaget's work has influenced researchers in domains extending beyond cognitive processes of a logical, scientific nature to those that are more social. Service-learning practitioners will find the following applicable: Kegan's (1982) discussion of Piaget's theory in relation to counseling; Power, Higgins, and Kohlberg's (1989) examination of moral education; Rosenberg's analysis (1988) of political psychology from a Piagetian perspective; and a series of works by Gardner (e.g., 1991) extending Piaget's theory with respect to education, creativity, and leadership.

Two of Piaget's key concepts — interaction and construction — both support and inform service-learning practice. Through interacting with their environment, developing individuals construct meaningful understandings of self and world (one often sees such claims in service-learning materials). Yet the process is not necessarily smooth or permanent. Individuals process environmental challenges using already developed cognitive structures, at times adapting — Piaget uses the term *accommodating* — these structures for a better fit. Such cognitive change is not without pain, as when a student's understanding of human nature or political equality is challenged during a service placement. The "function of cognitive growth," suggest Gruber and Voneche (1995), "is to produce more and more powerful logical structures that permit the individual to act upon the world in more flexible and complex ways" (xxxix).

Interaction for Piaget is distinct from maturation; it is the quality of experience that determines the directions of development (Whiteley 1980). Dewey also outlined an interactionist position, claiming that the challenge of education is "devising the conditions" that through interaction with the individual's internal potentials and "preferences" will "bring about transformation in the desired direction" (in Whiteley 1980: 248). Note that the process of determining "the desired direction" raises ethical questions, as does most educational practice, including service-learning.

That individuals are actively and continually constructing meaning should be a constant refrain (or reframe) of those who advance service-learning pedagogies. Brooks and Brooks (1993), in *The Case for Constructivist Classrooms*, argue from a Piagetian perspective that learning should be "understood as a self-regulated process of resolving inner cognitive conflicts that often become apparent through concrete experience, collaborative discourse, and reflection" (vii). Service-learning extends the classroom beyond traditional walls, providing rich opportunities for such experience and dialogue. The goal is to provide a balance of challenge and support while allowing individual differences to unfold. Some students serving in a soup kitchen may find their stereotypes of poor individuals confirmed, while others may begin to construct new understandings of root causes of poverty (see Yates and Youniss 1996b, for an interesting study of service-learning in such a setting).

Psychosocial Development

As we examine what (and how) students learn about themselves from the relational contexts of service involvements, the psychosocial theories of Erik Erikson are instructive. Service-learning advocates claim significant potential for the development of self. Self-reports from service-learning participants frequently include references to having "learned more about myself than I ever gave" (many claim this to be the primary benefit of the service experience).

Erikson (1950, 1975), who enhanced psychoanalytic theory by outlining the role of culture and social relationships in development, presents a consistent reminder that life history cannot be separated from the "historical moment," the influences of social context. For Erikson, development is an ongoing process of encounter with the social environment:

> *Personality can be said to develop according to steps predetermined in the human organism's readiness to be driven toward, to be aware of, and to interact with, a widening social radius, beginning with the dim image of a*

mother and ending with mankind, or at any rate that segment of mankind which "counts" in the particular individual's life. (1959: 52)

Thus, as with Piaget, interaction with the environment is key to development. Erikson suggests that inner mechanisms "create a *succession of potentialities for significant interaction*" with others (1959: 52). These potentials parallel challenges individuals face at successive stages of development, from establishing trust in the first year of life to searching for integrity at life's end (see Erikson's influential *Childhood and Society*, 1950, for a complete description of his eight stages of the life span).

Following Erikson's lead, we do well to understand service-learning efforts in the context of current cultural trends and challenges. In *Generation at the Crossroads: Apathy and Action on the American Campus*, Paul Loeb (1994) examines the reactions of what some have labeled "Generation X" to social and economic change as a new millennium dawns. How do youth who developed during the conservative era of the early 1980s, and whose parents advocated social change during the 1960s, understand current social and political challenges? According to Loeb, students of the late 1980s exhibited considerable apathy in political affairs, and developed a "mistrust of those who act" (16). Although interest in service-related activities has increased among a sizable minority in the 1990s, students consistently describe the need to focus on career and individual security in an age of declining resources and economic competition. Loeb suggests that service involvements may function for youth as an outlet for ideological development without the "messiness" of politics they have learned to distrust. Loeb's fear, echoed by other writers (e.g., Radest 1993), is that such service activity among youth may reinforce vague notions of individual concern or charity rather than attention to unjust or ineffective social structures, as when one student praised his service experience: "I hope that one day my grandchildren will get to have the same experience working in the same homeless shelter that I did" (237). In contrast to general voluntarism, service-learning offers opportunities for more disciplined social analysis, and has the potential to provide "intellectual scaffolding" (Loeb 1994: 219) and stimulate reflection upon complex structural concerns.

Service-learning also presents opportunities to foster understanding of self in relation to a changing culture. Erikson suggests that formation of identity is the key developmental task of youth (Yates and Youniss 1996b). Identity is a complex construct, with both psychological and popular renderings. For Erikson, identity formation is an ongoing "process of simultaneous reflection and observation" (1968: 22) in which individuals make judgments about themselves according to socially constructed criteria. Exploration of various "selves" and paths is, according to Erikson, necessary for establishing a mature identity.

Identity may be understood by examining component domains, including (1) perceptions of the physical body in comparison with others and the requirements of the culture; (2) conceptions of the personal self, its organization and direction; (3) career orientation and role assimilation; and (4) moral perceptions ("Am I a moral person?"). The individual's challenge according to Erikson is one of evolving from an embeddedness (both cognitive and social) in these domains toward a differentiated and integrated identity able to negotiate the demands of the current culture. Such an evolution is challenging even in relatively stable societies. As the social order undergoes dynamic change, as in America during this century, implications for identity formation are many. Erikson (1975) documents the impact on identity of the nuclear fact — that as a result of our own actions, society may cease to exist as we know it — and of the struggle for social equality witnessed most keenly in the civil rights initiatives of the 1960s. Today's youth face similarly complex challenges, and service-learning provides a means to enter into social contexts and explore aspects of self (personal, career, moral) in relation to the world.

In an insightful analysis, Yates and Youniss (1996b) suggest the relevance of community service to three aspects of identity formation: agency, social relatedness, and moral-political awareness. Although their focus is on high school youth in volunteer service contexts, their framework easily extends to service-learning among those in higher education. Central to the formation of identity — and building on the prior developmental stage in which personal "industry" is the focus — is a sense of agency (others may use the term *efficacy*). Traditional pedagogies often overlook activities that may foster a direct sense of personal capability. In contrast, Norton (1991) describes a community service experience during his youth that had long-term implications: "It indelibly imprinted in me the feeling that 'I can do it,' and it did so at an highly impressionable age. At some subterranean level that feeling has been with me ever since, and I have had countless occasions to be grateful for it" (69). Yates (1995) and Yates and Youniss (1996b) provide conceptual and empirical support that service activities have the potential to enhance agency.

With respect to social relatedness, Yates and Youniss (1996b) maintain that service involvements may enhance identity formation in relation to perceived sociability, family constructs, and institutional functioning. Finally, they suggest that service may enhance moral-political awareness as a component of identity.

How do individuals come to believe they are or are not moral or ethical, to establish what may be called *moral identity*? This is a critical question. Erikson points out, citing Piaget, that youth have the cognitive ability to take ideological stands, and often enjoy exploring them. Yet because of limitations in their thinking and experience, they often use a "totalistic logic" (Erikson 1975: 206). Service-learning has the potential to reinforce moral identity (even those who were required to serve often claim moral motivations upon completion) while offering opportunities to test "utopian convictions" and develop complex understandings of social concerns.

Moral Development

Service-learning places individuals in relational contexts, and thus presents numerous moral and ethical challenges. Psychologists have examined moral perceptions and behavior from a variety of viewpoints, including attribution theory, self-perception theory, and social learning theory. From a cognitive-developmental perspective, the work of Piaget (1932) and Kohlberg (1981) has been most salient. Building upon their efforts, Rest (1986) has developed a model outlining four components to morality: moral sensitivity, moral judgment or reasoning, moral motivation, and moral character. Rest points out that for Kohlberg, "behavior has an underlying structure; it is not an aggregation of disconnected responses triggered by external stimuli" (7). Moral behavior is influenced by dynamic cognitive structures that develop in complexity over time. Again, interaction with the environment is key.

Piaget's conception of autonomy in moral contexts is consistent with service-learning pedagogy. Philibert (1994) points out that unlike Erikson and Kohlberg, who frame autonomy more as individuation or separation from parental or societal convention, Piaget emphasizes mutuality: "For Piaget, then, autonomy means collaboration in a spirit of generous mutual interest" by developing an attitude "that holds others' values in esteem and asks for reasonable respect for one's own values" (79). Piaget (1932) focused on peer interactions in which mutual understandings among moral equals can be developed, and service-learning does well to build upon the friendship networks or "forms of community" (Parks 1986) that develop among service participants. Yet college-age youth, envisioning entry into the world of work, are also able to gain understanding from role models they observe in service agencies or individuals within the population served. Philibert suggests that a key to developing a mature sense of autonomy is dialogue, which can be enhanced through the creation of base communities, or "new structures of voluntary association" (1994: 84). Service-learning presents opportunities for such dialogue, both in and outside the classroom.

Boss (1994, 1995) has begun work to apply moral development theory to service-learning contexts. Noting that Dewey, Kohlberg, and others advocated real-world experience, she tested the efficacy of service-learning in an ethics course. Participants in this course showed greater gains on the Defining Issues Test (designed to measure principled reasoning in relation to

Kohlberg's scheme) than students who took the same course without service-learning components. Boss notes that students' pre-test DIT scores did not differ as a result of prior community service, and that students in both courses discussed a variety of moral dilemmas during class periods. Thus, Boss suggests that the *combination* of service experiences (which raise directly challenging moral issues) and classroom reflection and dialogue may maximize moral development. She suggests that a key factor in enhancing such development is *social* disequilibrium, provided by the service experience (both class groups were challenged by complex, controversial issues and thus potentially felt *cognitive* disequilibrium). The findings, Boss indicates, are consistent with the "suggestion that one's fullest potential in moral reasoning comes about through a successful integration of the Kohlbergian justice (cognitive) and the more feminine care (social/affective) perspectives" (1994: 191) outlined by Gilliga (1982).

In addition to the work of Boss, much can be learned from those who have applied moral development theory to educational contexts. Power, Higgins, and Kohlberg (1989) describe a variety of initiatives utilizing the moral questions that arise within classroom and school contexts. Service-learning further broadens the scope, enabling students to encounter complex social challenges in a direct, ongoing manner. At the highest (postconventional) levels of Kohlberg's theory, individuals are able to separate themselves from social conventions, see things from multiple perspectives, and use more complex problem-solving skills (Power 1992). Such abilities resonate with the goals of service-learning.

Meaning and Faith Development

A developmental framework for service-learning must account for the processes by which youth construct meaning in relation to the social contexts and developmental challenges they encounter. How do interactions lead to development, and what challenges are inherent to the young adult years that constrain or enliven?

Kegan (1982) and Parks (1986) emphasize that making meaning is what defines our humanity, what human organisms do: We organize meaning. Parks suggests

> that the seeking and defending of meaning pervades all of human life. Meaning-making is the activity of seeking pattern, order, form, and significance. . . . To be human is to seek to understand the fitting connections between things. To be human is to desire relationship. (14)

It is this "capacity and demand for meaning" that she seeks "to associate with the word *faith*" (xv). Note that Parks refers here to faith with a lower-case f. While specifically religious orientations may influence many youth (and lead to service involvements), Parks maintains that all individuals face the challenge of developing an adult faith, a set of coherent meanings by which they understand the world and their place in it. She invites an understanding of *faith* as a verb, and describes the challenges young adults face in working out a satisfying faith as they encounter a changing, complex society. Parks draws from Marstin (1979) in emphasizing that "not only is complex perspective taking essential to adequate moral reasoning . . . but the character and composition of the whole of reality (one's faith) will condition what one finds tolerable and intolerable" (Parks 1986: 67). Thus, seeing the world from another perspective (facilitated by service experiences) may not merely foster empathy; it has the potential to challenge a student's overall perspectives of social justice and life. This larger frame of reference is an important aspect and potential of service-learning. Going beyond brief volunteer service encounters, service-learning can provide the integration of experience, reflection, and analysis that will allow youth to develop (or recompose) a more complex and satisfying worldview or faith.

According to Parks, young adulthood is a critical period for the development of mature adult faith; and higher education, in which an increasing number of young adults spend critical years, has the potential for significant impact: "Every professor is potentially a spiritual guide and every syllabus a confession of faith" (1996: 134). Yet faculty are not always aware of such influence nor ready for such a role. Given that academic paradigms — emphasizing objectivity and value neutrality — still dominate, questions of meaning, of "ultimate reality" (135), are often considered off limits, beyond the role of the academy (though possibly part of extracurricular or residential life). Parks suggests we examine our epistemological assumptions, that we recognize the need for an epistemology in which "there is an ongoing process of interaction between the knower and the real," where there is movement beyond "unqualified relativism . . . into the composing of worthy commitments to self and society within a relativized world" (137). She claims that

> If higher education is to initiate the young adult into a conversation with the full force field of life, typically the student's experience must be enlarged. Faith is the place of experience and the imagination. The imagination must have plenty of experience to work upon if truth is to be apprehended. . . . This encounter is most powerfully achieved when the learner is not a detached observer but a responsible participant. . . . It is in the task, in the need to take responsible action, that the discernment of truth is rejoined with the moral act and that faith must be recomposed. Further, as students and their teachers experience the discernment of truth as indissolubly linked with act and its consequences, the dichotomies between

method and morality, theory and practice, knowledge and context, self and society, private and public — dichotomies that plague both higher education and society as a whole — are transcended, and the best impulses of the searching mind are honored. (143-144)

Without reference to it, Parks provides a developmental, epistemological, and practical argument for service-learning. Practitioners will do well to draw on her insights.

Support for experiential pedagogies can also be drawn from the work of Csikszentmihalyi (1990, 1993), who examines the conditions that lead to optimal experience, or states of *flow*. Csikszentmihalyi argues that positive development involves a spiral of differentiation (of self from other) and increasingly mature integration (joining with others in common pursuits). Drawing upon developmental theory, Csikszentmihalyi describes means by which succeeding stages of differentiation and integration may become increasingly complex, involving more elaborate meaning systems. He argues that mature growth involves the development of an integrated life theme or project that can guide decision making, focus energy, and sustain purpose. He notes that "a complex, negentropic life theme is rarely formulated as the response to just a personal problem. Instead, *the challenge becomes generalized to other people, or to mankind as a whole*" (1990: 233). Csikszentmihalyi in fact views our survival as a species to be dependent on our ability to foster such life themes; to the extent that we can align individual happiness and meaning with common purpose, our evolution can continue amid current challenges. Service-learning provides contexts for such individual and social development.

Ways of Knowing

Because service-learning represents an alternative to traditional classroom practices, it often prompts students to examine their own ways of learning. Some students become zealous converts, making sweeping claims that all courses should have service components or the like. Again, service-learning practitioners may draw from developmental theory to understand how individuals understand their own learning, and what may be done to foster lifelong learning skills.

What may be learned about learning, knowledge, and truth in a service context? That context matters, that stereotypes may not reflect reality, that multiple viewpoints have merit, that social problems have complex etiologies, and that solutions come from dialogue and cooperation. Such potential lessons have significant impact on students' inherent epistemological assumptions. In examining the relation between experience and education,

Dewey (1938) suggests that the "most important attitude that can be formed is that of desire to go on learning" (48). If service-learning can prompt an individual to continue the process of learning about social conditions through dialogue and relationships, its power as a pedagogy will be confirmed. Extrinsic motivation for learning (often the foundation for traditional pedagogies) may shift to intrinsic desire to learn as a means to contribute (Csikszentmihalyi 1990, claims that such a shift to intrinsic motivation is necessary for freedom, and may promote flow experiences).

Kolb (1984) notes that learning styles may change as a result of work experience and career development, and suggests increased attention to adult development and efforts to promote "lifelong learning and integrative development" (208). Yet little research has directly examined how service-learning participants learn about their own learning, how their epistemological assumptions may change as a result of service-learning (and in relation to other developmental influences). Though it does not examine service-learning directly, William Perry's research (1970, 1981) is informative. Few others have given such careful attention to how students understand knowledge — its genesis and implications — during higher education.

Through extensive interviews, Perry and his associates examined the "origins of knowledge and value" (1970: 204) among college students, and outlined nine positions along a path of intellectual and ethical development. Beginning with a dualistic frame of reference (we-they, right-wrong), students progress to a position characterized by multiplicity of viewpoints and relativism (authority is suspect, there are many truths) to one of commitment (in which choices to follow a particular value path are made despite the relativistic nature of the world). Perry's framework rings true for many educators, and a variety of instruments have been developed to assess individuals' positions in relation to the scheme. Consistent with pragmatism in the tradition of Dewey, Perry suggests that "students' ultimate purpose is . . . to find those forms through which they may best understand and confront with integrity the nature of the human condition" (1970: 201). Toward this end, he suggests that the educational "community's substantive provision of worthwhile things to care about is not enough. Nor is the provision on an expectation that the student will care. The student finds his greatest sustenance . . . in a sense of community in the risks of caring" (200). In service-learning terms, it is not enough for colleges to suggest in mission statements (as most do) that students should learn to be morally sensitive, or that important concerns be discussed in classes (as they are in many). Rather, Perry suggests that opportunities for involvement in which the risks of caring can prompt development are key. And the provision of such involvements requires risks on the part of educators (service-learning opportunities demand interaction and sometimes unplanned response on the part of faculty). Shared authentic involvement supports growth (Perry observes that teachers who visibly share their own challenges in making meaning and commitments are noted and appreciated by students). Perry concludes his major work (1970) by suggesting the importance of community in supporting students through the challenges of making responsible commitments:

> For the majority . . . the most important support seemed to derive from a special realization of community. This was the realization that in the very risks, separateness, and individuality of working out their Commitments, they were in the same boat not only with each other but with their instructors as well. (213)

Perry's comments, which parallel Piaget's notion of autonomy, serve as a reminder that service-learning is not simply a technique, nor an individually focused method, but a commitment of an institution in collaboration with other communities. Attention needs to be given to how dialogue contributes to growth, how we learn (construct truth) together, and how shared values develop in community. For related discussion of such issues, see Palmer's examination (1983) of learning as a community journey, and Senge's analysis (1990) of learning in institutional settings.

No discussion of experience in relation to learning would be complete without reference to the work of Paulo Freire. Freire reminds us that education is a political activity (service-learning is no exception, of course) and defines the challenges inherent to entering a group or community with the intention to help. In his influential *Pedagogy of the Oppressed* (1970), Freire encourages both dominant and oppressed persons to develop *conscientizacao*: the ability "to perceive social, political, and economic contradictions, and to take action against the oppressive elements of reality" (19). Freire critiques a "banking concept" of teaching, in which learning is deposited into relatively empty learners, advocating instead a "co-intentional education" in which

> Teachers and students (leadership and people), co-intent on reality, are both Subjects, not only in the task of unveiling that reality, and thereby coming to know it critically, but in the task of re-creating that knowledge. As they attain this knowledge of reality through common reflection and action, they discover themselves as its permanent re-creators. (56)

In a recent work, *Pedagogy of Hope* (1994), Freire describes his early understanding of learning, and the origins of his theories. A critical, formative incident for Freire — interestingly enough, as he lectured about Piaget's work on moral development — involved an interaction with an articulate poor man who challenged Freire to understand directly the perspectives of the poor and the conditions in which they live. Service-learning offers the potential for such interaction and perspective taking, with subsequent effects on value and epistemological development. Freire's work challenges service-learning practitioners and researchers to analyze the working assumptions (how we read the world) of both the relatively privileged service participants and those with whom they work.

Implications for Practice and Research

What has been (can be) learned, then, from developmental theory? This chapter has painted, using large brush strokes, an argument for service-based pedagogies grounded in theories of developmental psychology. In most cases, the theorists I employed preceded current specific service-learning initiatives (which strengthens the argument, it may be said). It would be interesting to gather, say, Dewey, James, Piaget, Erikson, Vygotsky, Kohlberg, Gilligan, Parks, and Freire for an extended discussion of the developmental merits and practice of service-learning. I trust there would be significant support (as outlined above), with various qualifications. In lieu of such imagined conversation, let me suggest implications for practice and research that may be drawn from the work of these theorists. Practitioners of service-learning will do well to:

1. Attend not only to external factors in the service-learning context (setting, type of work, opportunities for action and reflection) but also to internal factors: the epistemological, cognitive, moral, and identity dynamics within developing individuals.

2. Understand the developmental challenges inherent to youth and young adulthood, and the role these may play as participants interpret and respond to service-learning contexts.

3. Attend consistently to the quality of experiences offered, realizing, with Dewey, that all experiences are not equally educative. As Sprinthall (1980) asks, "Do we carefully select experiences, or do we simply accept the axiom that experience-based learning is intrinsically good?" (140).

4. Emphasize ongoing experiences (a strength of service-learning) rather than one-time exposures to social concerns.

5. Give opportunities for choice in the service-learning process.

6. Provide significant challenge (to enhance cognitive and social dissonance) and appropriate support.

7. Attend to what service-learning participants learn through and about community; attend to institutional and friendship supports.

8. Collaborate with related educational initiatives, including efforts to promote collaborative learning, active learning, and critical thinking within the classroom. Development is a many-faceted enterprise.

Although nothing may be so practical as a good theory, service-learning efforts often seem to begin in practice, an intuitive notion of the worth of service leading to a specific initiative. Swelling interest in service-learning provides an excellent opportunity to extend theory (and refine practice) through relevant research. Building on developmental theory, future research in this area should:

1. Examine what students learn about their own learning through service, how their epistemological assumptions change over time, and how their motivation for learning about social conditions is influenced.

2. Examine process variables (how individuals change through service initiatives) in addition to outcomes; see Yates and Youniss (1996a).

3. Examine naturally occurring transitions as students become involved in service-learning of increasing depth. Here, Delve, Mintz, and Stewart's (1990) "Service Learning Model" provides an important starting point.

4. Examine how youth construct meaning from service experiences, and study relative constraints and supports in such processes.

5. Employ longitudinal research designs that examine the long-term developmental implications of service-learning. Here, the work of McAdam (1988) and Fendrich (1993) examining the subsequent lives and attitudes of those involved in early civil rights efforts is instructive. Also, studies by Colby and Damon (1992) and Daloz et al. (1996) provide models for understanding how lifelong commitments to social and moral concerns are nurtured and sustained.

6. Examine the impact of social contexts (economic constraints, political threats) on the processes and outcomes of service-learning.

7. Integrate developmental theory with research in social psychology to examine how students' attributional tendencies and other cognitive patterns are influenced by service-learning experiences. For example, do their conceptions of the world as just or unjust change? See Bringle and Velo (1996) and Michlitsch and Frankel (1989).

The suggestions made above are consistent with recent calls (McCall 1996) for more relevant research focused on current social concerns. Such research may also have the reciprocal capacity to inform developmental theory overall.

As Dewey (1938) noted early in the century, the gap between the limited abilities of children and the complexities of adult society has led to a separation of learning from direct experience, resulting at times in educational methods that have limited vitality and capacity to stimulate interest. Service-learning offers a means to bridge this gap. As youth mature and approach adult responsibilities, service-learning may facilitate cognitive, social, and moral growth applicable to the social and leadership challenges of the next century.

References

Boss, J.A. (1994). "The Effect of Community Service Work on the Moral Development of College Ethics Students." *Journal of Moral Education* 23: 183-198.

——— . (1995). "Teaching Ethics Through Community Service." *The Journal of Experiential Education* 18: 20-24.

Bringle, R.G., and P. Velo. (June 1996). *Attributions About Misery*. Paper presented at the Campus Compact National Gathering, Indianapolis, IN.

Brooks, J.G., and M.G. Brooks. (1993). In *Search of Understanding: The Case for Constructivist Classrooms*. Alexandria, VA: Association for Supervision and Curriculum Development.

Colby, A.D., and W. Damon. (1992). *Some Do Care: Contemporary Lives of Moral Commitment*. New York: The Free Press.

Csikszentmihalyi, M. (1990). *Flow: The Psychology of Optimal Experience*. New York: Harper & Row.

——— . (1993). *The Evolving Self: A Psychology for the Third Millennium*. New York: HarperCollins.

Daloz, L.A.P., C.H. Keen, J.P. Keen, and S.D. Parks. (1996). *Common Fire: Lives of Commitment in a Complex World*. Boston: Beacon Press.

Delve, C.I., S.D. Mintz, and G.M. Stewart, eds. (1990). *Community Service as Values Education*. San Francisco: Jossey-Bass.

Dewey, J. (1938). *Experience and Education*. New York: Collier Books.

Erikson, E.H. (1950). *Childhood and Society*. New York: W.W. Norton.

——— . (1959). *Identity and the Life Cycle: Selected Papers*. New York: International Universities Press.

——— . (1968). *Identity: Youth and Crisis*. New York: W.W. Norton.

——— . (1975). *Life History and the Historical Moment*. New York: W.W. Norton.

Fendrich, J.M. (1993). *Ideal Citizens: The Legacy of the Civil Rights Movement*. Albany, NY: State University of New York Press.

Freire, P. (1970). *Pedagogy of the Oppressed*. New York: Continuum.

——— . (1994). *Pedagogy of Hope: Reliving Pedagogy of the Oppressed*. New York: Continuum.

Gardner, H. (1991). *The Unschooled Mind*. New York: Basic Books.

Giles, D.E., and J. Eyler. (1994). "The Theoretical Roots of Service-Learning in John Dewey: Toward a Theory of Service-Learning." *Michigan Journal of Community Service Learning* 1: 77-85.

Giles, D.E., Jr., E.P. Honnet, and S. Migliore. (1991). *Research Agenda for Combining Service and Learning in the 1990s*. Raleigh, NC: National Society for Experiential Education.

Gilligan, C. (1982). *In a Different Voice*. Cambridge, MA: Harvard University Press.

Gruber, H.E., and J.J. Voneche, eds. (1995). *The Essential Piaget: An Interpretive Reference and Guide*. Northvale, NJ: Jason Aronson.

Kegan, R. (1982). *The Evolving Self: Problem and Process in Human Development*. Cambridge: Harvard University Press.

Kohlberg, L. (1981). *Essays on Moral Development: Vol. II. The Psychology of Moral Development*. New York: Harper & Row.

Kolb, D. (1984). *Experiential Learning: Experience as the Source of Learning and Development*. Englewood Cliffs, NJ: Prentice-Hall.

Liu, G. (1995). "Knowledge, Foundations, and Discourse: Philosophical Support for Service-Learning." *Michigan Journal of Community Service Learning* 2: 5-18.

Loeb, P.R. (1994). *Generation at the Crossroads: Apathy and Action on the American Campus*. New Brunswick, NJ: Rutgers University Press.

Marstin, R. (1979). *Beyond Our Tribal Gods: The Maturing of Faith*. Maryknoll, NY: Orbis Books.

McAdam, D. (1988). *Freedom Summer*. New York: Oxford University Press.

McCall, R. (1996). "The Concept and Practice of Education, Research, and Public Service in University Psychology Departments." *American Psychologist* 51: 379-388.

Michlitsch, J.E., and S. Frankel. (1989). "Helping Orientations: Four Dimensions." *Perceptual and Motor Skills* 69: 1371-1378.

Norton, D.L. (1991). *Democracy and Moral Development*. Berkeley: University of California Press.

Palmer, P.J. (1983). *To Know as We Are Known: Education as a Spiritual Journey*. San Francisco: Harper & Row.

Parks, S. (1986). *The Critical Years: The Young Adult Search for a Faith to Live By*. San Francisco: Harper & Row.

Perry, W.G. (1970). *Forms of Intellectual and Ethical Development in the College Years*. New York: Holt, Rinehart & Winston.

——— . (1981). "Cognitive and Ethical Growth: The Making of Meaning." In *The Modern American College: Responding to the New Realities of Diverse Students and a Changing Society*, edited by A.W. Chickering, pp. 76-116. San Francisco: Jossey-Bass.

Philibert, P.J. (1994). "The Formation of Moral Life in a Mass-Mediated Culture." In *Mass Media and the Moral Imagination*, edited by P.J. Rossi and P.A. Soukup, pp. 71-84. Kansas City, MO: Sheed & Ward.

Piaget, J. (1932). *The Moral Judgment of the Child*, translated by M. Gabain. London: K. Paul, Trench, Trubner & Co. Ltd./Edinburgh Press.

——— . (1970). *Genetic Epistemology*, translated by E. Duckworth. New York: Columbia University Press.

Power, F.C. (1992). "Moral Education and Pluralism." In *The Challenge of Pluralism: Education, Politics, and Values*, edited by F.C. Power and D.K. Lapsley, pp. 1-14. Notre Dame, IN: University of Notre Dame Press.

———, A. Higgins, and L. Kohlberg. (1989). *Lawrence Kohlberg's Approach to Moral Education*. New York: Columbia University Press.

Radest, H.B. (1993). *Community Service: Encounter With Strangers*. Westport, CT: Praeger.

Rest, J. (1986). *Moral Development: Advances in Research and Theory*. New York: Praeger.

Rosenberg, S.W. (1988). *Reason, Ideology and Politics*. Princeton, NJ: Princeton University Press.

Senge, P.M. (1990). *The Fifth Discipline: The Art and Practice of the Learning Organization*. New York: Doubleday.

Sprinthall, N.A. (1980). "A Reply to Jim Rest: Doonesbury's Football Team and Deliberate Psychological Education." In *Developmental Counseling and Teaching*, edited by V.L. Erickson and J.M. Whiteley, pp. 140-143. Monterey, CA: Brooks/Cole Publishing Company.

Whiteley, J.M. (1980). "A Developmental Intervention in Higher Education." In *Developmental Counseling and Teaching*, edited by V.L. Erickson and J.M. Whiteley, pp. 236-261. Monterey, CA: Brooks/Cole Publishing Company.

Yates, M. (March 1995). "Community Service in Adolescence: Implications for Moral-Political Awareness." Paper presented at the Biennial Meeting of the Society for Research on Child Development, Indianapolis, IN.

———, and J. Youniss. (1996a)."A Developmental Perspective on Community Service in Adolescence." *Social Development* 5: 85-111.

———. (1996b). "Community Service and Political-Moral Identity in Adolescents." *Journal of Research on Adolescence* 6(3): 271-284.

Service-Learning and the Development of Expert Citizens:
Service-Learning and Cognitive Science

by Janet Eyler, Susan Root, and Dwight E. Giles, Jr.

Students who are very active in service-learning have impressed us with their commitment and their practical knowledge as they apply their insights about social problems to projects in their communities. These students' judgments about community issues seem qualitatively different from those of less experienced students or students analyzing social issues only in the classroom. For example, asked about a solution for the problem of poverty, a student who has participated for two years in a program that integrates community service with his college coursework responded:

> That's a difficult question. There are so many causes and so many ways of working on the solution, that there's no one clear answer. The way that our organization works is mainly to help families who are already poverty stricken, and so instead of working upstream on stopping the poverty, we're working downstream and helping people get off the streets once they're on the streets. We clearly need programs like ours to help people who are already stuck in the system, but I think I'd get more value and meaning out of it if I were to work upstream. And to do that, I think we need to revamp a lot of our systems. . . . [W]e might as well make it a system that works instead of making people go crazy jumping through hoops that are just going to leave them where they are.

The student went on to make a number of detailed recommendations about how to begin to solve the problem.

Contrast this response to a solution provided by a student engaged in her first service project, tutoring a child. After quickly identifying the cause of the school drop-out problem as lack of parental attention, she immediately jumps to a solution. It consists of "just telling" those involved in the problem to do better, a solution she is unable to support with procedural knowledge.

> I suppose it could be some kind of community program, getting the parents together and just telling them how it helps their children if they actually are involved in their lives and in their schoolwork and asking how things went in school, what they are doing, showing their schoolwork. But I don't

have any answers really about how you would do that. I just have ideas of what could be done and how it could be done.

Service-learning educators are interested in the development of an experiential pedagogy that will help students move from the naive and simplistic conceptions of how to approach community issues demonstrated by the second student to the more complex contextualized analysis demonstrated by the first. Furthermore, they are convinced that the combination of hands-on experience with structured reflection that is at the core of service-learning is the way to accomplish their objective. In recent years, cognitive psychologists also have devoted a good deal of attention to the issue of how factual knowledge, or what Anderson (1982) has called "knowing what," can be transformed to procedural knowledge that can be used in relevant contexts, i.e., "knowing how." Related to this, psychologists have studied the development of expertise, including the differences in the way that beginners identify and address problems compared with the way that those with extensive experience approach the same challenges. This work in cognitive psychology has some clear implications for service-learning practitioners. In this chapter we address three questions:

1. Is service-learning pedagogy consistent with what cognitive psychologists know about effective instruction for bridging the gap to "knowledge in use"?

2. Is there evidence to support the view that service-learning contributes to social problem finding or solving?

3. Are the differences in the patterns of problem analysis and solution demonstrated by students with varying degrees of service and service-learning experience consistent with differences identified in the expert/novice literature?

Cognitive Science and Service-Learning Pedagogy

There are a number of parallels between the way cognitive scientists and service-learning practitioners think about effective instruction. For example, Bransford and Vye (1989) argue that the best way to think about meaningful learning is to view it as a transition from memory to action. They, like other cognitive scientists, struggle with what has been called the "inert knowledge problem," i.e., the failure of students to use information acquired in the classroom when addressing real problems. They suggest that there are several defects in typical classroom instruction that lead to the problem of inert knowledge. One is that students receive little practice on how and when to apply factual knowledge. When problems are included in the curriculum, they are often bound by the content of a particular unit of instruction. Students working on problem solving are cued by the structure of the curriculum, and this drives their search for a method of problem solving. In the real world, of course, problems are not labeled; the first task is to recognize that there is a problem. The second task is to identify the nature of the problem and the relevant knowledge or skills to be applied. There is no chapter heading to tell us how to identify and approach an ill-structured problem in the real world, and solutions to real problems draw on multiple perspectives and disciplines.

In addition to cueing the response, the curriculum-bound nature of the problems used in classrooms may inhibit transfer. Some authors (e.g., Brown, Collins, and Duguid 1989; Lave 1989) posit that thinking skills cannot be separated from the contexts in which they are acquired. Abstract problems may not help students learn and use context-dependent tools for analysis and solution. Anchored instruction, which involves the use of guided problem solving within complex, concrete problem simulations, is one technique that cognitive psychologists are using to help students deal with problems in context. Bransford (1993) and his colleagues have found that these simulations facilitate the development of students' ability to transfer their skills to new situations. Repeated opportunities for identifying and solving problems in complex contexts enhance the likelihood of later use of the newly acquired skills and information. Using action-oriented case studies or simulations also engages students in the learning process more effectively than more didactic approaches.

Although solving problems in context is important, it is also important to provide structure and feedback for students. Lesgold (in Bransford and Vye 1989) describes this as "coached practice" rather than solitary practice and stresses the importance of helping students reflect on what they are doing and explore alternative approaches. As students confront difficult problems, part of their learning involves rejecting less adequate constructions of knowledge in favor of constructing new, more useful ways of looking at the world. Helping students to recognize the inadequacy of their existing constructs, to identify plausible alternatives, and try them out is a central role for the coach.

Like cognitive scientists, service-learning practitioners have long been convinced of the importance of "conditionalizing" learning by having students confront problems in rich contexts (Hamilton 1981; Moore 1981). In service-learning, however, the rich contexts for learning are placements in which students do real work with real people rather than simulations or case studies. Service-learning practitioners have embraced Dewey's concept of what makes experience educative. In addition to the need to generate interest, to present problems that awaken curiosity in students, and to allow for repeated experience and development over time, all of which are central concepts to psychologists committed to anchored instruction, service-learning educators have stressed the importance of Dewey's (1933) fourth criterion, which is that the activity must be intrinsically worthwhile. Although working on problems in the community gives the instructor decreased control over the information and issues confronted by the student, it has the advantages of both authenticity and high engagement in intrinsically worthwhile activity (Giles and Eyler 1994).

Service-learning practitioners, like cognitive scientists, also are committed to the importance of reflection as part of the process by which new constructions of reality occur. In fact, the presence of structured reflection is widely regarded as the factor that distinguishes service-learning from community service (Giles, Honnet, and Migliore 1991). Well-designed service-learning programs include a balance between action and reflection. Because service occurs in an authentic setting, providing appropriate feedback is more challenging than in classroom-based experiential programs; a good deal of the practitioner literature focuses on how to accomplish this task (Eyler, Giles, and Schmiede 1966; Silcox 1993).

Service-Learning and Improved Problem Solving

When we examine the service-learning literature, there is some evidence that this promise of service-learning pedagogy is realized: Students who are engaged in service-learning do show improved problem solving and may be better able to transfer learning. In an early study of service-learning and other field-based programs, Conrad and Hedin (1980) found that high school students who were involved in programs with frequent reflection opportunities and whose field experiences were with social issues similar to those used in problem-solving measures improved in the complexity of their problem analysis. Eyler and Halteman (1981) found that college students who served as legislative interns developed a more complex and realistic understanding of the legislative process than those whose study was limited to the classroom. Batchelder and Root (1994) examined problem analysis essays written by college students at the beginning and end of the semester. Those who participated in service as part of the class showed greater awareness of the complex and multidimensional nature of social problems and greater determination to act in the face of uncertainty than did the control group. As in Conrad and Hedin's study, these students showed more complex thinking on problems related to their service than on other social problems. Boss (1994) compared cognitive moral development scores of students who participated in a service-learning section of an ethics class and those who were in the standard course; service-learning students showed increases in moral reasoning compared with students limited to classroom discussion of moral dilemmas. In these last two studies, students experienced similar class sessions; the difference was that the service-learning students also experienced the issues under discussion in complex community contexts and participated in structured reflection to link their experiences and the subject matter of the course.

There is also some limited evidence that the quality of the service-learning experience, particularly the quality and intensity of reflection, may have an impact on cognitive outcomes. In a study of 1,500 college students, Eyler, Giles, and Braxton (1996) found that students in programs that integrated service and learning and had higher levels of structured reflection including complex written and oral assignments were more likely to view their service-learning classes as high quality, motivating, intellectually stimulating, and contributing to their learning than were students in programs with fewer of these characteristics. In another phase of this project, an analysis of hour-long pre- and post-semester interviews of 55 college students showed that students who participated in well-integrated and intensive service-learning courses were more likely to show growth in the complexity of their problem analysis, in their tendency to place problems in a broad systemic context, and in the quality of their strategies for addressing community problems than were students whose community service was not well integrated into the class for which it was undertaken (Eyler et al. 1997). Eyler (1993) also found that extensive levels of reflection were necessary in a field-based program if students were to transfer learning from the curriculum to new settings or tasks. Three groups of full-time college interns were compared. Two of the internship semesters immersed students in weekly intensive reflective seminars and required them to complete written assignments and projects and to make oral presentations in which they analyzed their organizations using concepts they had previously learned. One group completed the more informal reflection typical of such placements; they kept journals and occasionally met to share feelings and discuss concerns. When these interns each completed a letter of advice to a friend who has just accepted a job in a large organization, only the interns in the intensive reflection groups drew on the information and theories they had studied for four years as well as their internship experience; those with a less well integrated experience relied on the same general, clichéd advice such as "be yourself" offered by students who had yet undertaken the internship. That students in a curriculum with a strong commitment to experiential learning still failed to apply their knowledge without extensive structured reflection is consistent with cognitive science research that emphasizes the need for continuous and multiple opportunities for application as well as the importance of guided reflection.

Viewing Service-Learning From an Expert-Novice Perspective

Whereas research evidence links service-learning to gains in cognitive growth, there has been no effort to interpret the types of cognitive gains produced by service-learning from an expert-novice perspective. Yet the literature on expertise seems to be a particularly useful framework for understanding the cognitive changes experienced during service-learning.

Research on expertise attributes the level of skill of individuals' performance in a domain to specific abilities acquired through experience rather than to inherited or developmental characteristics, or more general knowledge or strategies. In a typical study, individuals at different levels of expertise are provided with representative tasks, such as recalling a case or a think-aloud problem-solving task. Their verbal or written protocols are decomposed into propositions and, depending on the goal of the study, are analyzed into concepts and relations, elements of problem solving, or other categories. A critical assumption of the research on expertise is that by analyzing expert-novice differences in performance, researchers can isolate the processes that mediate skilled performance and, eventually, the events that facilitate acquisition of those skills.

Expert-novice studies have been conducted in a range of fields, including chess, physics, computer programming, and teaching (Chase and Simon 1973; Chi, Feltovich, and Glaser 1981; Dalbey and Linn 1985; Swanson, O'Connor, and Cooney 1990). Although expertise differs in its particulars, these studies do suggest a general portrait of the expert that appears consistent with our observations of how students with a long history of community service think and behave. Experts have more extensive declarative knowledge of subject-area domains than do novices, and their knowledge is more coherent; there are more links among concepts. Experts' knowledge is likely to be organized around general principles rather than concrete examples. Experts have more extensive procedural knowledge than do novices; their knowledge of the domain is connected to rules for use and conditions of applicability. In problem solving, experts devote significantly greater amounts of time to problem representation, whereas novices tend to jump to a quick solution. Once a problem is clearly described, experts tend to engage in "forward" or data-driven reasoning, considering the specifics of a problem and then generating a solution, whereas novices tend to engage in "backward reasoning," creating a hypothesis relatively early in problem solving and then seeking confirmatory evidence.

To date, the majority of studies on expertise have attended primarily to domains in which a high percentage of the problems are well structured. Well-structured problems have clear goals and known constraints, and their solution paths are well established (Voss, Greene, et al.1983; Voss, Tyler, and Yengo 1983). In contrast, the problems encountered by students in service-learning experiences are apt to be ill structured, similar to the problems encountered by social scientists. As Voss notes (Voss, Greene, et al. 1983; Voss and Post 1988; Voss, Tyler, and Yengo 1983), social science problems usually involve a problematic situation, such as poverty or homelessness. Their solution lies in eliminating the causes; however, typically there is no consensus about the best solution. Because information essential to solving the problem, such as causes or constraints, is often unknown, problem solvers must often supply the information from their own knowledge of the problem topic (Voss, Greene, et al. 1983). Feedback about the efficacy of solutions to social science problems is not immediate, and there often is an absence of objective criteria by which to evaluate solutions. Thus, a significant task for problem solvers is to generate a line of argument in support of their solutions. A final characteristic of social science problems is that solutions are difficult to implement, often entailing the solution of subproblems (e.g., obtaining agreement by affected parties) before the primary solution can be implemented.

Voss and his colleagues have conducted a research program to examine differences in the social science problem solving of experts and novices. They have found that social science expertise is associated with several characteristics. Experts tend to explore their knowledge of the domain rather than the problem statement in constructing a problem representation. Experts typically recount the history of the problem in order to isolate its causes. Social science experts tend to adopt one of two heuristics for solving problems: (1) problem decomposition (breaking the problem into manageable subproblems), or (2) problem conversion (transforming the problem into a familiar problem with a known solution). They tend to provide general solutions to problems, followed by solutions to subproblems that are integral to the overall solution. Experts also generate solutions in which a large number of statements are devoted to "argument" (i.e., justifications for the proposed solution and consideration of alternatives). Finally, experts just know more about the problem and its context; they are able to formulate solutions based on their experience with similar problems and similar contexts; and they are able to apply that experience in novel situations.

Interviews With Students Who are "Novices" and "Experts" in Community Service

In a study, we sought to identify differences in community problem solving between college students with varying levels of experience in community service and service-learning to explore the relevance of the expert/novice construct to service-learning. We interviewed 24 college students at four institutions. Three students were not participating in service or service-learning; seven were beginners who were engaged in their first project; seven were "benchmark students," who had been involved in extensive service and were now identified as leaders in community service at their institution; and seven both had extensive service experience and were involved in a program that combined coursework with service. For our analysis, the responses of students in the first two groups were considered together as novice responses, and the students in the third and fourth groups were combined and considered to be experts. All were asked to identify and analyze the causes of a social problem related to their community service and to propose both a society-wide solution and a plan for individual action regarding the problem. Responses were audiotaped and transcribed. Using the literature on expertise as a starting point, we analyzed the transcripts for dimensions along which the problem-solving responses of novice and expert students differed. Particular attention was paid to how students described problems and whether they seemed to anchor their observations in a practical knowledge of how communities are organized to provide social services.

Four dimensions emerged that differentiated novice and expert student responses to questions about community problems: (1) the elaborateness of their representation of the community problem and whether they represented the problem in historical terms, (2) problem source or locus (whether the problem was attributed to an individual mental state or to the interaction of complex social processes), (3) the inclusiveness and depth of their solution (i.e., the extent to which the solution was vague or focused on discrete subproblems, or was an integrative solution inclusive of solutions to subproblems), and (4) the sophistication of their procedural knowledge regarding how to become personally involved in solving the community problem. The following section provides examples from the interviews of each dimension.

Elaborateness and Coherence of Problem Representation

A novice asked to identify a social problem in her community gave the following response:

> I came from . . . a very conservative type of community. There wasn't much
> . . . problems in terms of, you know, violence or any of that stuff. So in terms
> of that I guess we were kind of sheltered, but we were recently . . . in the
> past few years [we] . . . incorporated more, like, AIDS awareness type pro-
> grams throughout the school, more helping inner-city children type
> programs.

It is clear that this student had difficulty finding a community problem. Her efforts at representation involved not a search of her own knowledge of community but her recalling two programs that had been developed in her high school. She may not have had or been readily able to recall knowledge of her community relevant to the question. Compare her response with the extensive, historical presentation of a problem by a student with several years of service-learning experience:

> The most recent problem, I think, is classism. . . . What I've found in my experiences is that the bigger issue now is not prejudging people or oppressing people on the basis of their race as on the basis of their socio-economic status. . . . An example is poverty and homelessness. I always think of these things from an educational perspective . . . the quality of education that people get. Forty, 50, 60 years ago it could easily have been said that people of African-American background got for the most part inferior education compared to the education that most of the European-American people got, and that's why we had Brown vs. Board of Education and that's why we had busing.

This student uses both his experiences and sociopolitical knowledge to construct a representation of a problem: classism. He draws on his experiences in education to argue for disentangling the effects of two historically overlapping correlates of educational inequality: racism and classism. In addition, he supports his analysis of the problem with historical references to changes that have occurred in the United States in access to educational opportunity.

Problem Source: Individual Mental State vs. the Interaction of Social Processes

The following section includes quotations from two novices in a tutoring program. After identifying their problem as student underachievement, they located both the cause and solutions of underachievement in parents' psychological state — in the value parents assign to schooling and their commitment to their children:

> I think you need to have a parent who values education highly. I think in the schools, I don't want to blame the teachers because they have a really hard job. You can't expect them to be able to give individual encouragement to each of the kids. But I think encouragement and pushing the kids to read or learn is what really matters.

> I think that when people aren't committed to each other and to relationships and family, and I think before you have a life, you have a child, you

*really need to be, . . . maybe they don't even know themselves what they
are doing, then they have children.*

Although parents' attitudes certainly affect children's achievement, these
students fail to acknowledge either the contributions of others such as the
child or school or the social forces that might influence parental behavior.
Contrast these explanations with the response of a student who was concerned about the problem of underachieving students and who also had
been tutoring children for several years. While also expressing concern over
lack of parental attention, this student went on to discuss the effects of current economic trends on parents' capacity for involvement. This shift in the
locus of community problems from individual behavior to systemic and
structural contexts was typical of students with greater service and service-
learning experience:

> *I think the problem is parents aren't involved enough in their kids' lives. I
> think that this problem is one that is economically based because I think
> that if parents had less worries in other areas of their lives, they would
> have more time for their children. But I also think that a lot of it right now
> is that society is not putting that emphasis on the child.*

Similarly, the causal analyses of two expert students who respectively
selected community violence and poverty as central social problems also
emphasized the role of interacting institutional and social processes on individual mental state:

> *I have a really ecological way of looking at violence and I think it is a mix
> of everything from . . . individual psyches to the media presentation of peo-
> ple and violence. It has a lot to do with immigrants and low-income people
> and I think it is a real expression of disempowerment. . . . So I think it is
> just an expression of earning respect and power. . . . And also economic,
> because a lot of violence surrounds, like, drug selling and stuff, and that is
> a really acceptable way to make money when you don't know any other
> way.*

Note this student's "ecological" attribution of violence to a mix of institutions such as the media and its psychological effects (e.g., "disempower-
ment"). The following expert student also shows awareness of the different
groups affected by poverty and the ways in which societal factors have inter-
acted with each:

> *I can't narrow it down to one or two things, but some of the major prob-
> lems that we have in Boulder — we have a lot of migrant workers . . . sea-
> sonal working patterns . . . in the winter they're left without money . . . we
> have people who simply lose their jobs . . . we have people who fall through*

the social net . . . people who were receiving welfare but then decided to go and try to work harder . . . their welfare is cut, which leaves them without enough money to get by. . . . If you have two parents working, welfare won't cover things, whereas with one parent, it would . . . so it leaves you with breaking up the family. . . . Illness is a big one. We have people who had to deal with medical debt that they weren't expecting . . . lots of teenage mothers come in with their kids and have no place to go.

[Interviewer:] Are you pretty confident that the causes you identified are the causes?

I think I have somewhat of an idea . . . but I think that everything is interconnected, and that you can't just pinpoint a few things and say that works for everyone. . . . I'm sure there is more involved and it's more complicated than that.

Inclusiveness and Depth of Solution

In their solution statements, novice students often provide a single vague solution or a series of discrete solutions to concrete, low-level subproblems. For example, in response to the problem of lack of parental involvement, one novice's strategy involved exhorting parents to increase their sense of responsibility. How parents would change, why they might choose to listen, or specific actions helpers could undertake were not identified:

People need to reach out and educate them and make them aware of how important [parenting] is . . . kind of be there for them and direct them, and make them see that each life is precious . . . don't be a burden on the people around them, make them realize how important it is.

In the following discussion of underachievement, another novice reduced the problem to the specific problems of subgroups such as single mothers; he then was able to develop solutions to these particular problems:

It could be anything from tutoring, like, for instance, with single mothers . . . it could be, like, someone volunteering to take time out when the mother has to work to, like, look after the kid and tutor him and help him with his homework or whatever. Or it could be, like, the misplaced white kids who you see, like, not doing well in class . . . but you might see them have other interests, you might . . . direct them towards that.

Contrast these solutions to those of an expert student who, in discussing the problem of community violence, locates solutions in global underlying conditions (e.g., illiteracy, poor health conditions), which she calls "root" causes. This student appears to assume that these conditions foster violence and that her solutions would produce a series of consequences (e.g., literacy, better health), which would then prevent violence:

Right now I think the best thing we could do long term would be work more on . . . root things. Like work on literacy. I think we need to work on health care . . . we need to work on low-income housing. I would take a very well-ness approach to it . . . I think public representation is so important.

Another expert student proposed a solution to the problem of poverty that involved differentiating between types of poverty-stricken individuals and constructing an inclusive solution for each type's problems.

The first thing you would need to do . . . is to look at the diversity of home-less and poverty, because there's no one, single profile of people [who] are homeless and poverty stricken, and there's no one program that's going to work for everybody. . . . There are different types of poverty and different types of families and different types of people who need the assistance, and I think that's a real important first step . . . then after identifying who . . . you want to help, it would be: How can we help these people using the resources that are already available in the community? One thing that we do at Emergency Family Assistance is make sure we don't repeat services that other organizations do.

Sophistication of Students' Procedural Knowledge for How to Become Personally Involved in Solving a Community Problem

Novice participants in our study typically viewed community problem solving as an act of individual initiative. They seemed unaware either of the scale of most social problems or of their multidimensional nature, and thus had difficulty generating realistic, specific plans for becoming active in community service. They also tended to overlook the well-developed networks of volunteer organizations, political and social groups, and government agencies in the community. One example of this approach is the segment in the introduction to this chapter from the novice student: "I suppose it could be some kind of community program, getting the parents together and just telling them. . . . But I don't have any answers really about how you would do that."

The following response by a novice to the question of how she would become involved in helping the children in a community is also illustrative of this point:

I would find out who would help you and find out the easiest way to get in touch with these people and introduce yourself to this community and then get people to go with you and talk to the people and make them aware and let them know their options.

Contrast the vague and self-reliant nature of these action plans to the responses of two experienced students, who generated plans for involvement that took into account a number of contextual variables and their interactions. For example, in response to the question of how one could get involved in addressing the problem of racism, a student said:

> You know you don't just go into a community and say, "Hi, I'm your knight in shining armor; I'm here to help you." It just doesn't work that way . . . if there were leaders of certain groups . . . you'd have to find some way to say, "Well, it's to your benefit to overcome this problem." I have come to think of a lot of these things as strategies. Before you start solving any problems, you have to know who has the power, who has the ability to make the change and how you can get them talking.

A second expert student generated the following plan for how to become involved in solving the problem of community violence:

> I would say start building relationships, like building relationships with the people you want to serve and building relationships with the other agencies, not necessarily jumping in full force. . . . If I was going to go in and I was going to start from scratch, I would probably, like, waitress and meet people. Spend a lot of time doing one-on-ones with people in the community 'cause I don't think you really know how to service the community until you know what it is about.

Both students are aware of the need to understand the complexities of the particular community and to work with people on their own terms, and they are also aware that effective action takes into consideration existing agencies and programs and power arrangements.

Implications for Service-Learning Research and Practice

Service-learning is a pedagogy that exposes students to types of learning experiences that can foster the acquisition of more usable cognitive skills than does traditional classroom instruction. Students have multiple opportunities to confront ill-structured problems in rich community contexts and to participate in structured reflection on these experiences. The literature on the cognitive outcomes of service-learning supports this claim, indicating that participants in service-learning develop more nuanced, elaborate representations of social problems; more complex plans for solution; and a greater willingness than nonparticipants to act despite constraints.

While service-learning creates a context for student development, there is also evidence that the quality of the experience is important to achieve these outcomes. Because service-learning occurs in settings more difficult to structure and control than the anchored instruction models studied by cognitive psychologists, extra efforts must be made to align these experiences with what is known about effective learning. In choosing service sites, care should be taken to find community agencies that can engage students in meaningful work; it is important to match the students' experience in the field with the issues studied in the class; care must be taken to guide and support student inquiry as they raise questions based on their community experience. The integration of service and learning through reflection activities is not easy but it is critical for successful service-learning. Transfer of learning also rests on multiple opportunities to apply what has been learned, and those planning service-learning programs may want to think about creating a series of community options over the four years of the college program.

The field of expert-novice research may provide an especially useful lens through which to view the skills acquired through service-learning. In our qualitative analysis, students with long-term, active involvement in service and service-learning, like the "experts" identified in the expert-novice literature, conceptualized social issues in ways qualitatively different from beginners' and were able to define community problems and potential solutions within specific community contexts. Although this work is preliminary, it suggests that service-learning may be one mechanism by which students can develop a complex and useful grasp of the issues they will face as citizens, and that further attempts to understand community service expertise may be fruitful. More attention needs to be paid to defining citizenship "expertise" and identifying elements of expert community problem solving. And more attention should be paid to identifying activities and reflection techniques that help students develop higher levels of problem-solving skills within social contexts.

References

Anderson, J.R. (1982). "Acquisition of Cognitive Skill." *Psychological Review* 89: 369-406.

Batchelder, T.H., and S. Root. (1994). "Effects of an Undergraduate Program to Integrate Academic Learning and Service: Cognitive, Prosocial Cognitive and Identity Outcomes." *Journal of Adolescence* 17: 341-355.

Boss, J.A. (1994). "The Effect of Community Service Work on the Moral Development of College Ethics Students." *Journal of Moral Education* 23: 183-198.

Bransford, J.D. (1993). "Who Ya Gonna Call? Thoughts About Teaching Problem Solving." In *Cognitive Perspectives on Educational Leadership*, edited by P. Hallinger, K. Leithwood, and J. Murphy, pp. 171-191. New York: Teachers College Press.

————, and N.J. Vye. (1989). "A Perspective on Cognitive Research and Its Implications for Instruction." In *Toward the Thinking Curriculum: Current Cognitive Research*, edited by L. Resnick and L.E. Klopfer, pp. 173-205. Alexandria, VA: Association for Supervision and Curriculum Development.

Brown, J., S. Collins, and P. Duguid. (1989). "Situated Cognition and the Culture of Learning." *Educational Researcher* 18(1): 32-42.

Chase, W., and H. Simon. (1973). "Perception in Chess." *Cognitive Psychology* 4: 55-81.

Chi, M., P. Feltovich, and R. Glaser. (1981). "Categorization and Representation of Physics Problems by Experts and Novices." *Cognitive Science* 5: 121-152.

Conrad, D., and D. Hedin. (1980). *Experiential Education Evaluation Project. Executive Summary of the Final Report*. Minneapolis, MN: Center for Youth Development and Research, University of Minnesota.

Dalbey, J., and M. Linn. (1985). "The Demands and Requirements of Computer Programming: A Literature Review." *Journal of Educational Computing Research* 1: 253-274.

Dewey, J. (1933). *How We Think*. Boston: Heath.

Eyler, J. (1993). "Comparing the Impact of Two Internship Experiences on Student Learning." *Journal of Cooperative Education* 29(3): 41-52.

————. (November 1995). "The Impact of Alternative Models of Service-Learning on Student Outcomes." Paper presented at the National Society for Experiential Education meeting, New Orleans.

————, and B. Halteman. (1981). "The Impact of a Legislative Internship on Students' Political Skill and Sophistication." *Teaching Political Science* 9: 27-34.

Eyler, J., D.E. Giles, Jr., and J. Braxton. (April 1996). "The Impact of Service-Learning on Students' Attitudes, Skills and Values: Preliminary Results of Analysis of Selected Data From FIPSE-Sponsored Comparing Models of Service-Learning Project." Paper presented at the American Educational Research Association conference, New York.

Eyler, J., D.E. Giles, Jr., and A. Schmiede. (1966). *A Practitioner's Guide to Reflection in Service-Learning: Student Voices & Reflections*. Nashville, TN: Vanderbilt University.

Eyler, J., D.E. Giles, Jr., S. Root, and J. Price. (March 1997). "Service-Learning and the Development of Expert Citizens." Paper presented at the American Educational Research Association conference, Chicago.

Giles, D.E., Jr., and J. Eyler. (1994). "The Theoretical Roots of Service-Learning in John Dewey: Towards a Theory of Service-Learning." *Michigan Journal of Community Service-Learning* 1: 77-85.

Giles, D.E., Jr., E.P. Honnet, and S. Migliore. (1991). *Research Agenda for Combining Service and Learning in the 1990s*. Raleigh, NC: National Society for Experiential Education.

Hamilton, S.F. (1981). "Adolescents in Community Settings: What Is to Be Learned?" *Theory and Research in Social Education* 9(2): 23-38.

Lave, J. (1989). *Cognition in Practice: Mind, Mathematics, and Culture in Everyday Life.* New York: Cambridge University Press.

Moore, D.T. (1981). "Discovering the Pedagogy of Experience." *Harvard Educational Review* 51: 286-300.

Silcox, H. (1993). *A How To Guide to Reflection: Adding Cognitive Learning to Community Service Programs.* Philadelphia, PA: Brighton Press.

Swanson, H., J. O'Connor, and J. Cooney. (1990). "An Information Processing Analysis of Expert and Novice Teachers' Problem Solving." *American Educational Research Journal* 27: 533-556.

Voss, J., and T. Post. (1988). "On the Solving of Ill-Structured Problems." In *The Nature of Expertise,* edited by M. Chi, R. Glaser, and M. Farr, pp. 261-285. Hillsdale, NJ: Lawrence Erlbaum Associates.

Voss, J., S. Tyler, and L. Yengo. (1983). "Individual Differences in Social Science Problem Solving." In *Individual Differences in Cognitive Processes,* Vol. 1, edited by R. Dillon and R. Schmeck, pp. 205-232. New York: Academic Press.

Voss, J., T. Greene, T. Post, and B. Penner. (1983). "Problem-Solving Skill in the Social Sciences." In *The Psychology of Learning and Motivation: Advances in Research Theory,* Vol. 17, edited by G. Bower, pp. 165-213. New York: Academic Press.

The Helping Alliance and Service-Learning

by Jeremy Leeds

A focus on relationships is an important area in which service-learning and psychology overlap in concerns, and where some of the thinking in psychotherapy might provide useful insight for students and faculty involved in community service. A key issue in all service-learning involves the relationships developed between the "service providers" and those being served. These concerns are often appropriately tackled as conceptual issues and problems: Who are we? Who are they?

It has been my experience, both as a service-learning teacher and in speaking with numerous colleagues, that when addressing these issues, instructors often place themselves several steps apart from their students' experiences and motivations. The students' goal is often to establish relationships with people they meet in community settings and to have meaningful experiences based on these relationships. The "bigger" questions often end up being tangential to their actual experiences and disconnected from their immediate concerns. This need not be the case. Our concern with drawing lessons on a large scale from the individual's community activity must, and can, be posed so as to connect with the actual experience and motivations of the participants. A critical examination of relationships that develop in service settings is one concrete and important way to do so. Still another reason to focus on relationships is that many of the difficulties that arise in them in service situations (e.g., between students and community residents, students and staff, tutors and younger students) result from the relationships being poorly conceived. To ignore this sine qua non of the service experience puts learning at peril.

What can psychology and psychotherapy add to an understanding of relationships that will be productive for all involved in service-learning? This chapter will place the practice disciplines of psychology (clinical, counseling, educational) in the "service" of service-learning by using the concept of the helping alliance. In psychology, the concept of *helping alliance* or working alliance has become a shorthand, across theoretical perspectives, for the basic relationship upon which the actual work of counseling or psychotherapy rests (Greenson 1981a). The concept of the helping alliance has relevance for service-learning relationships in a way that both enriches service-learning and adds new understanding of helping alliances as well.

This chapter is divided into two sections. First, I present a history and conceptual background of the helping alliance concept and tie it to the concerns of service-learning. Second, I offer some examples from our research and practice to create an interface between psychology and service-learning around the helping alliance concept.

The Helping Alliance

The helping alliance or working alliance has had a long history in psychotherapy. Freud developed what Gill (1993) has called both a "one-person psychology" and a "two-person psychology." The one-person perspective views the person as "a closed system of forces and counterforces"; the two-person perspective looks at psychoanalysis as "a relationship between two people" (115). Over time and with clinical experience, Freud (1913) more directly addressed the relational aspects of psychoanalysis — both the irrational/resistance-based aspects, which were termed "transference," and the reality-based and attachment-oriented aspects. Freud's therapy involved an intense experience that by definition took place between two people and a close scrutiny of all that happened between and within them. Thus, whether or not the clinical relationship was originally conceived in this way, questions as to how to understand and categorize different aspects of it became central to the struggle to help people through psychotherapy.

A major advance in the consideration of relationships in psychoanalytic psychotherapy came with Greenson's papers on what he called the "working alliance." This is the "relatively nonneurotic, rational rapport which the patient has with his analyst" (Greenson 1981a: 320). He and others (Zetzel 1956) shifted attention to the real aspects of the relationship. In the taxonomy of relationships within psychoanalysis, a working alliance is a rational, but somewhat artificial, foundation for productive work. It is artificial because a rational, helpful stance may not at times be the natural reaction of either participant. There will be times when either party may need to step back and call forth a helpful, caring response by an act of will, when he or she might have a desire to do otherwise (Greenson 1981b: 90). These possible tensions between different feelings, and between feelings and the demands of a setting, are particularly relevant for understanding relationships in service-learning. Often the first, natural reaction of students in a service setting is not the helpful one.

In a seminal paper in 1979, Bordin radically expanded the idea of the working alliance, both within psychoanalytic therapy and into nontherapy contexts. He proposed that "the working alliance between the person who seeks change and the one who offers to be a change agent is one of the keys, if not *the* key, to the change process" (252). Bordin synthesized previous work on the working alliance into three core concepts: "an agreement on goals, an assignment of task or a series of tasks, and the development of bonds" (253). *Goals* can, depending on the kind of therapy undertaken, vary from enduring and long-term to focused and situational. *Tasks* represent the agreed-upon obligations and roles each participant will take on in the process. *Bonds* refer to the "nature of the human relationship between therapist and patient" (254). Bordin's general definitions, as he himself notes, make the working alliance applicable to all kinds of change processes (252). The three components may be present in different strengths depending on the quality and the context of the specific helping alliance. This goals-tasks-bonds triad is central to our operationalizing the alliance concept in service-learning.

Since Bordin's contribution, much work has been done on generalizing the working alliance concept to all kinds of psychotherapy. Luborsky was the first to develop an empirical methodology for assessing the "helping alliance," as he called it. His measure looked at two components of the alliance: "the patient's experiencing the therapist as helpful and supportive" and "a helping relationship based on a sense of working together in a joint struggle against whatever impedes the patient" (1994: 39). His summary definition states that "[t]he helping alliance is an expression of a patient's positive bond with the therapist who is perceived as a helpful and supportive person" (39). Note that the goals-tasks-bonds concepts are embedded in slightly different ways in this definition. Luborsky points out that this alliance can predict therapeutic outcome in theories other than psychodynamic theories (41).

The focus on the alliance between therapist and patient is now a relatively robust area of research that has moved in many cases from purely psychodynamic orientations to looking at this alliance as a common factor operating in all therapies (Henry and Strupp 1994: 51). However, Bordin's assertion that this alliance concept can be relevant to all kinds of helping situations, not just psychotherapy, has not been generally pursued. One possible reason is that it simply has not been an area of priority for psychologists. Another reason might be that even if it were disseminated, other disciplines would be wary of "therapizing" what they do. So, for example, service-learning teachers might be hesitant to use concepts originating in psychotherapy because they fear students might get the wrong idea and become too embroiled with those with whom they work.

There are two responses to this latter reservation. First, the alliance concept might have begun with psychotherapy but makes claims to all helping relationships. The broad definitions given by Bordin and Luborsky certainly can be applied to relationships outside of psychotherapy. Second, attention to the possibilities and limits of relationships is a key issue in service-learning experiences. Thinking about the nature and quality of alliances addresses central issues in what students learn, what they feel, and what barriers develop to accomplishing their goals.

The Helping Alliance in Community Service

We have begun to use the helping alliance framework to develop an academic component to student community activism and service at New York University, including training volunteers and service-learners in operational aspects of the helping alliance; beginning research on the students' perceptions of alliance issues and obstacles; and developing an action-research project, one component of which is to establish a working alliance with various agencies and their representatives.

One example of using the helping alliance came in training students to work primarily in settlement houses in Manhattan's Lower East Side and Greenwich Village neighborhoods (Leeds 1996). These students are organized as the President's Community Team ("C-Team"), which at present has more than 200 members. Settlement houses are neighborhood centers originally founded to provide a common ground for the "better off" members of society, such as students, and those who live in poorer communities (Addams 1892; Videka-Sherman 1992). Originating in England in the late 19th century, the first American settlements were founded in the 1890s on the Lower East Side. In their history and mission, as well as in the variety of activities they offer, they are perfect venues for both service and learning. Our students work with young people (ages 3 to 21) in a variety of programs for learning and recreation. Developing a single-session introduction/training for this variety of experiences was a daunting task. We decided to focus on providing the beginning tools for forming working alliances.

The first question to be addressed was: Who are the partners in the alliance? Most obvious are the students and the settlement house participants with whom the students work — in tutoring, recreation, and other activities. Other partners include the agencies themselves, the staff of the houses, the other volunteers, the C-Team, and other community residents. Putting the students' work in this many-sided context alerts students to the presence and the perspectives of others; it also enriches the day-to-day work by providing a broader framework.

The training begins with a video and discussion of settlement houses. We move from there to a series of role-play exercises that highlight different aspects of an alliance and possible pitfalls in its creation. The role plays have at different times been conducted by students in the Department of Applied Psychology, undergraduates in my service-learning class, and staff from the NYU Office of Community Service. Not all of these are experts and may themselves be C-Team participants and community service-learners. This points to one important lesson: Teaching is itself one of the best learning opportunities. Together, we develop scenarios of typical situations that pose challenges in the creation of alliances with the various players in the service setting. In performing these scenarios in training sessions, seminar participants think about the interplay of the helping alliance goals-tasks-bonds triad in the creation of productive relationships.

The role plays begin with one or more obvious and humorous "wrong" responses to a challenging situation. The audience is invited to critique and make suggestions, and perhaps to participate in redoing the scene. Finally, students provide some of the lessons to be kept in mind, and possible alternative ways to think about the situations. Below are examples of role-playing scenarios, along with a breakdown of learning objectives within the goals-tasks-bonds shorthand framework for the helping alliance.

Scenario 1

A young person asks a C-Team member to promise to keep a secret. This role play allows us to discuss the *role* of the college student in the agency, and the need to notify staff of difficult and troubling situations. It also addresses the roles of trust and secrecy in relationships. Students are urged not to make promises of secrecy that cannot be kept. Finally, it addresses the extent and limits of help itself; that is, the student may be most helpful by being able to bring an issue to the attention of someone who can actually provide more expertise and/or resources.

Goals: — maintaining a safe environment
       — providing help when needed

Tasks: — working together to develop responses to problems
       — service-learner has responsibility to work with staff to develop responses to problems, when necessary
       — service-learner is present to hear the concerns of the person

Bonds: — relationship has limits
       — how to maintain the helpful stance while suggesting something counter to the other's initial wishes

Scenario 2

A C-Team member cannot get the attention of a staff member about an important concern. This example involves some stresses in staff-student relations. Discussion can focus on understanding some of the pressures on staff: budget cuts, busy schedules, a need to prioritize on the run. We also address typical workplace issues — sometimes it's just a bad day; there are appropriate and inappropriate ways to communicate a concern. Most important, we discuss the need to take one's concerns seriously, and the responsibility to find a way to communicate the needed information.

Goals: — students and staff should work together for benefit of the programs and all those involved

Tasks: — volunteers must communicate with staff about difficult situations
　　　 — staff have a responsibility to respond to volunteers' concerns
Bonds: — both volunteers and staff need to recognize the difficulties that arise in their relationships that might lead to barriers in communication

We have also begun doing research on the helping alliance as it applies in our community service and service-learning context. Though the numbers of students involved and/or responding to the relevant helping alliance issues have thus far been small, there have been several suggestive findings that will lead both to further research and to new ideas about how the relationship/alliance plays out in this kind of environment. In a follow-up questionnaire, when asked what was important about the training, many students mentioned learning situational competencies and used verbs such as "deal," "handle," and "confront." For our purposes, we call these "competency" verbs. A preliminary finding of the study is that for relatively inexperienced and untrained helpers, a first concern and foundation for a productive alliance with program participants is a *feeling of basic competency in concrete situations* (Leeds 1995).

Another finding results from the work of a doctoral student in the Department of Applied Psychology who interviewed five tutors on the theme of their relationship with those they tutored. He used the "goals-tasks-bonds" framework in a semi-structured interview, and found that, without fail, all five tutors almost immediately mentioned "friend" as the key role they sought to play with their partners (Pellitteri 1996). This raises fascinating questions for psychology in general and for understanding working alliances in particular. By "friend," students were referring broadly to the "bonds" aspect of the alliance. Pellitteri suggests that this could be in conflict with goals and tasks, specifically the academic work toward which the program is geared. It is important, then, in training service-learning students and community activists, to set a framework for the recognition of all three aspects of the helping alliance. It is also important to note that there will be times when the aspects seem to be in conflict.

Areas for Further Inquiry

There are numerous issues associated with the helping alliance that require further thinking and research and that make this an exciting and useful concept to pursue. Perhaps the most important task is to look at concrete applications of the concept in nonpsychotherapy settings. Tutoring, mentoring, environmental activism — in short, the whole spectrum of service activities — are not psychotherapy. Here, relationships and alliances that are different in kind from those found in psychotherapy are to be expected, and indeed hoped for! The important *general* areas of inquiry about nonpsychotherapeutic helping alliances are: What constitutes a helping relationship? How is a particular relationship conceived of, formed, and evaluated from the perspectives of both/all participants? Another consideration might be: Does the relationship allow for the development of new kinds of helping and relating not originally planned for?

The measurement issue is important for further analysis and research. As mentioned above, the helping/working alliance in psychotherapy has been the subject of research using several measures. Horvath and Greenberg point out that there is a risk, much as in research on empathy, that different measures will not converge on the same definition of working alliance, and so compromise its construct validity (1994: 5). They also point out that the various measures, taken from the different possible perspectives (client-therapist-observer), do not show encouraging correlations with each other. Thus, even if research on nonpsychotherapy alliances uses existing or modified measures, researchers will need to proceed carefully. In any case, measures need to start from a solid and clearly enunciated concept of key alliance components and their development over time. This could begin with in-depth study of a series of these relationships over time, from as many angles as possible.

The measurement question is only the tip of the iceberg in a larger conceptual discussion. The alliance has been in general used as a construct, and in the process has perhaps lost some of its critical edge. The suggestion by Greenson, discussed above, that these helping alliances are somewhat artificial — based on the goals and needs of the situation — is a point that should not be forgotten in implementing the construct and in teaching about it. Relationships have many, sometimes contradictory components, which can vary over time in importance and prominence. Goals may be central at one time or in one situation, tasks in another. This raises fascinating areas of inquiry. How much helping is innate in people relating to each other? How do roles and responsibilities mediate help? What is the place of external social forces and contexts?

It is necessary to continue to look into the specifics of "friendship" as Pellitteri found in his interviews referred to above. This, after all, is the initial motive and expectation that many students bring to community work. What can we say about it? A great deal — but here I would like to make only three short points.

First, "friend" probably does not describe the bond people are envisioning. Differences in age, perhaps class, status, knowledge, and many other dimensions make the bond unequal and not conducive to what is generally meant by *friendship*. Perhaps "older sibling" is more accurate; or perhaps the key component is a positive emotional connection. Further investigation as to just what is meant, and how it plays out across a relationship's lifespan, is warranted.

Second, positive relationships that develop across differences in background are not typical in this society; in fact, studies of friendship and class show cross-class friendships to be rather rare (Garrett 1989). Thus, establishing and maintaining them takes inordinate effort and motivation. This aspect of bridging differences is worth recognizing, pursuing, and studying in service-learning. Attention to the opportunities for, and qualities of, these relations is crucial to students' experience, and is a key value for service-learning programs.

Finally, the psychology of friendships has much to contribute to a critical examination of what any of us means when we say we want to be "friends." Freud, for example, saw friendship as based in conflictual experience, perhaps as reflections of father/son relations of rivalry once removed (see Little 1989: 146-147). This is certainly not what undergraduates think of immediately when they say they want to be a program participant's "friend." A critical examination of the term and its psychology might prove thought-provoking. Following such a path demonstrates a central paradigm of service-learning: The experience provides a touchstone for new avenues of academic learning.

Another important strength of the helping alliance concept, and an area for further evaluation and inquiry, is that placing relationships in the spotlight and providing a psychological framework for studying them give us added conceptual tools to tackle typical service-learning dilemmas. The question of who is getting the most out of the experience can be seen in a dialectic with the same kinds of questions asked and answered in helping relationship theories. Does Rogers have the best vantage point on this? Freud? What do these theories lack that the encounters found in service-learning can illuminate?

Finally, the question can be turned around: What can psychology learn from the helping alliance in service-learning? We become service-learners ourselves when we bring concepts from psychotherapy out of the consulting room and into a wider context. An always vocal minority of psychologists and psychotherapists has called attention to the dangers of a narrow focus for psychology, leading to complacency, conformism, and a lack of awareness of our own context. Sarason (1982) notes that "Dewey saw clearly what psychology is still blind to: the substance of psychology cannot be independent of the social order. It is not that it *should not* be independent but that it *cannot be*" (236). Similarly, Fromm has argued that

> *Psychoanalysis was originally a radical, penetrating, liberating theory. It slowly lost this character and stagnated, failing to develop its theory in*

response to the changed human situation after the First World War; instead it retreated into conformism and the search for respectability. (1970: 16)

Service-learning holds the promise of contributing to the knowledge and practice of psychotherapy. Institutionalized connection with community action provides the opportunity to place psychologists in a context in which their theories can again come to life as "radical, penetrating, and liberating." A bit down the road, we may be able to reflect on how service-learning experiences have modified our understandings of helping alliances, and indeed our psychotherapeutic practice. We may also have a new basis for asking the big question: What is it about relationships that makes them so important to us, and yet so difficult? I cannot think of a service-learning experience or course that would not be enriched by giving this some thought.

References

Addams, J. (1892). "The Subjective Necessity for Social Settlements." In *On Education*, by J. Addams, pp. 49-63. New Brunswick, NJ: Transaction Publishers.

Bordin, E.S. (1979). "The Generalizibility of the Psychoanalytic Concept of the Working Alliance." *Psychotherapy: Theory, Research and Practice* 16: 252-259.

Freud, S. (1913). *Further Recommendation on the Techniques of Psychoanalysis. On Beginning the Treatment*. Standard Edition, Vol. 12. London: Hogart Press.

Fromm, E. (1970). *The Crisis of Psychoanalysis*. New York: Henry Holt and Company.

Garrett, S. (1989). "Friendship and the Social Order." In *Dialectics of Friendship*, edited by R. Porter and S. Tomaselli, pp. 130-142. London: Routledge.

Gill, M. (1993). "One-Person and Two-Person Perspectives: Freud's 'Observations on Transference-Love.'" In *On Freud's "Observations on Transference-Love,"* edited by E.S. Person, A. Hagelin, and P. Fonagy, pp. 114-129. New Haven, CT: Yale University Press.

Greenson, R.R. (1981a). "The 'Real' Relationship Between the Patient and the Psychoanalyst." In *Classics in Psychoanalytic Technique*, edited by R. Langs, pp. 319-330. 1971. Reprint, New York: Jason Aronson.

———. (1981b). "The Working Alliance and the Transference Neurosis." In *Classics in Psychoanalytic Technique*, edited by R. Langs, pp. 87-96. 1965. Reprint, New York: Jason Aronson.

Henry, W.P., and H.H. Strupp. (1994). "The Therapeutic Alliance as Interpersonal Process." In *The Working Alliance: Theory, Research, and Practice*, edited by A.O. Horvath and L.S. Greenberg, pp. 51-84. New York: John Wiley & Sons.

Horvath, A.O., and L.S. Greenberg. (1994). "Introduction." In *The Working Alliance: Theory, Research, and Practice*, edited by A.O. Horvath and L.S. Greenberg, pp. 1-9. New York: John Wiley & Sons.

Leeds, J. (June 1995). "Training Community Volunteers: A Preliminary Follow-Up." Poster presented at the Fifth Biennial Conference, Society for Community Research and Action, Chicago.

———— . (1996). "Training Student Volunteers for Community Service: A Model Collaboration." *Journal of Community Practice* 3(2): 95-102.

Little, G. (1989). "Freud, Friendship and Politics." In *Dialectics of Friendship*, edited by R. Porter and S. Tomaselli, pp. 143-158. London: Routledge.

Luborsky, L. (1994). "Therapeutic Alliances as Predictors of Psychotherapy Outcomes: Factors Explaining the Predictive Success." In *The Working Alliance: Theory, Research, and Practice*, edited by A.O. Horvath and L.S. Greenberg, pp. 38-50. New York: John Wiley & Sons.

Pellitteri, J. (1996). *"The Working Alliance and the Tutor-Student Relationship."* Unpublished candidacy paper, Department of Applied Psychology, New York University.

Sarason, S.B. (1982). *Psychology and Social Action: Selected Papers.* New York: Praeger.

Videka-Sherman, L. (1992). "New-Style Settlement Houses." *Bulletin of the Rockefeller Institute,* Tenth Anniversary, 41-44.

Zetzel, E.R. (1956). "Current Concepts of Transference." *International Journal of Psychoanalysis* 37: 369-376.

Professor McKenna Teaches Introductory Psychology

by Donna K. Duffy and Robert G. Bringle

Professor McKenna is preparing to teach Introductory Psychology for the 30th time. She sighs as she gathers her notes and materials: What can she do to energize herself as well as her students? The variety of material in the introductory course provides a plethora of teaching possibilities, but Professor McKenna is discouraged by offering only surface coverage of so many topics. Professor McKenna feels overwhelmed as she reflects on the diversity in her classroom. She considers herself an above-average lecturer and she receives good student satisfaction ratings. However, she realizes that her traditional approaches are not motivating many of her students, yet she is not certain what strategies would be more effective.

She remembers hearing a presentation about service-learning at a recent APA conference. Service-learning is an approach that links community service, academic content, and structured reflection activities. The presenter at the conference reported that his students valued the opportunity to learn in a setting outside of the classroom, searched the course material for its relevance and limitations, talked more to other students and to him, raised more critical questions in class, and developed a deeper understanding of the course concepts because of their concrete experiences in community agencies. Professor McKenna was intrigued by the presentation and now wonders whether service-learning could work in her course. What would be unique about the learning that occurs when students, faculty, and communities intersect?

Along with some of her colleagues in higher education, our fictitious Professor McKenna is beginning to question both the content and the processes she uses in teaching her courses. As Rice (1996) suggests, higher education is in the middle of major paradigm shifts from (1) focus on knowledge to a focus on learning, (2) faculty autonomy to institution building, (3) individualistic work to collaboration, and (4) isolation to greater faculty responsibility for public life. These transitions present new opportunities for her to redirect her professional energies in ways that can have a more meaningful impact on her students and her community.

Psychology has a rich tradition of using practice-based education, including laboratories, practica, and internships. Practica and internships focus on teaching and refining professional skills and are typically reserved for advanced and graduate courses in psychology. Professor McKenna knows that service-learning has been integrated effectively into internship programs (Motiff and Roehling 1994), but she realizes that her introductory students do not have adequate training for many clinical settings. She must find service opportunities in the community that both engage the skills of students appropriately and enhance their learning of course content in a meaningful way.

Professor McKenna has found her own community service experiences professionally enriching. As she volunteers at a shelter for homeless women, she readily sees ways in which her involvement provides examples of concepts and theories presented in her courses. In this work, she regularly confronts complex issues in the lives of individuals that challenge the wisdom and relevance of material in a basic psychology course. She realizes along with others (Prilleltensky 1994; Sarason 1996) that psychology's focus on the individual is only a part of the answer; psychologists need to consider social policies and inequities existing within the broader society as they work to solve problems. But although Professor McKenna's students may be enthusiastic about going into the community, they do not possess her background and the conceptual framework within which they can readily make connections between course content and community experiences. Hence, she is drawn to the fact that in service-learning courses students benefit from regular opportunities to engage in reflective activities that allow them to practice making connections between community work and course content. With practice and experience in reflecting on their experiences, her students could enhance their critical-thinking skills, examine their values, and develop civic responsibility (Eyler, Giles, and Schmiede 1996; Hatcher and Bringle 1997; Silcox 1993).

But despite her growing suspicion that service-learning would indeed be useful as a means of enhancing her Introductory Psychology course, she still has many questions about exactly how she could incorporate it. Should the service be required? Should students locate their own placements? Who will prepare them for the service setting? As she considers revising her syllabus, she discusses these issues with a psychology professor at a nearby college who has integrated service-learning into several psychology courses. She then decides that for the first semester, she will make service-learning an option that students can choose instead of writing a term paper. This will allow her to begin on a small scale. She also decides that she will present a list of potential service sites to the students and will talk with the relevant agencies prior to the beginning of the semester to discuss the particulars of service-learning and to explain how service-learning differs from the typical volunteer programs with which they are familiar. As it turns out, agency personnel are very receptive to her ideas, and she begins to realize just how valuable a resource those agencies represent — both educationally and administratively (e.g., orientation, training, supervision, evaluation). Finally, she decides on the reflection activities for those students electing the service-learning option: Every other week they will submit two-page typewritten papers linking their service experience to the course content, and then write a longer paper at the end of the semester that describes their service experience, relates it to the course content, and relates it to their values and goals.

Altman (1996) has suggested that service-learning leads to *socially responsive knowledge,* a kind of knowledge that has not been emphasized recently in higher education. There are three goals for socially responsive knowledge: "First, to educate students in the problems of society; second, to have them experience and understand firsthand social issues in their community; and third, and most importantly, to give them the experiences and skills they need to act on social problems" (Altman 1996: 375-376). In Altman's view, socially responsive knowledge should be an integral part of the undergraduate curriculum, along with *foundational knowledge* (content and cross-disciplinary knowledge) and *professional knowledge* (practitioner skills and content).

Service-learning is effective in helping students develop socially responsive knowledge; it may also facilitate learning in the more traditional domains of content and skills. In thinking about her Introductory Psychology course, Professor McKenna has often experienced frustration about the ever burgeoning content of the course. Students can be exposed to a wide range of information, but what do they really understand? Langer (1989, 1993), Perkins (1992), and Gardner (1991) all discuss knowledge acquisition; they agree on the necessity of considering problems from several perspectives in order to reach genuine understanding. Gardner (1993) defines genuine understanding as the capacity to take information and concepts and apply them to new situations for which that knowledge is appropriate (also see Eyler, Root, and Giles, beginning on p. 85 of this volume). He maintains that much of the learning in educational institutions is superficial, and he encourages teachers to consider covering less content while focusing on true understanding. Students in an introductory course who work in a setting outside of the classroom will have more opportunities to apply course information to new situations; they also will be exposed to perspectives different from those of their professor and classmates.

Throughout her years in higher education, Professor McKenna has reflected on her goals for teaching psychology. She wants students to question ideas and to consider multiple ways to explain the complexity of human behavior. She worries most about students who form premature cognitive commitments, fixed beliefs that result from the "mindless acceptance of information as true without consideration of alternative versions of that information" (Langer 1993: 45). Students with firsthand experience in the community are more willing to question ideas and concepts that do not fit with their experiences. Service-learning experiences and appropriately selected reflection activities encourage students to move through the four processes of Kolb's (1984) learning cycle: concrete experience, reflective observation, abstract conceptualization, and active experimentation. In Kolb's view, students who move through activities in all four phases of the cycle will learn more effectively than if they focus on only one or two of the phases. Enns (1993) suggests that using Kolb's model provides a framework for integrating separate and connected knowledge and for helping professors create a "multifocal, gender-balanced, inclusive approach to teaching psychology" (12).

In reviewing the American Psychological Association's learner-centered psychological principles (1993) as well as principles of effective teaching (Angelo 1993; Chickering and Gamson 1987; Katz and Henry 1988), Professor McKenna realizes that service-learning supports four key principles: (1) focus on active rather than passive learning; (2) recognition of individual styles of learning; (3) increasing communication and connections among students and between students and faculty; and (4) opportunities for early and frequent feedback on learning success. Service-learning aligns well with principles for a student-centered classroom, but Professor McKenna is curious about the specific impact that a service-learning course will have on *her* students.

She has become increasingly aware of the importance at the national level of assessing outcomes in higher education (Banta and Associates 1993); she is also familiar with recent initiatives in her department and college. As she considers incorporating service-learning into her course, she outlines a plan: write measurable objectives for the service component, create activities that will reflect the objectives effectively, assess student learning, and use the findings to improve practice. Professor McKenna already employs several types of classroom-assessment techniques (Angelo and Cross 1993; Brown, Rust, and Gibbs 1994; Rando and Lenze 1994) to monitor student learning regularly throughout the semester. By using a variety of formative assessment approaches, she can learn what is confusing to students, which concepts are being mastered, and how to improve instruction. Because she plans to experiment with service-learning, she confirms to herself the importance of using these techniques so that she can obtain regular student feedback and make adjustments.

She is also interested in knowing about the changes that occur in students over the course of a semester. Thus, she will plan to do not only classroom assessment but also course assessment. This will include the traditional forms of course assessment that regularly are a part of her instruction (e.g., learning, satisfaction) as well as forms to capture changes uniquely related to the service-learning experience. After examining other evaluation studies of service-learning courses (Bringle and Kremer 1993; Cohen and Kinsey 1994; Conrad and Hedin 1982, 1989; Giles and Eyler 1994; Markus, Howard, and King 1993), she is aware of the vast array of possible dependent variables that could be included in such a study. Because of the particular nature of her class and its placements, she has decided to select several measures that seem particularly relevant and compile them into a questionnaire that can be given to students at the beginning and end of the semester.

However, because of Professor McKenna's understanding of experimental design, she realizes how limited this information is in its ability to clarify why changes occur. Even if she expands this procedure to include another section of the course that did not engage in service-learning, not controlling for assignment of students to sections would still prevent her from determining why certain changes occurred. In order to answer the why question, a more sophisticated experimental design will be necessary. This could be accomplished through random assignment of students to sections, which would be impractical, or through random assignment of sections of her course to levels of a variable (e.g., type of reflection activity) — a more realistic option.

Pondering why students change during a service-learning course brings her to an additional array of research possibilities. For example, the why question leads to a consideration of motives of volunteers (students or generally), issues of moral development and how students might be affected by service experiences, cognitive topics including how students problem solve at their service sites and the kinds of attributions they make about their clients, the nature of the relationships that develop between the helper and the helped, and what is it in the service experience that produces learning and changes the students' attitudes, beliefs, behavior, and values. She realizes that psychology provides not only the measurement and design tools needed to help answer these types of questions, but it also has a wealth of theories and empirical findings that are relevant to these questions.

Professor McKenna has renewed excitement for her curriculum development efforts involving service-learning. Not only does she see how it integrates her service interests and those of her students with her teaching, but she also sees how it has the potential to be integrated with research on teaching and theoretical research. Thus, engaging in classroom assessment, course evaluation, and research becomes a reflective exercise through which she can gain new insights into her professional work and transform her own learning (Cranton 1996). Furthermore, students can become partners with her in the design and execution of these applied and basic research studies, adding a new dimension to how students can learn from service-learning.

Naturally, she also recognizes that she will have to take some risks as she questions and changes her approach to teaching Introductory Psychology. Working in partnership with agencies in the community may require more flexibility, but it may also lead to concrete ways in which her research can be applied to social problems. Teaching Introductory Psychology 29 times has made it rather predictable; teaching it the 30th time with a community service component will present novel challenges. But, they strike her as good, constructive challenges that she is looking forward to.

Professors who have adopted service-learning in their classrooms have used a variety of courses and approaches. Some have required service components, whereas others have made the service optional. It has been adapted to a five-week semester, a regular semester, and a full-year immersion curriculum. Whether service is a recent addition to a course, or a long-standing program, each instructor has struggled with concerns regarding appropriate placements, reflection activities, and assessment. Like Professor McKenna, each one wondered whether service-learning would work in his or her course; now they all are exploring the uniqueness of the learning that occurs when students, faculty, and communities intersect.

References

Altman, I. (1996). "Higher Education and Psychology in the Millennium." *American Psychologist* 51: 371-378.

American Psychological Association. (1993). *Learner-Centered Psychological Principles: Guidelines for School Redesign and Reform*. Washington, DC: APA.

Angelo, T.A. (April 1993). "A 'Teacher's Dozen': Fourteen General, Research-Based Principles for Improving Higher Learning in Our Classrooms." *AAHE Bulletin* 45(8): 3-7, 13.

———— , and K.P. Cross. (1993). *Classroom Assessment Techniques: A Handbook for College Teachers*. 2nd ed. San Francisco: Jossey-Bass.

Banta, T.W., and Associates. (1993). *Making a Difference: Outcomes of a Decade of Assessment in Higher Education*. San Francisco: Jossey-Bass.

Bringle, R.G., and J.F. Kremer. (1993). "An Evaluation of an Intergenerational Service-Learning Project for Undergraduates." *Educational Gerontology* 19: 407-416.

Brown, S., C. Rust, and G. Gibbs. (1994). *Strategies for Diversifying Assessment in Higher Education*. Oxford: Oxford Centre for Staff Development.

Chickering, A.W., and Z.F. Gamson. (March 1987). "Seven Principles for Good Practice in Undergraduate Education." *AAHE Bulletin* 39(7): 3-7.

Cohen, J., and D. Kinsey. (1994). "'Doing Good' and Scholarship: A Service-Learning Study." *Journalism Educator* vol. 4: 4-19.

Conrad, D., and D. Hedin. (1982). "The Impact of Experiential Education on Adolescent Development." *Child and Youth Services* 4: 57-76.

——— . (1989). *High School Community Service: A Review of Research and Programs*. Madison, WI: National Center on Effective Secondary Schools.

Cranton, P. (1996). *Professional Development as Transformative Learning*. San Francisco: Jossey-Bass.

Enns, C.Z. (1993). "Integrating Separate and Connected Knowing: The Experiential Learning Model." *Teaching of Psychology* 20: 7-13.

Eyler, J., D.E. Giles, Jr., and A. Schmiede. (1996). *A Practitioner's Guide to Reflection in Service-Learning: Student Voices & Reflections*. Nashville, TN: Vanderbilt University.

Gardner, H. (1991). *The Unschooled Mind*. New York: Basic Books.

——— . (1993). *Multiple Intelligences: The Theory in Practice*. New York: Basic Books.

Giles, D.E., Jr., and J. Eyler. (1994). "The Impact of a College Community Service Laboratory on Students' Personal, Social, and Cognitive Outcomes." *Journal of Adolescence* 17: 327-339.

Hatcher, J.A., and R.G. Bringle. (1997). "Reflection: Bridging the Gap Between Service and Learning." *Journal of College Teaching* 45: 153-158.

Katz, J., and M. Henry. (1988). *Turning Professors Into Teachers*. New York: Macmillan.

Kolb, D. (1984). *Experiential Learning: Experience as a Source of Learning and Development*. Englewood Cliffs, NJ: Prentice-Hall.

Langer, E.J. (1989). *Mindfulness*. Reading, MA: Addison-Wesley.

——— . (1993). "A Mindful Education." *Educational Psychologist* 28: 43-50.

Markus, G., J. Howard, and D. King. (1993). "Integrating Community Service and Classroom Instruction Enhances Learning: Results From an Experiment." *Educational Evaluation and Policy Analysis* 15: 410-419.

Motiff, J.P., and P.V. Roehling. (1994). "Learning While Serving in a Psychology Internship." *Michigan Journal of Community Service Learning* 1: 70-76.

Perkins, D. (1992). *Smart Schools: From Training Memories to Educating Minds*. New York: Free Press.

Prilleltensky, I. (1994). *The Morals and Politics of Psychology: Psychological Discourse and the Status Quo*. Albany, NY: State University of New York Press.

Rando, W.C., and L.F. Lenze. (1994). *Learning From Students: Early Term Student Feedback in Higher Education*. University Park, PA: National Center on Postsecondary Teaching, Learning, and Assessment, Pennsylvania State University.

Rice, R.E. (January 1996). "Making a Place for the New American Scholar." Paper presented at the AAHE Conference on Faculty Roles & Rewards, Atlanta, GA.

Sarason, S.B. (1996). *The Barometers of Social Change: Essays on Individual, Institutional Change in the Post World War II Era.* San Francisco: Jossey-Bass.

Silcox, H. (1993). *A How To Guide to Reflection: Adding Cognitive Learning to Community Service Programs.* Philadelphia, PA: Brighton Press.

Strategies for Service-Learning:
Internalization and Empowerment

by Carol M. Werner

Service-learning provides students with opportunities to make a difference in their communities. It can also lead to changes in values about our roles as citizens, changes in students' self-concepts and personal efficacy, and changes in community members' actions and beliefs. Unfortunately, in some cases it can also be discouraging to students or have negative impacts on the very individuals the students intend to help. This chapter outlines a philosophical approach to service-learning that emphasizes long-term positive impacts for both students and community. It is based on psychological literatures on self-efficacy, intrinsic motivation, empowerment, and internalization of values. It adopts a holistic perspective, meaning that service-learning projects should be viewed not as isolated events but rather as parts of the total community system. Another assumption is that people have both individual and social identities, and service projects should provide opportunities for enhancing both — they should make people feel good about themselves as individuals, and they should allow people to feel part of a group (Werner and Altman in press; Werner, Brown, and Altman 1997). Thus, as a social psychologist interested in internalization of values and attitudes, I emphasize service-learning approaches that guide students to adopt a service lifestyle and encourage citizens to assume more control over their local environment.

At the University of Utah, I offer service-learning opportunities in two classes, introductory environmental psychology and advanced (Environment and Behavior). Both classes require a term paper describing how an exercise or project fits with some aspect of course content. Both are advanced classes, so students bring knowledge about methodology, data analysis, and psychological content. Service projects take advantage of these

The philosophy articulated here has benefited enormously from discussions with my colleagues Irwin Altman, Barbara Brown, Irene Fisher, Linda Bonar, and Cathy Zick; my service-learning teaching assistant, Ryan Russell; and, of course, the students in my classes. My service experiences would not have been possible without the psychological and financial support of the university's Bennion Community Service Center.

Correspondence concerning this article should be addressed to Carol M. Werner, University of Utah, Psychology Department, Beh. Sci. Bldg., 390 S. 1530 E., Room 502, Salt Lake City, UT 84112-0251.

skills and build new ones. Examples of projects are "The Urban Forester" (three projects that helped increase participation in a volunteer Urban Forester program) and "University, City, and County" (six projects that supported recycling efforts). Although my primary experience with service-learning has been in the area of environmental psychology, I believe the lessons I have learned can be generalized to other areas as well.

This chapter begins with a section on my philosophical orientation. The first part, "Why Service-Learning?," explains why I believe in service-learning; the second, "How Service-Learning?," suggests how service-learning can empower students and citizens. These are followed by a section on practicalities, such as locating opportunities and keeping projects manageable. The chapter ends by encouraging others to explore service and define their own goals and philosophy.

Philosophical Orientation

Why Service-Learning?

Projects, not exercises. Before service-learning, students wrote papers about "exercises," applications of course content that demonstrated mastery of the literature and an ability to apply it but served no broader purpose (e.g., critiques of children's parks that were not shared with park management). Now they write about *projects,* similar applications but now involving the community and using the knowledge gained to improve a real situation. Too often, students put a lot of effort into term papers that are filed away and forgotten. I would rather students take the same amount of effort and produce both a term paper and a project that serves a community need. Furthermore, we give the best term papers on a project to the relevant community organization, providing feedback and information that can have short- and long-term impacts.

Pedagogy. There is an old saying about teaching: "Explain and I'll forget; show me and I'll remember; involve me and I'll understand." Most students respond in exactly this way to a service-learning project. Although many also respond this way to a nonservice paper assignment, projects carry more responsibility and have the potential to increase a student's depth of commitment and understanding. Most students would be horribly embarrassed to reach out to someone in the community, promising information of worth, but then to have nothing to offer.

My experience has been that students involved in service-learning projects usually read the material more carefully, think about it more deeply, and challenge the parts that seem weak. Many read beyond the assigned material, either drawing in material from other courses or seeking additional articles from the library. Their term papers are a joy to read (and students enjoy writing them!). The cumulative effect is improved education (see Perkins 1992, for an extended discussion). Students who choose to work as a group learn to function effectively in a group, developing skills desired by more and more employers. Indeed, projects involving groups of students benefit from their multiple perspectives, different domains of expertise, and scrutiny of one another's ideas, producing the best work possible. As an added benefit, students often make lasting friendships while working together.

Social responsibility. Is service to community a social responsibility? Do universities have the right — let alone any obligation — to change the beliefs of students who grew up believing in "rugged individualism"? Do we have a right to require service-learning? And if it is required, does it meet the spirit of true service? There are arguments on both sides. Let me list a few that suggest it is our business to teach students social responsibility: Universities *should* challenge students' traditional beliefs; *all* members of a society are interdependent, and each of us has benefited enormously from the support and services of others; "rugged individualism" is a myth; certainly, people need to build individual skills, strive for individual goals, and seek individual recognition, but we also need to contribute to the group in order to keep it viable (Werner and Altman in press).

Although I endorse the previous contentions, I do not require service in my classes. First, I am reluctant to impose my values on anyone else. Second, I believe that required service is not service after all, although sometimes it provides good, free labor for a worthy cause. And finally, as research on motivation attests, requiring a behavior is usually a good way to reduce any intrinsic interest in it (e.g., Lepper and Greene 1978). My own strategy is to make service opportunities available, knowing that not everyone will want or be able to participate. Across the quarter, I try to make the service projects so attractive and important that by the end of the term, nonparticipants are *envious* of the service-learning students. I hope to show that service-learning students are putting in no more work but are bringing home more rewards. In this way, I underscore the contributions of service-learning students and encourage future giving by others.

Another way to underscore the importance of service-learning is to hold class presentations highlighting service projects. I invite agency personnel and introduce them to the class; they take the opportunity to thank the students and commend their work. Further legitimacy comes on the final exam, where an essay question asks students to describe an effective research or community intervention. Although they could use any example from the class, many use one of the service projects. Students describe the project, state its purposes, and explain why it exemplifies good research and practice. This further legitimizes the service projects and provides an opportunity for all students to rehearse and remember them.

Ethics of service-learning. Although I am willing to encourage students to develop service lifestyles, I am less willing to tell them what values their service projects should support (e.g., students who favor livestock grazing in national forests should not be required to participate in anti-livestock activities). They should have alternative, equally appropriate options available. Certainly, students should be exposed to alternative points of view, that is one function of a university education. But they should not be required — for a grade — to support something they find morally wrong.

How Service-Learning?

Service-learning projects should be undertaken in ways that empower both the students providing the service and the community members who benefit from it. Service-learning should be internalized by students; they should come to believe in both personal responsibility (their obligation to contribute) and personal effectiveness (their belief that they can make a difference). Choice and control are key.

Service-learning empowers rather than undermines the recipients. "Empower" may be an overused term, but it is an important one. Considerable psychological research on learned helplessness suggests that people who lose the sense of control over one aspect of their lives become passive in other domains as well. "Helping" that involves doing everything for a person rather than expecting the person to do for him or herself can actually undermine the person's sense of control and increase dependency on others. Community psychologists who study empowerment suggest that the best community programs are those that *expect* participation and contributions by the recipients (Zimmerman and Perkins 1995). Service-learning projects should involve the community as well as the students. Students choose which projects to undertake and which agencies and people to involve; similarly, agencies and community members choose which problems to address and which projects they will support in their community.

Service-learning leaves mechanisms in place to maintain a project. As suggested by the holistic perspective that I advocated in the opening paragraph, empowering citizens is only part of community involvement. The positive individual experiences will fade unless the larger sociopolitical system provides support. Institutionalize the project. Leave in place structural mechanisms that continue to support and provide opportunities for relevant behaviors. For example, in recycling projects in organizations, it is important to get commitments from building users, managers, and custodial services to make sure that signs containing prompts or persuasive messages are left in place, that recycling equipment is maintained, and that the collected goods are actually recycled.

Service-learning makes a difference. Selecting a service-learning project is much like deciding on a research project — one needs to keep the project manageable. Of all the opportunities that can be addressed, it is important to select those where meaningful changes can be made and left in place. Limits are imposed by the academic calendar, number of students available, number of local people available to participate, and the sheer scope of the problem. A good way to discourage everybody, students and citizens alike, is to start a project and not complete it. This is a value judgment. Is "manageable" too cautious? Does it by definition limit the amount of impact? Perhaps. However, using the criterion of "impact" or "meaningful change" in selecting projects sets sufficiently high standards that caution is rarely a problem. I prefer to err on the side of manageability, success, and self-efficacy.

Service-learning empowers the students and encourages continued service. This point is related to earlier concerns, but is sufficiently important to warrant highlighting. It assumes that colleges and universities have responsibilities to sensitize students regarding their role in society and raise the possibility of continued service after graduation. It relates to the above discussion of keeping service-learning projects to a manageable scope. One way to ensure that students feel empowered is to give them a sense of success about the project. One obvious strategy is to use highly visible projects where students can point not only to the total project and its significance to the local community but also to their unique, individual contribution. By leaving in place effective mechanisms, students can also see that their efforts were not short-term, but will have long-term impact. And finally, students need to feel as though they have had control over and impact on how the project was undertaken. Being a "grunt" is okay for some aspects of the project, but students can experience learned helplessness or lose interest in the activity if they lack control and do not feel a sense of psychological ownership.

Practical Examples

Gaining Access: Relationships With Community Agencies

I have found it useful to work with established community agencies for two general reasons. On the practical side, the agency provides an existing structure in which students can function — this can expand the scope of the project, extend its reach into otherwise inaccessible areas of the community, give insights into the particular workings of a neighborhood, and provide one way of leaving mechanisms in place to continue the program after student involvement ends. On the philosophical/ethical side, working with an established organization sanctions the students' activities. It embeds the service in a known group whose own involvement provides legitimacy for the service project.

Locating opportunities. Many organizations are eager for student volunteers. Locating one with a manageable project that fits with course content can be a challenge. Some campuses, such as mine, have centers that facilitate matches between organizations needing service and faculty seeking service opportunities (our Bennion Community Service Center is fabulous!). Another route I stumbled upon is to offer myself to serve. As a member of the Mayor's Recycling Committee, I met government and private/non-profit personnel eager for help and willing to work within our educational constraints. I still serve on and am friends with several people from that committee.

One problem with selecting opportunities beforehand is that a manageable project that fits with course content is not always attractive to students. I try very hard not to lead an organization to expect student participation unless I am very certain that students will actually want to undertake that project. I have learned to state project guidelines up front with new organizations: relevant to course content, manageable, provide a genuine learning opportunity including freedom for creativity, and of interest to students. If I do not have some opportunities already lined up at the beginning of the quarter, students often cannot complete a project in our short, 10-week term. An alternative is to let students spend some precious weeks seeking an appropriate opportunity. I should note, students who go out and find their own opportunities and solutions seem to have the strongest and most positive service-learning experiences. One colleague of mine is planning to offer a two-quarter course — a creative solution to balancing structure and time constraints with student autonomy, creativity, and commitment.

Maintaining good relations. Student qualities such as responsibility, commitment, follow-through, and honesty are essential for maintaining positive relations with the organization. Students choose to get involved in a project, and their decision must reflect, at least in part, their willingness to accept the responsibility of meeting commitments, doing their best, and staying on top of the project. I also stress their responsibility to future classes: If they alienate this organization, other students may lose out on similar opportunities.

Confidentiality is another important aspect of good working relationships. When working with children, if students learn personal information about family members or if the child discloses a secret as though to a friend, the students must keep this information confidential (naturally, information about abuse, by law, would be passed on to authorities). Promises of confidentiality to survey participants must be kept.

Feedback to the agency/dissemination of information. The agency or organization endorses the project and deserves feedback about it. I invite representatives to attend student class presentations on their projects. Not only does this allow the organizations to absorb the information in a relatively quick way, but it also allows them to ask questions and gain clarification about particular points. Students' papers are due after the presentation so that they have time to make changes in response to agency and class input. As noted earlier, I send the very best papers to the agency as a permanent record of the project. And finally, for many projects, we prepare a manuscript for publication so others may benefit from what we learned (e.g., Bell et al. 1996; Werner, Rhodes, and Partain 1996).

Student-Faculty Relations

Grading. The term papers describing the projects contribute 33 percent (introductory course) or 67 percent (Environment and Behavior) to the students' final grades. Even in group projects, each student writes a separate paper. Individual papers ensure that everyone understands the project and how it fits with the course. Students must describe the rationale of the project and cite relevant literature; they must explain what they learned; and they must discuss theoretical and practical implications of the project. I deemphasize competition between students, because I prefer a cooperative work group. I do not talk about explicit comparisons between papers, but I make it clear that I expect independent work. I also tell them that the best papers (plural, to reduce competitiveness) will be sent to the organization. Although I base project grades only on individual papers, there are strategies for managing and grading group projects that emphasize group and individual accountability (e.g., Goodsell et al. 1992; Johnson, Johnson, and Smith 1991). I use these strategies in other classes and may also apply them to service-learning.

Faculty involvement. I believe that students need to select and design their projects in order to be fully committed, as well as to feel fully responsible for their successes. At the same time, students are not experts, and they can make decisions that reduce a project's quality and impact. They can also run into political hassles and interpersonal problems that undermine their goals. After a few unfortunate experiences, I decided to stay more involved in the projects by attending students' organizational meetings and some of their work days. I also have taken advantage of our Bennion Center's Service-Learning Teaching Assistant Program. The assistant helped students identify potential sites and potential topics, helped them work effectively with community members, "reflected" with them to make sure they were benefiting from the experience and not experiencing problems, and in general facilitated the service aspects of the project. However, he was not responsible for a project's academic content. By meeting with the group to discuss their plans and how those would translate into acceptable papers, I was able to stay involved with the students, remark on their successes, and ensure that their project and papers would fulfill the course assignment.

Discussion

This chapter lays out one route to service-learning. It emphasizes a philosophy and practical techniques intended to increase commitment and empowerment among students and community members, show respect for individual values, and ensure the long-term impact of projects. Not all of my service projects have achieved these goals, and I continue to determine the best ways for ensuring that students will be involved in projects in which they can feel autonomous and successful, proud of the work they have done, and satisfied that they have made important contributions to their community.

My projects typically have a "green" component, but other colleagues provide services that address other aspects of the environmental psychology curriculum. For example, Barbara Brown and her students helped a new hospital understand how its design created stress among visitors and patients and made suggestions for improving the situation. As this book attests, there are numerous arenas for service-learning. The more familiar we are with our communities, the more service opportunities we find there.

References

Bell, M., K. Gaufin, K. Neugart, S. Chamberlain, D. Kaili, K. Miller, R. Russell, V. Seeley, M. Simons, and D. Smith. (1996). "Community Self-Help: Jackson Elementary Builds a Nature Study Center. In *Public and Private Places: Proceedings of EDRA 27*, edited by J.L. Nasar and B.B. Brown, p. 219. Edmond, OK: Environmental Design Research Association.

Goodsell, A.S., M.R. Maher, V. Tinto, B.L. Smith, and J. MacGregor. (1992). *Collaborative Learning: A Sourcebook for Higher Education.* University Park, PA: National Center on Postsecondary Teaching.

Johnson, D.W., R.T. Johnson, and K.A. Smith. (1991). *Active Learning: Cooperation in the College Classroom.* Edina, MN: Interaction Book Company.

Lepper, M.R., and D. Greene. (1978). *The Hidden Costs of Rewards: New Perspectives on the Psychology of Human Motivation.* Hillsdale, NY: Lawrence Erlbaum Associates.

Perkins, D. (1992). *Smart Schools: From Training Memories to Educating Minds.* New York: Free Press.

Werner, C.M., and I. Altman. (In press). "A Transactional/Dialectical Approach to Neighborhoods." In *Children, Cities, and Psychological Theories,* edited by D. Gorlitz, H. Harloff, J. Valsiner, and G. Mey. Berlin: De Gruyter.

Werner, C.M., B.B. Brown, and I. Altman. (1997). "Environmental Psychology." In *Handbook of Cross-Cultural Psychology, Vol. 3. Social Behavior and Applications,* edited by J.W. Berry, M.H. Sigall, and C. Kagitcibasi, pp. 255-290. 2nd ed. Needham Heights, MA: Allyn and Bacon.

Werner, C.M., M.U. Rhodes, and K.K. Partain. (1996). "Designing Effective Instructional Signs With Schema Theory: Case Studies of Polystyrene Recycling." Unpublished manuscript.

Zimmerman, M.A., and D.D. Perkins, eds. (1995). *American Journal of Community Psychology* (Special Issue: Empowerment Theory) 23(5).

Service-Learning: From Process to Impact

by Randall E. Osborne, Kenneth Weadick, and James Penticuff

Psychology faculty members wishing to incorporate service-learning into their courses will quickly discover that many issues need to be considered before the service activities are developed. To aid in this process, we provide an outline of issues to consider and offer suggestions for their successful resolution. In its complete form, this analysis will take psychology faculty through the basic development of service-learning ideas from process to impact.

Why Use Service-Learning in a Course?

Every college course is designed to fulfill a set of learning objectives. Whether these objectives are explicitly stated or implied, they serve as the framework around which the course is designed. Indiana University East has recently required that course learning objectives be explicitly stated on the course syllabus. As we began to write these objectives for our psychology courses, we noted that many of the courses had learning objectives that centered around awareness of how disorders affect individuals' lives and developing skills for interacting with individuals with diverse problems and challenges. As we struggled with developing course assignments to aid student understanding of these issues, it became obvious that a service-learning component was an ideal way to approach such issues.

Throughout this article, we will be referring to one of our own service-learning courses to illustrate issues we confronted and methods we use within the course to approach those issues. The reader is encouraged to use information we provide about this course as an example of ideas that are involved in creating service-learning opportunities within courses in general and psychology courses in particular. The sample *opposite* of the learning objectives listed in the syllabus for our Emotional and Behavioral Disorders of Childhood and Adolescence course illustrates the reason service-learning is such a valuable asset to the course.

Service-learning experiences that place students in community agencies that work with youth are particularly appropriate to facilitate students' integration of course content with applied and professional aspects of psychology. Faculty members can then make the case that the service-learning experience within a given course is meant to mirror the linkage between learning about something and actually doing it. If faculty members feel that engaging in community service makes them more aware of contemporary

Sample Learning Objectives

Emotional and Behavioral Disorders of Childhood and Adolescence

1. Understands the Difference Between "Emotional" and "Behavioral" Disorders

   1.1 defines "abnormal"

   1.2 explains the difference between "developmental" and "societal" norms

   1.3 explains the importance and problems of using definitions

   1.4 explains the current National Mental Health and Special Education Coalition definition for "seriously emotionally disturbed"

2. Understands the Causal Factors That Create and Perpetuate the Disorders

   2.1 describes the family factors

   2.2 describes the school factors

   2.3 describes the cultural factors

   2.4 explains the possible interactions between these causal factors

3. Can Apply Course Principles to the Profession

   3.1 describes relationship between course material and the psychology profession

   3.2 describes specific youth mental health needs within the community

   3.3 explains course content that relates to possible solutions to community mental health "problems"

   3.4 can utilize course principles to propose solutions to community youth mental health needs issues and, therefore, makes them better teachers, then the same connection should be made between the experience in the course, the content of the course, and expected student learning outcomes.

Many students do not know the degree to which faculty engage in professional service and certainly know even less about the reasons why faculty do. Faculty members who are asking students to engage in community service could present their own service contributions and how these activities have enhanced their growth as professionals. Helping students understand that a psychology faculty member has made service commitments establishes the instructor as a role model for these activities. Through service-learning, then, both campus and community become involved in the education of students (e.g., Cotton and Stanton 1990).

In a similar vein, contemporary issues in psychology are often reflected in the service choices that faculty members make. Rather than *assuming* what the psychological needs of a community are, those engaged in service within the community are in a much better position to *know* those needs. When this connection has been established, students doing service-learning in a psychology course can expect that they will come out of the experience with something of great value to their education and their professional future.

As far as that professional future is concerned, many undergraduate psychology programs expect their majors to engage in some form of cooperative placement. It is expected that being placed in an agency or organization that does psychology-related work will aid students in understanding the bridge between what they have learned in their courses and the application of that knowledge. We also have a traditional placement course, Cooperative Work Experience in Psychology, which requires 84 hours of service to an agency, a daily work journal, and a course paper connecting the experience to what students have learned in their other psychology courses.

Although students find this course interesting, the course paper can be a major challenge because there are no specific learning goals connected to it. We see service-learning as an opportunity to expose our psychology majors to this connection between content and application many times throughout their coursework. Because the service-learning is linked to the specific goals of each course, it is much easier to help students connect what they are learning in the course to what they are doing with the service activity.

Explicitly linking service goals and learning objectives takes the guesswork out of what students will be responsible for knowing and also reinforces the rationale for including the service activity. In our Emotional and Behavioral Disorders of Childhood and Adolescence course, for example, we discuss the role of service in professional development and discuss how the service-learning experience ties into the major learning objectives for the course. In this fashion, students discover that the service-learning experience is designed to enhance both their learning and their developing psychological skills.

Issues Involved in Designing Service-Learning Experiences

Some faculty members make a serious mistake when developing service-learning within their psychology courses when they take groups of students to an agency, drop them at the agency's door, and ask students to write course papers stating what they learned as a function of the experience when the semester is over. These papers, then, serve as the major *project* through which students integrate the service experience with the content of the course.

But projects of that type are poorly defined. Most not-for-profit agencies (where most psychology-oriented service-learning activities will be conducted) are understaffed even before they are asked to help a faculty member with a service-learning course. Projects that "dump" students into an agency, or only superficially involve students with an agency, are not good service-learning experiences. What determines whether an assignment, project, or product can be defined as a "good" service-learning experience?

This question should be considered before the psychology faculty member considers the unique challenges of incorporating service-learning into a psychology course. According to Howard (1993), a good service-learning unit embodies the following principles: (1) academic credit is for learning, not service, (2) the unit does not compromise academic rigor, (3) the faculty member has set learning goals for students, (4) the faculty member has established criteria for the selection of community service placements, (5) the faculty member has provided educationally sound mechanisms to harvest the community learning, (6) the unit provides supports for students to learn how to harvest the community learning, (7) the unit minimizes the distinction between students' community learning role and their classroom learning role, (8) the faculty member has rethought the faculty instruction role, (9) the faculty member is prepared for uncertainty and variation in student learning outcomes, and (10) the unit maximizes the community responsibility orientation of the course. These principles served as our guiding framework in developing the service-learning aspects of the Emotional and Behavioral Disorders of Childhood and Adolescence course.

Time is a critical resource in not-for-profit agencies. Training students and working through the activities will place a substantial strain on their already overtaxed resources. A faculty member needs to address how that investment in time will result in a benefit to the agency, the community, and the students. Taking the time to do this cost-benefit analysis prior to placing students in the agency will help convince the agency that having student volunteers is worthwhile.

Because of the sensitive nature of much of the work that lends itself to service-learning in psychology (projects at clinical, counseling, and advocacy-oriented sites), a psychology faculty member may have to do considerable advance preparation. Prior to placing students in an agency, he or she must address issues of rights, confidentiality, and protection of the agency. Another strategy is to include a significant discussion of rights, confidences, and professional settings and relationships within the fabric of the agency orientation and training. In either case, the faculty member and the agency will need to verify the details of each institution's insurance coverage and take care to define the rights and responsibilities of the students during their placements. Some schools have adopted a policy of not placing students in clinical settings until they reach upper-level courses to avoid potential pitfalls.

One of the reasons for developing service-learning opportunities is to allow students to witness psychology in action. In most cases, however, students have little or no background in clinical skills, maintaining confidentiality, or developing professional relationships. Service-learning experiences should be designed to ensure that students will not be asked to make client-oriented decisions.

Developing Projects That Are Appropriate for a Given Course

Certainly not all service-learning experiences are appropriate for any course. In a personality psychology course, it would make little sense to place student groups at the local library teaching literacy courses. It could make sense, however, for those same students to work with a mental health association to develop a self-esteem program for local youth. It would be best to approach an agency, explain the nature of the service-learning concept, and, if the staff expresses strong interest in the idea, work with it to develop an appropriate list of potential activities given the focus of the course and the needs of the agency.

The faculty member needs to ensure that the service activities that are selected meet several criteria. First, the activities should encourage students to use material from the course. This is critical, because one rationale for adopting service-learning strategies in psychology courses is to provide students with a learning experience that makes the course content more relevant and useful. Second, in most courses it is wise to ensure that the activities will result in an "identifiable" product that the students can then deliver to the agency. Third, it is a good practice for the faculty member to be a strong liaison between the students and the agency to ensure that the service activities can be completed within the time frame of the course. This liaison role also helps the faculty member ensure that students are gaining insights into how to integrate the service experience with the psychological content of the course.

We have chosen to make service activities a component that accounts for most of the course's nonexam points. Other faculty may choose to provide a service-learning track that students can choose (see Werner, beginning on p. 119 in this volume; Bringle and Hatcher 1996; Enos and Troppe 1996; Troppe 1995).

Incorporating Service-Learning Into Course Arrangements

Each faculty member will have to consider how best to integrate the service activities into the course and into classroom activities. Because much of the content in psychology courses is conducive to application, there are many opportunities for connecting the course content to the practical experiences provided through service activities. To get students started in our course, we randomly assign them to five-person groups. At the beginning of the semester, we provide in-class time for groups to meet so they can get to know their members and reflect on their concerns about the service-learning activity. We provide these opportunities in several class periods at the beginning of the semester so students can discuss potential activities that can be chosen, ask questions about the agencies involved, and build enthusiasm for what they will be doing.

A second aspect of weaving service-learning into the class deals with making decisions about how many points the activities will be worth, how many hours of service will be required, what the assignments related to the service activities will be, how student effort on these activities should be translated into points for the course, and how the impact of the service activities should be assessed. Students in psychology courses are just as likely as any other students to question the significance of the learning the faculty member believes will come from the service experience if the related assignments are worth only a fraction of the points available for the course.

In our Emotional and Behavioral Disorders course, 10 hours of volunteer service per student are required, and the service assignments are worth at least as much as an exam. Another arrangement that could be used to incorporate service assignments is to allow students to replace their lowest exam grade with the combined scores on their service-learning assignments.

We encourage students to reflect on the service activity in multiple ways throughout the semester. Not only do these reflection activities reflect

Howard's (1993) principles of good service-learning, but they also emphasize the importance of service-learning as a critical aspect of the course. *Opposite* is a copy of reflection assignments included in the syllabus for Emotional and Behavioral Disorders of Childhood and Adolescence.

Student comments on end-of-semester course evaluations provide information that is beneficial to revising the course. Some of our commuting students drive as many as 90 miles to campus. One student suggested we might form student groups based on where students live, rather than creating random groupings, in order to facilitate out-of-class meetings. Another student reminded us that it is difficult to fulfill the service requirement when all agencies close by 5:00 pm. This led to ensuring that at least one agency placement offers evening hours.

Balancing the Need for Content With the Goals of Service-Learning

Some faculty believe that content will have to be sacrificed to free up time for service activities. If, however, one believes in the significance of the learning that can come from utilizing a service-learning activity, this is not always a serious concern. The key is to develop service-learning activities and assignments that reinforce specific segments of the course content. In Emotional and Behavioral Disorders of Childhood and Adolescence, for example, we normally present material about applying the course content to environments in which one would encounter children with emotional and behavioral disorders. Because students are now working in agencies dealing with children with disorders, we ask students to discuss applications of lecture content during their Updates.

In this fashion, the service-learning activities enhance the instructor's ability to teach the content of the course. During our discussion of the concept of *reciprocal influence* in the course, we ask students to do individual five-minute Thought Papers on how this concept applies to their service-learning activity. One student noted that "reciprocal influence is important in understanding the self-esteem problems of youths because the whole family feeds into the problem and, therefore, should be a part of the solution." In this student's group assignment, the group subsequently recommended a method for involving the entire family in a self-esteem enhancement program.

One of the primary goals of service-learning is to allow students to see academic issues in action in the community. The course, then, should focus on developing student understanding of those issues and providing students with an opportunity to witness that connection firsthand. Because the service-learning activity becomes a primary focal point for the course con-

Reflection Assignments

Emotional and Behavioral Disorders of Childhood and Adolescence

Individual Reflection Assignments

1. <u>Exit Cards</u> -- At the end of each class period (once projects have started), you will be asked to take a few moments and reflect on the content currently being covered in the course. In particular, you will be asked to answer the following question, "How does information from today's class period relate to your service project/experience?" 3 points each x 17 class periods = 51 points maximum

2. <u>Thought Papers</u> -- Throughout the semester, you will be asked to complete four 1-page "Thought Papers" (10 points each). I call these Thought Papers because I want you to discuss with me some aspect of the course and/or the service project that has stimulated your thinking. Be sure and include answers to the following questions:
   - How has this situation/information challenged or changed your way of thinking?
   - What might you do differently now that you have confronted or encountered this issue?

3. <u>Essay Question(s) on Exams</u> -- At least one essay question will appear on each of the three exams. These questions will ask you to consider a dominant issue from the current section of material and discuss that issue as it relates to the service project you are doing. These will be worth a varying amount of points on each exam but at least 15 out of the 100 points.

Group Reflection Assignments

1. <u>3-Minute Updates</u> -- Once each month, groups will take about 3 minutes of class time and give a very brief update of progress, obstacles, goals, etc. You will need to choose a spokesperson for each of these, and a given student can only give one of these updates. Each group member present during the update class periods will earn 5 assignment points for the update given by the spokesperson.

2. <u>Final Updates</u> -- Groups will schedule and present a final project update during final exams week (note we do not have a regular final exam). Each group member must be involved in this presentation, and a copy of the final project product must be turned in to the instructor at the completion of this presentation. Except in extreme circumstances, only those group members present during the presentation can earn Final Updates points. Final Updates are worth up to 50 points and should include expanded coverage of the same items requested in 3-Minute Updates plus strong integration of course content.

3. <u>Project Products</u> -- These are the culminating event for the course. These products should illustrate what you did for the agency, your resolution to the agency's problem or stated need, an analysis of major course content as it applies to the work you did, applicable references (minimum of 15), and individual reflections from each group member about the experience and specific ways the project affected their learning. These products will be graded as a group and are worth up to 100 points.

tent, it creates many teachable moments.

In the Emotional and Behavioral Disorders course, we examine factors that cause disorders. Because students are working with agencies that specialize in dealing with individuals with these disorders, students reflect on the causal factors of disorders they have encountered in their group service-learning activity. Herein lies the most important reason we have discovered for using service-learning in psychology courses: Students can continuously apply course content to their assignments. Faculty members teaching psychology courses quickly discover that students will try to apply every theory, diagnostic category, and treatment regimen in terms of their own lives and individuals they know. Connecting specific course content to agency projects provides students with structure and guidance in their application efforts.

Most groups also will be reviewing relevant literature, and therefore have access to more information than what is being provided in the core course content. As a result of reviewing additional literature and the application of course content to their service activities, students become better critical thinkers. They develop discipline-specific but generalizable critical-thinking skills because they are required to ask and answer questions about how certain theories and findings relate to their assignments and/or individuals at the agencies.

Exit Cards (described in the "Reflection Assignments" handout) encourage thinking that each class period links course content to applied experiences, without using more than a modest amount of class time. Two links noted by students were a discussion of how certain treatment approaches were used by counselors within the agency, and a suggestion that the behavior modification techniques in an agency classroom were counterproductive because they utilized negative reinforcement to attempt to eliminate problem behaviors. As the student so wisely noted, "negative reinforcement will actually increase the behavior, not decrease it."

Coordinating Service-Learning Demands With Other Responsibilities

Incorporating service-learning into courses requires effort. For example, establishing a working relationship with psychology-oriented agencies will require multiple meetings prior to and during the semester. Once these relationships have been established, however, one can find many ways to make service-learning assignments more time efficient for the instructor, agencies, and students. One of the most successful techniques is to provide upper-level majors the opportunity to earn field experience or other independent study credit for serving as service-learning course coordinators. These students serve as liaisons between the primary staff person at an agency and the student groups assigned to that agency, and help to coordinate schedules, problem solve, furnish supplies, and aid students as they relate their service activities to course content and requirements.

A service-learning coordinator has to be at least a junior-level student who either has done a service-learning project in an upper-level psychology course or has completed our Cooperative Work Experience in Psychology course. This three-credit-hour course includes training on issues of confidentiality, professional relationships, and time management and requires 84 hours of service, a daily work journal, and a course paper. In the course paper, students are required to reflect on content and theories from their major psychology coursework that are relevant to their placement experience.

A service-learning coordinator can also play a key role in generating potential agency service-learning activities. The educational objectives for student service-learning coordinators vary depending on each student's professional goals. A student interested in the mental health field, for example, could reflect on the agency's programs and issues involved in the development, implementation, and evaluation of these programs.

Another program component that can help orient new service-learning student groups is an orientation video that answers typical questions students have about agencies. Once students have decided on particular service-learning activities, a more specific orientation can be provided.

Evaluating the Impact of Service-Learning Courses

One may incorporate service-learning into a course because of a belief that such experiences will provide students with a level of learning that cannot be accomplished any other way. But the rationale for using such experiences is only as sound as the impact such experiences have on the students and their learning. The faculty member needs to consider both the desired impact and how that impact will be evaluated (e.g., Hesser 1995). For example, a majority of our students state on entrance surveys that they are unsure that they can succeed as college students. Statements such as these as well as data on self-esteem in general suggest that many of these students have shaky self-confidence about their abilities. It is our belief that psychology courses can enhance student self-esteem as well as increase retention. Thus, we decided to gather data to provide information about the impact that service-learning might have on each of these issues.

Self-esteem, self-confidence, and self-perception data were collected from students in a service-learning course at the beginning and end of a semester. The same data had been collected from students enrolled in the same course offered without a service-learning focus during an earlier semester. Both courses were taught by the same instructor. Demographically, the students from the two sections were indistinguishable. The average age of students in both sections was 28. In both sections, 65 percent of the students were female and 98 percent of the students were Caucasian.

Comparison of the two groups showed that students in the service-learning section showed significantly more improvement in self-esteem and self-confidence scores across the semester than did their counterparts in the non-service-learning section (see the table *opposite*). A comparison of self-perception data provided by students at the end of the semester showed a higher percentage of self-descriptors focusing on interpersonal characteristics for the service-learning students versus more intrapersonal descriptors for those students in the non-service-learning section of the course.

The Rosenberg Self-Esteem Scale measures general perceptions of self-worth and is the most widely used self-esteem measure. Sample questions include "I feel that I am a person of worth, at least on an equal plane with others" and "On the whole, I am satisfied with myself." The Texas Social Behavior Inventory asks questions about an individual's perceptions of self-worth in relationship to social situations. Sample items include "I feel confident of my social behavior"; "I have no doubts about my social competence"; and "I feel comfortable approaching someone in a position of authority over me." It is important to note that student scores did not differ significantly between the two sections of the course on these measures taken at the beginning of the semester.

As far as course retention is concerned, divisional data from our campus shows an average attrition rate of 10 percent of students in 300-level and 400-level courses. The non-service-learning section of this course showed exactly that same attrition rate. Of 35 students who started the course, 31 finished. In the service-learning-oriented section of the course, 32 students started the course and all 32 finished. Although these data are quite limited and certainly could be influenced by the instructor's attitude, they are a starting point for documenting the impact service-learning may have on students and the institution.

Conclusion

Howard's (1993) principles of good practice provide an important guiding framework for developing service-learning activities in psychology courses. As we encountered various challenges and issues in developing service-learning experiences, they mirrored the issues raised by Howard's principles. As we resolved the issues, the course became stronger and the service activ-

Self-Esteem and Self-Confidence Scores in
Non-Service-Learning and Service-Learning Courses

Pre Scores

	Non-Service-Learning	Service-Learning
Rosenberg Self-Esteem	30.00	30.55 [a]
Texas Social Beh. Inventory	65.00	63.00 [b]
Self-Perceptions	91.50	90.00 [c]

Post Scores

	Non-Service-Learning	Service-Learning
Rosenberg Self-Esteem	31.00	34.72 [a]
Texas Social Beh. Inventory	67.00	71.16 [b]
Self-Perceptions	94.00	100.34 [c]

Superscript letters represent pre and post scores utilized in t-test analyses:

[a] $t(1,31) = 5.94$, $p<.05$ [b] $t(1,31) = 10.84$, $p<.05$ [c] $t(1,31) = 12.11$, $p<.05$

ities became more successful and had more impact. By focusing academic credit on learning and not service, for example, reflection became an important tool for encouraging students to demonstrate how their service activities enhanced their understanding of course content. By articulating learning objectives in the course syllabi, and explicitly describing reflection requirements, student learning goals were well identified. The reflection requirements also reinforced integration of course content with service activities and satisfied Howard's principle of helping students harvest their community learning. In this fashion, academic rigor was not compromised, because we had the same (or even higher) expectations for students in the service-learning section of the course as we had in the nonservice section.

By integrating service activities into the fabric of the course and by making both service and reflection activities account for a significant portion of the course grade, we were able to fulfill Howard's suggestion of minimizing the distinction between the community learning role and the classroom learning role. The use of student service-learning coordinators minimized the uncertainty that can accompany such activities, and the reflection requirements minimized variability in student learning outcomes. Finally, we followed Howard's advice of maximizing the focus on the community by requiring students to deliver to the agencies final products that could potentially be utilized.

In the end, the issues raised in the design, implementation, and evaluation of this course illustrate the fundamental concepts to be considered and addressed when integrating service-learning into psychology courses. If there is a moral to the story, it is to suggest that service-learning activities in psychology courses should be developed according to a systematic model. This attention to detail (the process side of service-learning) may then enhance the success of the activities and the effect these activities have on student learning and the community being served (the impact side of service-learning).

References

Bringle, R., and J. Hatcher. (1996). "Implementing Service Learning in Higher Education." *Journal of Higher Education* 67: 221-239.

Cotton, D., and T. Stanton. (1990). "Joining Campus and Community Through Service Learning." In *Community Service as Values Education*, edited by C. Delve, S. Mintz, and G. Stewart, pp. 101-110. San Francisco: Jossey-Bass.

Enos, S., and M. Troppe. (1996). "Service-Learning in the Curriculum." In *Service-Learning in Higher Education: Concepts and Practices*, edited by B. Jacoby and Associates, pp. 156-181. San Francisco: Jossey-Bass.

Hesser, G. (1995). "Faculty Assessment of Student Learning: Outcomes Attributed to Service-Learning and Evidence of Changes in Faculty Attitudes About Experiential Education." *Michigan Journal of Community Service Learning* 2: 33-42.

Howard, J. (1993). "Community Service in the Curriculum." In *Praxis I: A Faculty Casebook on Community Service Learning*, edited by J. Howard, pp. 3-12. Ann Arbor, MI: OCSL Press.

Troppe, M., ed. (1995). *Connecting Cognition and Action: Evaluation of Student Performance in Service-Learning Courses*. Providence, RI: Campus Compact.

Human Relations:
A Service-Learning Approach

by David B. Johnson

A number of convergent societal forces emphasize the need for more effective education in the areas of communication and conflict-resolution skills,
workplace literacy, and civic responsibility. Cocooning families watch 175-
channel satellite-linked TVs in alarm-rigged homes behind bolted doors.
"Dormitory lounges are being carved up for clusters of computers, student
unions are declining as gathering places, and computer-wired dorm rooms
are becoming, in some cases, high-tech caves" (Gabriel 1996: A12). We are
losing touch with our fellow human beings, and our human relations skills
are deteriorating. Students need a learning experience that addresses these
problems by encouraging them to develop a greater sense of personal
responsibility, improved human relations skills, a commitment to civic
engagement, and an accelerated movement toward becoming effective and
decent human beings. For it to be successful, it must make the connection
between human relations theories and students' attitudes, beliefs, and
actions. It also needs to connect the discipline of the intellect with the habits
of the heart. The application of a service-learning teaching strategy in a
human relations course can make that connection and produce the desired
outcomes.

The Human Relations course at Miami-Dade Community College was
designed to effectively utilize the reciprocal process of service-learning in
which the classroom lectures, presentations, and discussion would inform
the service, and the service experience would inform the class. It was
designed so that the classroom experience would draw from (1) research
findings in the areas of human relations and social psychology to ensure an
understanding of theory, (2) the wisdom literature of the ages to discover
mythical and cultural themes, and (3) students' stories to provide insight
into the complexity of relationships. Class time would be devoted to developing a deeper understanding of the concepts and principles of human relations as well as engaging in specific exercises designed to develop skills in
areas such as communication and conflict resolution.

The service component of the course would move students beyond the
cognitive domain of the classroom into the real world of action. Instead of
only thinking about issues, students would confront a variety of social problems with whatever knowledge and skill they possessed and would experience immediate feedback in terms of real consequences (Permaul 1993). The
content of this experience, rich in examples of the paradox and perplexity of

human relations, would then "come tumbling into the classroom" as an "object of reflection" (Stanley 1993: 61).

Structured and guided reflection in the form of journals and reflective dialogue would make the connection between the classroom content and the service. The combination of text, service, and reflection would enable students to consciously create meaning from their experience by progressing through the cyclical process of concrete experience, reflective observation, abstract conceptualization, and active experimentation described by Kolb (1984).

From Vision to Reality

The first step in moving from the drawing board to the classroom was to get administrative approval to implement the service-learning strategy in the course. Some are suspicious of the pedagogy's academic integrity, fear liability issues, or question its match with specific disciplines; therefore, it was important to fully explain the strategy and present as much information as possible regarding its effective implementation in the discipline.

The next challenge was getting students to enroll. Initially, I felt it was important that students knew, before registering, about the community service commitment. I therefore required a registration override to get into the course. This was a mistake, because it drove students to course sections not requiring the extra effort of obtaining an override. Thus, experience to date suggests that prior knowledge and consent to participate in a service-learning class is unnecessary. For the past two terms, students have not been informed of the service requirement before registration, and no increase in student complaints or drop rates has occurred. The service requirement should be viewed the same as a library research project or any other pedagogical strategy employed by faculty to meet course objectives.

The effective application of service-learning requires considerable design and planning on the front end so that all participants know what to expect and how to achieve the desired results. Because Human Relations was a new preparation, the course provided an opportunity to consider texts that effectively present the content and are suitable for the pedagogy. Atwater's *Human Relations* (Prentice-Hall, 1986) was chosen as the principle text because of its comprehensive focus on both content and skills and its conversational style. Dass and Gorman's *How Can I Help? Stories and Reflections on Service* (Knopf, 1993) was also selected to provide an unconventional perspective on the service experience. This text characterizes service as a path where "we are constantly given feedback which helps us along the greater journey of awakening," and which "reveals a larger vision of life . . . the inherent generosity of our heart . . . and allows us to meet our fears and resistances" (p. 225). It seemed the perfect companion to the more traditional social science orientation of Atwater. The third text was an in-house *Service-Learning Student Handbook*, which provides an introduction to and overview of service-learning, its benefits, students' rights and responsibilities, and a collection of forms for site application, site confirmation, accumulated hours, agency reports, and student feedback.

In deciding on specific textual content, one must be very careful to establish logical consistency between the students' community learning role and their classroom learning role. Because students are being asked to adopt an active "learner-leader role" in the community, the same has to apply in the classroom (Howard 1993: 8). Therefore, in this course, students select the chapters they want covered and then take responsibility for presenting the selected material to each other. While ultimate responsibility for sufficient and appropriate content still rests with me, the classroom format emphasizes a student-controlled information-processing mode. To make this successful, students are encouraged to use interactive and collaborative strategies for their presentations. Various presentation techniques and approaches such as skits, "stand and declare," and videos are explained, and students are supported in their early efforts to decide upon and develop a format. From the first time this class was offered to the present, students have readily accepted this role and have expressed enthusiastic satisfaction with the learning experienced from such a format.

Students perform a minimum of 30 hours of community service to complete the requirements of the course. While an "unattractive" alternative of a lengthy library research paper is available to those absolutely opposed to service, none so far has chosen this option. The service component of the course is coordinated by the campus Service-Learning Center. The center has been critical to the success of the course and the college's service-learning program in general. A network of more than 100 community placements offers a wide variety of meaningful service activities and flexibility in terms of hours and location. The variety practically eliminates the standard student excuses of transportation problems, schedule conflicts, and lack of interesting alternatives.

Because of the ubiquitous applicability of human relations concepts, students are allowed to choose any type of service experience from the Service-Learning Center's list. This variability leads to less certainty and homogeneity in student learning outcomes, and as Howard (1993) has noted, it makes the content of class dialogue and analytic papers less predictable and thus more difficult to evaluate. However, it also makes the service requirement easier for students to fulfill and provides a valuable variety of context and experience.

The syllabus begins with a brief statement of the course philosophy and scope, followed by a list of required and recommended texts and critical readings. The requirements for class and service attendance, papers, and journals are then presented, along with the guidelines for the nonservice alternative paper. Finally, grading requirements are listed: two take-home analytic papers/exams (40%), service journal (30%), group presentations (10%), and attendance and participation in reflective dialogue sessions (20%). The syllabus makes it clear that while no specific credit is given for service, completion of the commitment is necessary to satisfactorily meet the reflective dialogue, journal, and analytic paper requirements.

Implementation: Teaching and Learning

Human Relations has now been offered five times, each of which has been a unique adventure. I have drawn from all five classes to present a composite of the typical course progression.

During the first two class meetings, students explore the concepts of experiential education, the need for community service, and the connections between this service and learning about human relations. The next class is devoted to an exploration of the conventional wisdom of human relations through a discussion of codes, aphorisms, commandments, and clichés and the paradoxes and perplexity they can create regarding our choices (i.e., "Two heads are better than one," "Too many cooks spoil the broth," "Birds of a feather . . ."). The following two sessions focus on developing a general model of personal and interpersonal effectiveness. Steven Covey's *Seven Habits of Highly Effective People* (Simon & Schuster, 1989) serves as a starting point, and the students are encouraged to begin developing their own constructs as we plunge into our texts and the service experience.

Sometime during the first weeks of class, student ambassadors from the Service-Learning Center visit the class to speak about their service experiences and to highlight the most attractive opportunities on the center's annotated placement list (distributed to each student). They explain how to get started and provide tips for getting maximum benefit from the service experience. Throughout the term, these ambassadors and the center's staff check on student progress, intervene when problems occur, and provide me with necessary feedback. At the end of the term, they provide reports of hours, agency feedback, and student satisfaction. This comprehensive effort is key to course success.

By the third week of the term, most students have begun their service. At this point, we focus on developing skills of reflection. Here the contributions of Kendall and Associates (1990) and Silcox (1993) have been most instructive. Preservice reflective work consists of discussing expectations and goals: How do they hope to serve? What do they want to learn? Students must identify and submit, in writing, at least three specific service and learning objectives. This is a critical point in establishing the linkage between service and specific learning objectives related to human relations. Many students have difficulty making this connection, so time spent here is crucial for the future success of the reflective process. To provide further guidance and structure, a handout describes the purpose and techniques of journaling and lists specific questions to direct students' observations and writing to the more cognitive aspects of the course objectives. Examples of effective journal entries based on these questions are presented and discussed.

All sessions, up to week five, are devoted to the presentation of conceptual and textual information. The classroom format includes lecture/discussion, student presentations, and open dialogue. These sessions are usually quite animated, especially those focused on the topics of communication, gender, conflict, separation and loss, and career exploration. Students have been effective in their "learner-leader" roles, using a variety of creative strategies such as panels, videos, skits, and other engaging techniques to make their presentations.

During the fifth week, when students have had at least a few service experiences, the structured reflective dialogue sessions begin. In order to facilitate participation, the class is divided into two or three groups defined by common service objectives or recipients (e.g., children, elderly, the environment). These groups, limited to between eight and 15 students, then meet on alternate Thursdays (one group per week). While Tuesday classes continue to focus on text-related presentations, Thursday sessions are now devoted to small-group reflective dialogue.

The Thursday reflective sessions take a variety of forms. Some begin with journal reading or story telling. Others focus on specific questions from the journal handout or on specific chapter topics as they relate to service. Regardless of focus, these sessions are always rich in meaning and feeling resulting from the intensity of student involvement with the powerful and perplexing issues they are confronting in their service. I struggle to keep the focus in the cognitive domain, but admit that often the affective takes over. My students in the midst of a story will sometimes mimic me: "I know, how does this relate to human relations concepts?"

This pattern of Tuesday presentation/Thursday reflection continues for the remainder of the course. By midterm, students are more knowledgeable and are enthused about their service. How do I know, however, if students are learning, and how can I measure it? At week seven, I give the first examination — a take-home analytic paper that requires students to create a developmental model of human relations integrating the texts, lectures, presentations, and service experiences they have had to date. Typically, most of the students are able to develop a meaningful personal construct from these varied sources of knowledge. Some, however, struggle with this test format, due to their unfamiliarity with such an active-learning mode and lack of the research and writing skills needed to complete a take-home examination. To deal with this problem, I begin offering a test-coaching session during exam week for those needing help. More than three quarters of the class shows up on their day off.

A week later, the first entries of the journals are collected for grading. I have already reviewed selected entries before this to make sure the students are on track; but now, halfway through the course, I am evaluating the quality of their journals. This is where I pay the price for the lack of homogeneity in service experiences. The variety of activities, coupled with the different abilities of students to draw meaning from experience, creates a special evaluative challenge. How do I evaluate a student's brilliant account of an Everglades environmental project that is focused mainly on intrapersonal, spiritual, and political issues not even mentioned in the reflection handout (but certainly in the domain of human relations)? With limited control of input, it is difficult to standardize or measure outcomes (Howard 1993). However, objective assessment is quite possible, and literature on the subject is available (Brown, Rust, and Gibbs 1994; Troppe 1995). In the case of journals, grades are based on students' success in translating their specific service experiences into meaning as it relates to course objectives and their effective communication of the linkage.

At the end of the term, the evaluation process described above is repeated. The completed journal is submitted with approximately 15 entries, or one per service episode. Usually, as a result of the first review, these entries are much more sophisticated and appropriately cognitive in focus. The second analytic paper asks for a comprehensive statement of how the texts, class, and service experiences have influenced students' knowledge of human relations. This final set of papers is rich in content and documents real learning. By the end of the course, students are often transformed by the experience and are as eager to share their insights as I am to hear them. This is where the payoff comes — the evidence that something real and meaningful has happened. Service-learning is a front-end-loaded effort, with the benefits often not evident until close to the end. When they come, however, they are powerfully gratifying.

Results

Traditional measures of course outcomes such as withdrawal rates and grade distributions are generally in line with other courses I have taught and other sections of this same course taught by my colleagues. The service requirement does not seem to elevate the drop rate, but it does seem to correlate with a skewed grade distribution toward A's and B's. I view this as a reflection of the increased motivation and learning produced by the pedagogy.

One statistical result unique to service-learning courses is the significant contribution of service to the community. During the past five terms, students from the course have provided a total of more than 3,000 hours of enthusiastic, high-quality, free service to the community. Feedback from agencies, many of which say they could not survive without student help, reveals their genuine appreciation and confirms the value of the service.

Student Reactions

Student reactions as recorded in their journals, papers, and end-of-term feedback instruments reveal how they view the pedagogy and how it supports learning, creates personal meaning, and transforms both the student and recipients. Most students support incorporating a service requirement and find their experiences valuable in terms of their academic, vocational, and personal development. As one student said: "The lectures in the class backed up what we were seeing for ourselves. Whether it's working with people, communication skills, problem-solving techniques, stress, or even coping with loss, we were out there and these things were happening." Another said: "The service-learning experience gave me a new outlook on helping out the community, and by going to school to reflect on this experience, I learned social and leadership skills. I even gained a sense of effective citizenship in my community." I imagine everyone who uses this strategy sees or hears comments like these, but they certainly have reinforced my commitment to the pedagogy.

Classroom Research

In addition to such qualitative feedback, I have also been interested in measuring the specific effectiveness of the service and reflection experience in bringing about mastery of conceptual material. To determine this, I designed an instrument that listed the nine major conceptual content units of the course. Students were asked to check only those areas in which understanding and skill had been enhanced specifically by the service and reflection experience (beyond learning from the texts and lectures). The survey results from four class sections (N=77) indicated that the service experience was successful in deepening understanding and skills in all nine of the conceptual areas. The clearest content/skill beneficiary was "effective communication," with a 96.1 percent positive response; 92.2 percent indicated the positive effect of service on enhancing learning in the areas of "achieving independence and interdependence" and "perceiving others." "Handling conflict" was better understood by 83.1 percent, "stress management" by 79.2 percent, "the nature of friendship and intimacy" by 76.6 percent, "exploring the workplace" by 72.7 percent, and "gender issues" by 68.8 percent. The weakest connection between the service and course content was in the area of "love and marriage," with only 46.8 percent recognizing any enhancement from the linkage. When asked to comment on the most significant human relations lesson learned from the service-learning experience, the most common responses were communication, empathy, and self-awareness.

Instructor's Reactions

Since the service-learning approach is the only way I have taught Human Relations, I do not have a personal benchmark for comparison. However, I can say that these classes have been both my most personally rewarding and my most emotionally draining teaching experiences. The service-learning pedagogy is a natural for a course focused on developing intra- and interpersonal awareness and skill, so the design and application are relatively straightforward. The execution, however, is complicated. Without the Service-Learning Center to assist in establishing, developing, and maintaining placements for more than 50 students a term, it could be overwhelming.

This pedagogy creates a much deeper personal involvement with students, which results in greater admiration as well as increased frustration with those who refuse to engage. I have been thrilled to watch students who might not excel in traditional lecture courses become stars through their written and oral reflective work. Their comments, journals, and papers were full of transformational insights. However, the few students who refused to truly engage or who in a few instances actually misrepresented their service have been particularly problematic. In a traditional lecture class, the contrast would not have been as obvious or bothersome.

Undoubtedly, this pedagogy has changed my teaching style from disseminator to facilitator. Once I began to use active-learning models, I was gratified to find students taking responsibility and using effective strategies for teaching and learning. At first I was uncomfortable with this, concerned that students in their more active role might perceive me as not doing my job, a fear expressed by others (Morton 1993). As stated earlier, many of the benefits of service-learning are not evident until nearly the end of the term when students have reflected on their service and thought about its effect on their learning. At the midterm, when our course evaluations were conducted, a few students were still unhappy about the extra requirement and expressed this in their anonymous evaluations. I now know to anticipate this.

Service-learning is a natural pedagogy for the human relations curriculum; in my view, there is no better way to teach a course in this area. By providing students with an opportunity to enter into a special relationship of service with others, it allows them not only to discover and experience laws and generalizations about the action patterns of individuals and groups but also to encounter a part of themselves that transforms them into more aware, decent, caring, and effective citizens. As one student put it, "You can learn a lot more from a service-learning experience than you ever will from a textbook. There are some points no book will ever cover." In helping to both broaden the mind and deepen the heart, service-learning provides an optimal teaching strategy for human relations.

References

Brown, S., C. Rust, and G. Gibbs. (1994). *Strategies for Diversifying Assessment*. Oxford: Oxford Centre for Staff Development.

Gabriel, T. (November 11, 1996). "Computers Help Unite Campuses But Also Drive Some Students Apart." *The New York Times*, A12.

Howard, J. (1993). "Community Service in the Curriculum." In *Praxis I: A Faculty Casebook on Community Service-Learning,* edited by J. Howard, pp. 3-12. Ann Arbor, MI: OCSL Press, University of Michigan.

Kendall, J.C., and Associates, eds. (1990). *Combining Service and Learning: A Resource Book for Community and Public Service.* Raleigh, NC: National Society for Experiential Education.

Kolb, D. (1984). *Experiential Learning: Experience as the Source of Learning and Development.* Englewood Cliffs, NJ: Prentice-Hall.

Morton, K. (1993). "Reflection in the Classroom." In *Rethinking Tradition: Integrating Service With Academic Study on College Campuses,* edited by T. Kupiec, pp. 89-97. Denver: Education Commission of the States.

Permaul, J. (1993). "Community Service and Intercultural Education." In *Rethinking Tradition: Integrating Service With Academic Study on College Campuses,* edited by T. Kupiec, pp. 83-87. Denver: Education Commission of the States.

Silcox, H. (1993). *A How To Guide to Reflection: Adding Cognitive Learning to Community Service Programs.* Philadelphia, PA: Brighton Press.

Stanley, M. (1993). "Community Service and Citizenship: Social Control and Social Justice." In *Rethinking Tradition: Integrating Service With Academic Study on College Campuses,* edited by T. Kupiec, pp. 59-62. Denver: Education Commission of the States.

Troppe, M., ed. (1995). *Connecting Cognition and Action: Evaluation of Student Performance in Service-Learning Courses.* Providence, RI: Campus Compact.

Bringing Undergraduate Service-Learning Into a High-Risk, Urban Environment

by Maurice J. Elias and Gregg Gambone

This chapter describes the development and administration of a service-learning pilot program that is a one-credit adjunct to the three-credit Community Psychology course and Atypical Child Development course. The project began in the spring of 1995 and is the first service-learning course affiliated with Rutgers University's Department of Psychology. In three semesters, it has involved more than 100 undergraduates in nine Head Start centers in Middlesex County, New Jersey. Having generated a great deal of student interest and support at the placement sites, this program now accounts for more than 3,000 hours of supervised service-learning and in Fall 1996 was formally added to the undergraduate psychology curriculum.

There are numerous elements of course design and management that have contributed to the overall success of this project (Coles 1993; Melton 1991). The following five elements seem to be particularly important:

1. Participants are a subset of students enrolled in courses focusing (in part) on the purpose and value of service-learning.

2. Participants share the same service-learning environment.

3. Quality of supervision is geared toward the facilitation of educational goals.

4. Pedagogical focus is on practical and realistic goals at the individual level.

5. Student evaluation is multidimensional.

In addition to these organizational elements, implementation of this program attempted to respect three personal and contextual processes that we consider essential for effective learning: (1) the importance of individual identity, (2) creative flexibility, and (3) the lasting emotional changes that can result from well-structured experiences. Our view of the operation of these elements and processes is interwoven throughout the following pages.

Participants Are a Subset of Students Enrolled in Courses Focusing (in Part) on the Purpose and Value of Service-Learning

Of the approximately 150 students enrolled each semester in the target three-credit courses, about one third have chosen to add the adjunct service-learning component. This level of involvement may, in part, be attributable to recruitment procedures. During the first or second week of each semester, the education coordinator and the disability coordinator for the local Head Start program address the entire class about Head Start's role as our nation's primary systematic early childhood-, family-, and school-focused antipoverty program. They also identify the need for weekly volunteers in area Head Start centers. All students (participating and nonparticipating) receive specific information about the characteristics of the targeted population, the responsibilities and commitments necessary to work with this population, and the rewards likely to be gained through this type of service-learning. Students are then provided with a schedule and are encouraged to make a decision about their involvement during the following week.

This recruitment process may hold down dropout rates by allowing interested students to evaluate their availability for service-learning and reorganize their personal schedules with a thorough understanding of program requirements and expectations. More important, this recruitment provides the foundation for a learning environment that includes both participating and nonparticipating students, fosters peer support and responsibility, and establishes the service-learning component as a "natural laboratory" for the course.

Because conditions that contribute to unrealized personal potential, sociopathy, and poor health are prevalent in urban areas, and because the incidence rates of poverty, crime, mental illness, and undereducation are highest in these areas, they have been deemed "high-risk" and become the target of many preventive social, educational, and health programs. Many courses in psychology and other social sciences focus on these high-risk, urban environments.

A focus on high-risk, urban environments is particularly relevant to courses in community psychology and atypical child development. However, most undergraduates have no familiarity with such urban settings. Moreover, the possibility that artificial classroom presentations or exercises could compensate for these deficits is quite small. An invaluable asset for such courses, therefore, is the ability to provide regular interaction with people who have personal contact with these communities. Incorporating service-learning students, as a subgroup of the entire class enrollment, provides exactly that advantage (Coles 1993). Through course discussions of their weekly experiences with Head Start classes, teachers, and parents, service-learning participants become "resident experts" who provide firsthand views of children in high-risk environments. This arrangement provides a natural laboratory setting in which the undergraduates can explore, develop, and test models related to their specific interests.

A second advantage of this arrangement comes from the ease with which students who are not engaged in the service-learning component can identify and relate to those who are so engaged. Undergraduates often experience difficulty in being able to imagine themselves engaged in the types of prevention activities described in textbooks. This condition may inhibit student motivation, learning, and goal development. In the current program, however, this inhibition is minimized because the people who do the service-learning are the classmates of those for whom the models are provided. Peer identification, therefore, enhances the impact of this modeling.

Because it combines service-learning participants and nonparticipants in a single class, the current course design is thought to have the following unique benefits:

1. The development of a sense of citizenship is reinforced for both participating and nonparticipating students. The concept of civic responsibility, particularly toward less fortunate (yet equally deserving) segments of society, is potentially strengthened, in every class period, by the presence of fellow students who have committed their time to the service-learning experience.

2. The collegial atmosphere of this arrangement bolsters a spirit of enthusiasm for the entire class. Because service-learning students are important in-class information resources, dialogue and feedback between participating and nonparticipating groups establish an active-learning environment.

3. Emotional and maturational rewards of working with an underserved population are experienced directly and indirectly. Both service-learners and nonparticipating students, particularly those who are unsure about future goals or who have difficulty seeing themselves as role models, may be encouraged to value themselves as mainstream culture bearers and, more important, as educated adults.

4. Students understand the psychological commonalties of all developing children, especially sensitivity to the potential risks of environmental threats. The significance of environments that foster a sense of psychological and interpersonal equity is established. Here, the notion is that adequate support, guidance, security, and opportunity, despite natural ability, are necessary components for developing human potential, and that, unfortunately, these elements may not be equally available for all Americans (Melton 1991). Again, the combination of service-learners and nonparticipating students in a single class fosters critical dialogue and conceptual clarity for all students.

5. The course fosters a sense of commitment, an understanding of the complexity of social problems, and optimism in light of evidence that the efforts of individuals can make differences for other individuals. All too often, attempts to deal with complex problems lead to feelings of being overwhelmed and discouraged. The supportive environment of the present

program, while not guaranteeing success, maximizes opportunities for students to see their efforts make a tangible difference in the lives of underprivileged children through Head Start. Beyond what would be expected from purely academic classes, this program extends the motivation of service-learners, the supportiveness of nonparticipating students, and the hope of all involved (Barber 1995; Berman 1990).

In general, we have found that the natural laboratory model of service-learning encourages critical thinking, self-evaluation, dialogue, and problem solving for real-world, resource-constrained situations. Overall, this program enhances both the practical and the academic experiences of all students by focusing on the common interests, values, and experiences of service-learners and nonparticipating students. The next two sections identify specific elements of this commonality that have been incorporated into our program.

Participants Share the Same Service-Learning Environment

Of particular significance in the design of this program is the inclusion of a single type of setting for all service-learning students. Although this was initially a matter of convenience, it is now thought to be a key element in the program's success. Students are not scheduled to work at the same time; however, many do share the same Head Start centers and, on different days, the same classrooms and participating teachers. This creates an environment for course discussion and service-learning supervision that provides students with exposure to the firsthand perspectives of other students about settings with which they are already familiar. Repeated exposure to the varied perspectives of other service-learning students heightens group awareness of the scope of targeted issues at both conceptual and pragmatic levels. Simultaneously, multiple exposure leads to increased awareness, empathy, and support for the personal struggles and growth of other individual service-learning students. The design of this course creates an environment in which support and understanding for the program's goals reciprocally reinforce support and understanding for the individuals attempting to realize those goals.

Along with their parallel intragroup experiences, students are also encouraged to identify and define parallels between their own experiences and those of nonparticipating students, the professor, the service-learning supervisor, and the Head Start students and staff. Class discussion, question-and-answer activities with "resident experts," group projects, and supervision all provide opportunities to identify such parallels. Throughout the program, the importance of developing supportive, helping relationships is emphasized. We suggest that these relationships are grounded in the recognition of interpersonal similarities in learning, planning for the future, teaching, role modeling, and effecting positive change in oneself and others.

This approach may have an added benefit in that it provides the opportunity for a check on both the experiences of participating students and the reactions of nonparticipating students. In class discussions, students are able to make frequent and informal comparisons of their own service-learning experiences with those of others. This facilitates an identification of the normal range of experience and reactions, and encourages dialogue about unusual situations or responses to be considered in light of that normal range.

Given the common circumstances experienced by many participating students, especially with regard to personal adjustments, problem situations, and relationships with Head Start staff and pupils, the opportunity to exchange ideas with other students fosters an appreciation of the importance of resource assessment and management. Students are encouraged to consider issues of time, transportation, money, stress, tolerance levels, personality, cultural diversity, physical environment, student maturity, and societal expectations when discussing their service-learning experiences. Through focused dialogue, cooperative problem solving, and group and individual projects, students become aware of the benefits of realistic and practical thinking in the pursuit of academic and professional goals.

Logistical Considerations

Up until now, this discussion has focused on the class as a whole. We will now shift our attention to elements of the service-learning component itself. It may, at this point, be beneficial to briefly discuss the logistics of managing this program. With 40 or more participants, all of whom are required to complete 10 visits at one of nine Head Start centers, and four on-campus training/supervision sessions within a 12-week time frame, this task can easily become overwhelming. Briefly, the planning and management of this program includes the following:

Recruiting service-learning sites and initial planning. This involves contacting and meeting with regional (Head Start) administrators to (1) ascertain the need for service-learning students, (2) identify available placement sites and participating teachers, (3) define student and placement-site responsibilities (including academic and legal documentation), (4) outline a program time line and develop a working schedule, (5) establish assignment procedures, (6) organize the transfer of assignment information and contracts, (7) plan and set agendas for university visits, and (8) arrange for regular feedback contacts.

Student recruitment and registration. Student assignments must be confirmed in time to meet university registration deadlines, thereby avoiding possible financial penalties. Although universities do provide initial add-drop periods, there is a great deal to accomplish in a limited time. Students need to be informed of the locations of placement sites, the time slots available for service sessions, and the number of openings at each site. They also must have access to information regarding public transportation, ride sharing, parking facilities, school holidays, and snow-emergency procedures. For the present program, this information has been organized and presented effectively through the use of a simple bulletin board that was clearly labeled and placed in the back of the lecture hall.

Record keeping and feedback procedures. Students are assigned to sites and time slots on a specified day following a course lecture. Head Start administrators are invited back for this period to facilitate answering questions and making special arrangements for interested students. Student assignments are entered on a master spreadsheet designed to track site visits, supervision sessions, and completed written work. Head Start administrators are given a finished copy of this spreadsheet for their records and contacted thereafter on a weekly basis for purposes of student tracking and feedback.

Supervision scheduling. Supervision is scheduled in repeated units, allowing flexibility of attendance without loss of content. Times for supervision include daytime and evening hours in order to accommodate student schedules. Procedures for individual supervisor contact must also be established. The present program uses its designated bulletin board to display and update this information as needed.

Quality of Supervision Is Geared Toward the Facilitation of Educational Goals

Student supervision is a particularly important element in the success of the program. Although the logistics of group supervision are important, it is the spirit of supervision that seems most relevant to the present discussion. At all levels of this program, and especially with regard to supervision, we have stressed "five C's": compassion, communication, connection, comprehension, and closure. These elements are thought to have significance for all of the relationships and situations defined by this program.

The value of compassion may be most evident when directed toward the life-situations of the underserved populations found in Head Start programs. However, within the context of service-learning supervision, compassion has significance with regard to the kinds of adjustments and difficulties undergraduate students may face during their involvement with the program that may influence their academic performance. Supervision for these service-learning students, therefore, is likely to be most effective when it takes into account individual differences at the personal and academic levels. The assessment of these individual differences requires well-established lines of communication conducive to the sharing of concerns both personal and those of the supervisory group. Accordingly, the regular availability of individual and small-group meetings is a necessity.

Service-learning supervisors must facilitate an atmosphere of trust and patience that extends beyond supervision to the Head Start placement sites. Individual difficulties, or those experienced generally by the group, are, therefore, addressed through cooperative problem solving. The identification of common values and concerns between supervisor and student, as well as recognition of similar experiences and parallels in their emotional and intellectual processes, fosters the personal connection necessary for effective supervision. Secondarily, this relationship provides a·model that students can apply in their own service-learning work, as well as with student peers.

More than an appreciation for interpersonal similarities, comprehension is the goal of service-learning supervision. Background readings, specific to both placement sites and target populations, provide essential information to service-learners. In addition, critical group analysis of causal mechanisms that explain what students experience at their placement sites and the cooperative development of strategies to implement intended changes are key to effective service-learning supervision.

Finally, because commitments to service are thought to foster personal growth and change that should not go unnoticed, there is a need for closure. Here, we do not suggest a simple recapitulation, but rather a comprehensive reformulation of the significant thoughts, feelings, and experiences that students have had while doing service. Students are encouraged to evaluate and define how this program fits into the current chapter of their life story, and what changes they have experienced in themselves, their attitudes and assumptions, and their expectations and hopes for the future.

Parallel to this, students are directed to facilitate the same kind of closure with their Head Start classes. Specifically, they must design and implement a "good-bye" lesson that focuses on valuing formal education and includes a creative class activity that reinforces individual and group identity.

Pedagogical Focus Is on Practical and Realistic Goals at the Individual Level

At the core of service-learning is the idea that educational benefits can be attained through the responsible performance of service tasks. To maximize learning in the present program, students are given many opportunities to act responsibly. Students are expected to attend one orientation session, three group supervision sessions, and all regular course lectures. In addition, they are expected to complete directed readings, engage in group discussions (with both participating and nonparticipating students), submit a structured weekly journal of their site visits, and design and implement a "good-bye" (closure) project for their Head Start class. This is all done in 12 weeks, and all for one credit.

Together with program design and supervision, reflecting upon and interpreting course content can influence students' service-learning performance. A student journal accomplishes this with particular effectiveness. In each journal entry, students target specific Head Start service-learning experiences as the focus of a structured problem-solving process. Targeted concerns can be client-, self-, or site-focused (e.g., dealing with a noncommunicative child, handling personal feelings of frustration or anger, difficulties in getting art supplies). Students complete nine journal entries for which individual and group feedback is made available. Although each journal entry records a separate site visit, students are encouraged to identify and write about ongoing problems and related progress. Journal entries follow a structured problem-solving process that involves five steps. Each of these steps is described in a journal entry subsection of approximately 100 to 200 words in length. The steps include (1) problem/task definition, (2) brainstorming for a solution, (3) solution strategy selection and implementation, (4) outcomes and evaluation, and (5) personal reflection.

Throughout training and supervision, within the context of group and individual problem-solving sessions, there is a focus on the identification of practical goals (Bransford and Stein 1993; Segal 1995). Students are encouraged to identify and problem solve the smallest of changes that might create progress toward client, personal, and systemic goals, rather than target larger changes that (although warranted) may be unattainable. This dual focus on attainable change and the problem-solving process has positive effects on students' efficacy and productivity.

Student Evaluation Is Multidimensional

Any evaluation of student performance is implicitly an evaluation of the effectiveness of the total student experience. Nowhere is this more significant than in service-learning. Because of the fluidity of human interaction and the variety of individual placements and schedules, no two students ever experience the same learning set. This means that there can be little regulation over the consistency of student experiences. Consequently, evaluation needs to be structured along personal performance dimensions that are sensitive to individual student progress.

In this program, performance dimensions include student expectations and self-reflections, critical-thinking skills, schemata for problem solving, and, in general, students' ability to address the unknown successfully. Although these individual characteristics are not formally assessed, initial informational contacts between student and supervisor can establish estimates of personal strengths and target areas for improvement and growth for each student. These early estimates are then compared with progress that students demonstrate throughout the program. This approach requires ongoing direction, challenge, encouragement, support, and feedback, all of which depend on the complex relationships between student, course professor, and service-learning supervisor.

Service-learning students respond to multiple challenges at multiple levels and times. In this program, therefore, evaluation is a process that includes the following:

1. Ongoing availability for feedback and guidance. This requires a somewhat flexible schedule for meeting times and attention to individuals' abilities, circumstances, and needs.

2. A variety of student responsibilities that reflect the complexity of task demands associated with their service-learning experience, including actual service hours, individually contracted activities, assigned readings, verbal and written reports, meeting project deadlines, and representation of service-learning to other classes and organizations.

3. Measures of student output that reflect program participation, academic and professional development, and growth along personal performance dimensions, including placement-site attendance records, weekly journal entries, closure ("good-bye") projects, training and supervision attendance, class cooperation, and student dialogue.

4. Student feedback for program refinement, improvement, and future development. A final responsibility of students is that they share their insights into ways in which the service-learning experience might be improved. Although not always achievable, their suggestions are invaluable for continuing efforts to design and administer programs in which students may find fulfillment, resonance, and meaning in the service of others.

Conclusion

In the future, colleges and universities will need to take the lead in effectively combining the American values of individuality and freedom with the responsibilities of citizenship and democracy. We believe that service-learning programs meet the complementary needs of both the underserved and the undergraduate, and we encourage all universities to continue to develop and support such programs.

References

Barber, B.R. (April 15, 1995). "Workshops of Our Democracy." *Education Week,* 34.

Berman, S. (1990). "Educating for Social Responsibility." *Educational Leadership* 48(3): 375-380.

Bransford, J., and B.S. Stein. (1993). *The Ideal Problem Solver.* 2nd ed. New York: W.H. Freeman.

Coles, R. (1993). *The Call of Service.* New York: Houghton Mifflin.

Melton, G.B. (1991). "Socialization in the Global Community." *American Psychologist* 46: 66-71.

Segal, E. (April 15, 1995). "Becoming People Who Find Solutions." *Education Week,* 35.

Service-Learning Through Action-Research Partnerships

by Georgia Nigro and Stanton Wortham

Student research and community service are core experiences for many undergraduates at small liberal arts institutions such as Bates College. Student researchers often turn to local communities as useful sources of data for their own projects, and as a result the students develop research skills. Students also volunteer time to fill community needs, and as a result develop civic consciousness, moral character, and job skills. Rarely are student research and community service combined, such that student research itself becomes service provided to the community (Harkavy 1993). In this chapter, we describe a course in which undergraduates learned from and with members of the local community by doing research that contributed to the solution of significant community problems involving services to children. Student researchers collaborated with local practitioners on research questions that originated in the practitioners' settings. In some cases, the research built on practitioners' own recent attempts to do research; in others, the research had awaited the assistance that student researchers could provide. In every case, the collaborations created partnerships that benefited our students, local practitioners, and the children in our community.

Service and Service-Learning

Student service is booming on college campuses across the country. Yet Levine (1994) argues that student commitment to service is low because service activities are often separate from and unrelated to college coursework. Service-learning corrects this problem through its emphasis on service that is integrated into and enhances the academic curriculum, as well as through the inclusion of structured time for students to reflect on the service experience (Zlotkowski 1996). The revival of service-learning over the last 10 years has been stimulated by Campus Compact, a national organization

This work was supported in part by grants from the Maine Campus Compact and the Center for Service-Learning at Bates College. The authors thank Dean James Carignan, Peggy Rotundo, and Liz McCabe Park for their generous support and encouragement.

Correspondence concerning this chapter should be addressed to Georgia Nigro, Department of Psychology, Bates College, Lewiston, ME 04240; gnigro@bates.edu.

formed by college and university presidents to foster citizenship skills and values in students through active involvement in collegiate-based public and community service. More than 500 institutions, including our own, belong to Campus Compact.

According to Levine (1994), working with children is one of the most popular service activities on college campuses today. This interest suggests that developmental psychology and related courses are opportune sites for service-learning components (McCluskey-Fawcett and Green 1992; Raupp and Cohen 1992). Our course capitalized upon student interest in working with children in its selection of projects involving services to children.

Action Research

Action research refers to systematic inquiry by practitioners about their own practices (Cochran-Smith and Lytle 1993). In psychology, the term dates back to Kurt Lewin (1946), who believed that knowledge should be created from problem solving in real-world situations. In Lewin's formulation, action research involves a spiral of cycles of planning, acting, observing, and reflecting. Drawing on Lewin's work, Argyris and Schön (1991) describe action research as follows:

> *Action research takes its cues — its questions, puzzles, and problems — from the perceptions of practitioners within particular, local practice con-texts. It bounds episodes of research according to the boundaries of the local context. It builds descriptions and theories within the practice context itself, and tests them through intervention experiments — that is, through experiments that bear the double burden of testing hypotheses and effecting some (putatively) desired change in the situation. (86)*

The double burden that Argyris and Schön refer to — a concern with both research (creating valid knowledge) and action (improving practice or effect-ing social change) — makes action research particularly appealing to those undergraduates who find laboratory research too removed from the reality it seeks to understand.

Within the field of education, the problem-solving focus of action research has attracted many followers. Robinson (1993) describes the need for a problem-based methodology in educational research as follows:

> *Much research has failed to influence educational problems because it has separated problematic practices from the pretheorized problem-solving processes that gave rise to them and which render them sensible to those who engage in them. Once practice is understood in this way, the theoriz-*

ing and reasoning of practitioners becomes a key to understanding what sustains problematic practice. (256)

The practitioners that Robinson refers to are, of course, teachers, and action research within the field of education is usually called "teacher research."

Two features of teacher research are relevant to this discussion — its epistemology and its politics. The titles of several recent volumes allude to the epistemology of teacher research: *Inside/Outside: Teacher Research and Knowledge* (Cochran-Smith and Lytle 1993), *Studying Your Own School: An Educator's Guide to Qualitative Practitioner Research* (Anderson, Herr, and Nihlen 1994). Teacher research generates knowledge from within; knowledge is not created outside schools and then disseminated or transferred into schools to be implemented by practitioners. Instead, practitioners themselves are researchers. This epistemology makes inquiry and reform intrinsic to teaching, and it blurs the traditional distinction between theory and practice.

Closely related to this epistemology is the politics of teacher research. In their recent book on teacher research, Anderson, Herr, and Nihlen (1994) argue that practitioner research is "best viewed as a vehicle for the empowerment of practitioners, students, and communities toward a goal of institutional and social change from the inside" (36). Similarly, Cochran-Smith and Lytle (1993) see teacher research as a way to reprofessionalize teaching in the face of increasing attempts to turn teachers into technicians whose role is to implement the research findings of others in the areas of instruction, curriculum, and assessment. Soltis (1994) captures both the epistemology and the politics of teacher research when he describes the "new teacher" as one who demonstrates genuine intellectual engagement in his or her practice; collaborates with other teachers, college and university people, and students; and sees teaching as embedded in a larger social context in which power, dominance, and social injustices exist.

Combining Action Research and Service-Learning

Action research and service-learning complement each other well. In both cases, the participants (local practitioners and students) learn by trying something in an actual setting, reflecting systematically on what happened, and then modifying their practice. The two also differ from the more traditional model in which researchers or teachers develop knowledge and then dispense it to practitioners or students. Thus, action research and service-learning both depend on a theory-practice dialectic instead of a more traditional, linear application of theory to practice.

Action research and service-learning also involve less-hierarchical relationships between researcher and practitioner and between teacher and student. Local practitioners are empowered to develop knowledge about their practice without mediation of experts, or in genuine collaboration with experts. Similarly, in service-learning, students are less beholden to professors; they can go out and see psychological phenomena for themselves. In this way, professors become more like facilitators and less like experts.

So action research and service-learning may be complementary, but why combine them? There are several good reasons. One is that although few psychology students go on to become laboratory-based experimentalists, many find jobs in which they are called upon to carry out some form of empirical inquiry — very often in complex, real-world situations (Robson 1993). Action-research partnerships can give students firsthand experience in these complex research situations while they learn methods for achieving rigor and trustworthiness in their inquiries. Another good reason to combine action research and service-learning is that practitioner research benefits from developing supportive institutional partnerships. Lieberman and Miller (1994) note the importance of networks, collaborations, and coalitions for creating a culture of inquiry that permits teacher research to flourish in schools. They describe many benefits to practitioners of these networks, collaborations, and coalitions: opportunities to share ideas and perspectives; support for experimentation, questioning, and risk taking; opportunities to develop leadership skills; and professional learning.

The unique feature of the action-research partnerships we created was pairing college research students with local practitioner-researchers. Wells (1994) and Noffke, Mosher, and Maricle (1994) have described successful partnerships between university researchers and teachers. Harkavy (1993) has documented the successes and challenges of a university-community partnership between West Philadelphia and the University of Pennsylvania that includes participatory action research by undergraduates. Our project combines research generated by practitioners with college students doing research as service.

A Course in Action Research

Pairing student and practitioner-researchers took place in the context of an action-research course we taught during our institution's five-week spring term. To ensure that students and local practitioners collaborated on projects that fit the length of the term, we met with local teachers and service providers in the months preceding the course to help them formulate research questions that were ready for investigation. These meetings took several forms: We provided inservice training in schools, attended staff meetings, took local practitioners to a teacher-research conference, and facilitated an ongoing practitioner-research group that formed after a conference we held at the college. Funding from the college as well as a grant from the Maine Campus Compact supported these efforts.

The table on the next page provides a brief description of the projects. Students received a list of these projects, including the settings and names of local collaborators, on the first day of the course. They also received a syllabus that contained the usual information about texts, requirements, and schedule. Our major text was Robson's *Real World Research* (Blackwell, 1993). Class meetings introduced students to qualitative and quantitative research methods, especially those we knew would be particularly suited to the research questions of the local practitioners. These included survey design, ethnography, and single-subject design. Class meetings also served as a time to reflect on the research work. Local practitioners were welcome to attend class meetings, which were scheduled at different times to fit their schedules.

The unique nature of the five-week short term shaped our course in various ways. For example, students were matched to projects on the first day of the term, and by the end of the first week they turned in detailed action plans formulated in conjunction with their collaborator. The research had to be completed in three weeks, so that the last week of the term could be devoted to writing and presenting research reports. Because students take only one course during the short term and are expected to devote themselves to it full-time, this schedule worked, although some of the projects could have used more time. We do not think a course such as this depends on a structure like our short term, though. In fact, we have recently adapted the course to fit Bates College's regular 13-week semester.

To give a sense of the scope and substance of the research projects, we describe two in more detail below. Although these projects were substantial enough to involve two student researchers each, they represent the work accomplished in other projects.

Example 1: Violence Prevention in Schools

This project involved two students with an agency, Advocates for Children, that provides sexual abuse prevention programs to schools in Androscoggin County, Maine. The agency was interested in expanding its services to violence prevention, but first wanted to know more about the nature of violence occurring in local schools and about any current efforts at prevention. Although some individual schools had begun to keep statistics about violent incidents and had implemented some violence prevention strategies, the data about violence and prevention strategies across schools were haphazard. Thus, agency staff and the two students agreed that the first step was to design a survey to be sent to principals and guidance counselors.

Action Research Projects

- The EAT (Educational Assessment Team) at an elementary school hoped to find out what parents, students, and staff believe is working and not working at the school.

- A guidance counselor at a school wanted to assess second graders' fears.

- Teachers at an alternative elementary school wished to assess their new curriculum based on Howard Gardner's theory of multiple intelligences.

- A French teacher at a middle school wished to develop and administer an oral test of proficiency and compare students' oral scores with their written scores.

- A third-grade teacher was interested in understanding children's motivations to write.

- A high school teacher wanted to assess student satisfaction with the new 80-minute periods.

- A high school math teacher wanted to investigate the career paths of women and men who took his calculus course.

- A nursery school teacher was interested in obtaining an observational record of the teacher-child and peer interactions of a troubled three-year-old student.

- A preschool teacher wanted an observational study of how children utilize time and space during choice periods.

- A child abuse prevention agency hoped to survey all schools in the county about current levels of violence and efforts at violence prevention.

- A youth agency wished to know if its transitional living program increased protective factors for the at-risk youth it serves.

- A youth agency hoped to learn more about the experiences of female juvenile offenders before and after they go through its after-care program.

Using their text as a guide to survey design and the college library as a source of materials about the theoretical bases and nature of violence prevention programs, the two students quickly drafted a survey that they and their collaborators revised and mailed out to all elementary and secondary schools in the county. After one week, 50 percent of the surveys had been returned, a sample deemed satisfactory for data analysis. The two students entered the data into SPSS and with their collaborators examined the results for interesting trends. Concerned that the picture gleaned from the surveys may have been skewed because of the narrow cohort chosen (principals and guidance counselors), the students and agency staff decided to collect more information — from students and staff in one school district in focus groups with the various constituencies. The students ran these groups and summarized the data, which did, indeed, differ from the survey data in several important ways. For example, student opinions about the efficacy of different approaches to violence prevention diverged markedly from principals' and guidance counselors'.

The agency used the data gathered from this multimethod approach to apply successfully for state funds to support a violence prevention pilot program in which the students led focus groups.

Example 2: A Multiple Intelligences Curriculum

This project involved two students and six teachers at an ungraded K-3 school. The teachers had developed a curriculum based on Gardner's (1983) theory of multiple intelligences that they planned to implement for six weeks. The curriculum included six stations, based on six of the intelligences, and the plan called for children to spend one week at each of the stations during the period set aside each afternoon for the project. For example, a child would spend an hour each afternoon for a week at "music smart," making an instrument, composing a song, or comparing and contrasting different styles of music. The next week, the same child might spend the time at "picture smart," participating in activities designed to foster spatial intelligence, such as making block prints and solving visual puzzles. The teachers had several research questions they hoped to answer, and different plans in place for answering them. Our students were able to assist them in two ways. First, by observing eight particular children with family, behavioral, academic, and self-esteem problems, our students could offer the teachers insight into the effectiveness of the curriculum in raising these children's self-esteem and perhaps reducing some of their behavioral and academic problems. Second, the students would observe and interview the teachers, to provide an external perspective on what staff were learning from the curricular innovation. In particular, the teachers wished to learn whether they were acquiring new tools for managing the children's differences.

Taking an ethnographic approach, the two students observed and interviewed the eight children and interviewed the six teachers individually and in a group. They learned that many children did discover new strengths, although observations were often clouded by the enjoyment level at certain stations and by the interpersonal dynamics among children grouped together at a station. Both teachers and children noticed students' nontraditional strengths more, and teachers came to appreciate different learning styles more than they had before.

Despite the success of the research, there was a depressing postscript to this project. After teachers planned a more elaborate project for the following year, they learned that the district had decided to close the school to save money.

Our Own Action Research

To see whether our course had the desired effects for students and local practitioners, we examined students' and practitioners' evaluations of the course, as well as the research reports prepared by the students. Several significant findings emerged. Students appreciated the direct experience they got with complex community problems and the sense that they possessed or could acquire specific skills that would help solve the problems. They also enjoyed the control they had; they thought we provided the latitude that allowed them to take initiative and think on their own. Practitioners appreciated getting multiple perspectives on their practices. They found it engaging and energizing to step back from their quotidian concerns and see their work through the students' eyes. They also appreciated the students' time and expertise, as many completed projects the practitioners could not have conducted on their own. Finally, many practitioners expressed gratitude for the particular information they received on their practices, and they expected that it would help them serve children better. One year later, teachers still remark to us that without the students' help, they would never have discovered that some of their classroom practices were counterproductive.

Some of the problems and challenges we faced are instructive as well. Both students and practitioners wished for more time and guidance in formulating research questions. Practitioners also wished for greater involvement in the research tasks that followed question formulation. In some cases, they simply had to hand off a research question to the students and wait for an answer. Many practitioners could not attend class meetings and learn more about research strategies. Finally, the nature of the college calendar meant projects came to an end after only a few weeks. Practitioners regretted the loss of relationships with our students, and students did not always get to see the changes practitioners made in response to the data.

Although we have not devised solutions to all these problems and challenges, we hope our work in building ongoing practitioner-research networks will address some of these concerns. Also, we hope that by moving the course to one of the 13-week semesters, we will create more satisfying collaborations.

These problems and challenges aside, we believe that service-learning through action-research partnerships is a valuable part of the psychology curriculum. In addition to the many worthwhile outcomes we outlined above, service-learning has the added benefit of connecting research, teaching, and service for the faculty members involved. With this benefit comes another challenge though, as Zlotkowski's 1996 article on service-learning indicates: The professional importance of service-learning has yet to find its way into the personnel practices of committees for promotion and tenure. This is a significant challenge, because service-learning depends critically upon faculty commitment.

References

Anderson, G., K. Herr, and A.S. Nihlen. (1994). *Studying Your Own School: An Educator's Guide to Qualitative Practitioner Research*. Thousand Oaks, CA: Corwin Press.

Argyris, C., and D. Schön. (1991). "Participatory Action Research and Action Science Compared: A Commentary." In *Participatory Action Research*, edited by W.F. Whyte, pp. 85-96. Newbury Park, CA: Sage.

Cochran-Smith, M., and S.L. Lytle. (1993). *Inside/Outside: Teacher Research and Knowledge*. New York: Teachers College Press.

Gardner, H. (1983). *Frames of Mind: The Theory of Multiple Intelligences*. New York: Basic Books.

Harkavy, I. (1993). "University-Community Partnerships: The University of Pennsylvania and West Philadelphia as a Case Study." In *Rethinking Tradition: Integrating Service With Academic Study on Campuses*, edited by T.Y. Kupiec, pp. 121-128. Denver: Education Commission of the States.

Levine, A. (July/August 1994). "Service on Campus." *Change* 26(4): 4-5.

Lewin, K. (1946). "Action Research and Minority Problems." *Journal of Social Issues* 2(4): 34-46.

Lieberman, A., and L. Miller. (1994). "Problems and Possibilities of Institutionalizing Teacher Research." In *Ninety-Third Yearbook of the National Society for the Study of Education: Part I. Teacher Research and Educational Reform*, edited by K.J. Rehage (Society ed.) and S. Hollingsworth and H. Sockett (volume eds.), pp. 204-220. Chicago: National Society for the Study of Education.

McCluskey-Fawcett, K., and P. Green. (1992). "Using Community Service to Teach Developmental Psychology." *Teaching of Psychology* 19: 150-152.

Noffke, S., L. Mosher, and C. Maricle. (1994). "Curriculum Research Together: Writing Our Work." In *Ninety-Third Yearbook of the National Society for the Study of Education: Part I. Teacher Research and Educational Reform*, edited by K.J. Rehage (Society ed.) and S. Hollingsworth and H. Sockett (volume eds.), pp. 166-185. Chicago: National Society for the Study of Education.

Raupp, C.D., and D.C. Cohen. (1992). "'A Thousand Points of Light' Illuminate the Psychology Curriculum: Volunteering as a Learning Experience." *Teaching of Psychology* 19: 25-30.

Robinson, V.M. (1993). *Problem-Based Methodology: Research for the Improvement of Practice.* Oxford: Pergamon.

Soltis, J. (1994). "The New Teacher." In *Ninety-Third Yearbook of the National Society for the Study of Education: Part I. Teacher Research and Educational Reform*, edited by K.J. Rehage (Society ed.) and S. Hollingsworth and H. Sockett (volume eds.), pp. 245-260. Chicago: National Society for the Study of Education.

Wells, G. (1994). "Introduction: Teacher Research and Educational Change." In *Changing Schools From Within: Creating Communities of Inquiry*, edited by G. Wells, pp. 1-35. Portsmouth, NH: Heinemann.

Zlotkowski, E. (January/February 1996). "Linking Service-Learning and the Academy: A New Voice at the Table?" *Change* 28(1): 20-28.

Service-Learning and Cross-Cultural Psychology

by Iva GreyWolf

Three years ago at Concordia College (MN), I began developing a cross-cultural psychology course with a unique pedagogy. The approach was a combination of feminist and Native American pedagogy. This meant everyone in the class, including the teacher, was in the process of "becoming." Learning was an active, ongoing process. Each participant experienced an equal voice in the classroom, respect and power were shared, stories were used to teach, and there were many experimental learning opportunities (GreyWolf, Lintleman, and Postema 1995; Kirkness and Barnhardt 1991; Muller 1993; Pepper and Henry 1986; Sawyer 1991). Special emphasis was placed on cooperative learning exercises. I wanted to do more than give facts and expand the students' knowledge base. The style of education focused on thinking problems out rather than transferring and regurgitating information. It was not a top-down ordering or linear presentation of information. Students and teacher were jointly responsible for a process in which all grew by in-depth reflection on the readings, lectures, discussions, videos, and service-learning.

The first year the class was taught, service-learning was not included, and the class did not strictly follow a nontraditional learning model. It was, however, apparent that the students needed to move beyond a sterile cognitive examination of culture and psychology. To do so, they needed an in-depth experience, one with real impact, and it was along these lines that I rethought and restructured the course. I became very cognizant of how "authentic reflection considers neither abstract man nor the world without men, but men in their relations with the world" (Freire 1970: 69). Consequently, one challenge was presenting the students with problems that both related to them personally and interrelated with the world around them.

Concordia College is a homogeneous campus (white, middle-class, Christian, Midwestern), so I wanted to open the students' eyes to the world of differences around them. The only way to effectively encourage a thorough exploration of other cultures was to expose them to other cultures — not just through reading but also through experiences with people from other cultures. I wanted to expose them to a level of uncomfortableness sufficient to nudge them to respond to the challenge of working with someone from another culture to solve a significant problem. Hence, I decided to incorporate in the class community service to nonwhite cultures. The students would then be faced not just with theoretical dilemmas but also with the real problems of real people from other cultures who had moved into the students' community.

Cross-Cultural Psychology is a senior-level class that integrates the students' liberal arts experiences. Students are exposed to a more global psychological perspective. This promotes their recognition that the majority of psychologists have been trained in Western theories and methods, while the majority of the world is not white and may not value a Western perspective (Segall et al. 1990). Students need to learn that there are many versions of human behavior, as opposed to a single best version. Studying cross-cultural psychology requires acknowledging the limitations and culture-bound nature of the disciplines. Students' intellectual perspectives are broadened by investigating themes, problems, historical periods, and behavioral differences, as well as common experiences, around the world.

Initially, I set goals for the students that included engaging in problem solving with people from other cultures, recognizing ethnocentric biases, demonstrating an understanding of what cross-cultural psychology encompasses, increasing awareness of global psychological issues, and recognizing the local impact of those issues. Next, I identified the content to be covered and devised a plan that would engage the students.

During the first year of my learning process, I brought in speakers from other cultures and other religions to talk about their lives and to answer questions. Students wrote response papers clarifying what they had gleaned from the presentations, examining how what they had learned related to their readings, and identifying issues and/or feelings the presentations brought up for them. The second year I wanted a more challenging experience for them so I expanded my working relationship with the Sources of Service (SOS), the service-learning organization on our campus, which had an English-as-a-second-language (ESL) program for adults in the community and a Lutheran Social Services (LSS) refugee program. Nurturing a positive cooperative relationship with the service-learning office was essential. Its staff coordinated student interaction with the relevant agencies; they also helped students with guidelines for maximizing the benefit of their service-learning activities (e.g., journaling, and reflection groups called "mirror sessions") and provided a record of the number of hours students logged.

The ESL program involved students in conversation groups that provided an exchange of cultural information while the ESL participants practiced their conversational skills. Students talked about many topics including courtship practices, holidays and celebrations, the weather, and politics. The LSS refugee program matched students with refugee families and individuals. Students oriented the refugees to the local community by helping with basic English, transportation, working with bureaucracies, shopping, cooking, paying bills, working with schools, and so on. In partnership with the refugee program, the students responded to the needs of the refugees that LSS identified. The campus SOS program coordinated many of these efforts, and it also matched some student-volunteers with international students on our campus. Meetings with SOS, ESL, and LSS were built into the syllabus and scheduled throughout the semester so students never had the impression that community service was an add-on but was instead an integral part of the learning experience.

Having the students involved in the struggles of other human beings was essential to a second-year plan to prepare them to do a comparative analysis of belief systems. In the course of working with individuals from other cultures, the students exchanged information and were encouraged to examine their own beliefs, to question themselves, to be self-critical without flagellating themselves, and to clarify and support their positions. I hoped that in this way they would develop an increased tolerance of differences, an increase in empathy, a sense of fairness, and a clearer understanding of our interconnectedness with others in the world. They needed to see the interrelationships between culture and behavior if they were to understand human behavior and mental processes.

The third year, my approach was more refined. We learned from the students that the refugee experiences and the ESL conversations were most helpful. Concordia's international students did not need the students from the Cross-Cultural Psychology course students as much as the LSS and ESL participants did. I had used the campus SOS program in all my other classes to coordinate service-learning projects, and I continued to use their philosophy and some of their methodology in the cross-cultural class. I also added to the course assignments. During the second year, students had evaluated their experiences in a long reflection paper at the end of the semester. The reflection paper required them to connect the readings, lectures, presentations, and videos, examining concepts and personal reactions. The third year, they kept a class journal in addition to the reflection paper.

Class journal entries were all anonymous. Each student was required to choose a pseudonym and put it on a 3x5 card along with his/her real name. The 3x5 card was placed in a sealed envelope. These envelopes all were put in a larger envelope, and it was sealed in front of the class. Students also turned in journal entries written during three 1-hour segments of class time set aside for that purpose. The class journal was kept in the psychology office in a three-ring binder. It was agreed that the envelope with the identifying information would not be opened until the end of the semester, so that both the teacher and the students would not be aware of who was responsible for which entry. Such anonymity allowed for more honest discourse. At the end of the semester, the anonymity issue was addressed directly by a student who said: "I would like to raise the possibility that some people from the journal may not want to reveal their identities. I have no problem with it, but I can see where others might. We should be given the choice whether we want to reveal ourselves or not." After a discussion, it was decided that only the teacher would have access to the identity of the journalists.

Students were required to make two-part entries in the class journal once a week: (1) one section responding to other entries, and (2) a second section reacting to anything presented in the class, readings for the week, or the service-learning project itself. The journaling helped identify the beginning point of growth for each of the students. For example, two entries read:

> Many of the writers commented about their ignorance of other cultures and the homogeneity of the people from their home areas.

> A recurrent theme I noticed while reading the entries was one of "I feel naive/ignorant about other cultures," paraphrasing Sammy, White, 3834, and Snickers. I must admit, I feel the same. There is a definite underexposure to other cultures and backgrounds in our country, even though we are supposedly a diverse nation.

The anonymity of the journal allowed the students to confront each other's ethnocentrism and to ask for clarifications of their thinking. The following are some examples of this process:

> To me, Snicker's comment illustrated the blind belief in the superiority of America.

> Often I felt that many of the entries were superficial (such as one entry in which the writer tried to compare how it feels to be a minority in skin color with how it feels to have white, untanned skin while among people who had dark tans). The way I see it, trying to relate to a very real issue in such a shallow manner is in accordance to apathy (you don't really care about the issue) and maybe even mockery.

> I was very disappointed in one of our presenters in the first group of presentations. Before closing her presentation she said, "I am glad I am American and I don't have to go through that" . . . imply[ing] that what you are and [what you have] is much better than others. We should be careful trying to compare our lives with other cultures I think.

> Does cross-cultural psychology emphasize learning of others or of oneself? 'Phoebe the Cat' believes it of oneself, and I agree that I too have gained considerable knowledge of who I am from our class, but I believe it was because of learning about others that let me do this. I would like to know other people's comments on this. What have you learned most, in class (others) or (yourself)?

In explaining their views to their peers, students found it necessary to examine and evaluate the values that functioned in their decision making in addition to recognizing the role their disciplinary training (e.g., psychology, political science, business) played in forming their positions. I have witnessed students' thinking change from initially being dualist (e.g., identifying absolute truths, a set of facts to be learned, rights and wrongs) to relativist (e.g., identifying a framework within which facts are interpreted) to a deeper understanding of complexities. Students were able to make connections between their anecdotal experiences and classroom information. They were thinking and questioning more.

The service-learning work with the refugees was done in teams of four, so the team could decide the emphasis to be taken with a refugee family and divide the work and time commitment. The students determined their own teams after class discussion about the needs of the refugees, the size of the refugee families, and the time frames when students would be needed and available. Students worked a minimum of two and a half hours a week on their service projects. This also helped with a fairer division of labor and helped address safety issues.

Outside assistance is a vital part of the refugee program. The students worked with the refugees to improve their telephone etiquette, increase their social network, help them budget expenditures for entertainment, and help them understand the public transportation system, shopping, cooking American foods, seasonal activities, and safety. The activities were necessary to help the refugees adjust to their new environment. The students were witnessing the struggles and challenges of living in a foreign environment and were contributing to the refugees' adjustment in a meaningful way.

Class size was small (14), so it allowed for close monitoring of experiences. Because this was a frightening project for some students, it required a lot of structure. Expectations as well as concrete ideas needed to be clarified in order to help students reach their goals (e.g., using coloring books to teach vocabulary, making up a game to learn the bus system). Weekly communication between the LSS coordinators and me was necessary as were telephone contacts with the students to ferret out difficulties they were facing.

During this semester, the O.J. Simpson trial reached a conclusion; Prime Minister Yitzhak Rabin was assassinated; and there was a racial incident in our community that received national attention. Constant communication and processing was necessary because the students sometimes felt helpless to make a difference in the world or were emotionally overwhelmed by the dilemmas of the refugees. Many of their journal entries included comments about the wide range of emotions they were experiencing.

Students were always encouraged to work together. They worked in teams to support each other. In studying study-guide questions, in completing their take-home tests, and in working with their refugee families, they learned to learn cooperatively. This allowed them to raise questions, support each other, and again challenge each other. However, they were required to write their own papers and take their own tests.

A balance needed to be kept between knowledge, awareness, and skill building so students could gain the greatest benefit from their service experience (Pederson 1988). A focus solely on increasing knowledge would minimize the human component and lack compassion. Mere awareness of the scope of differences can overwhelm without including skills to effectively address those differences. Techniques of how to work with other cultures without background knowledge of those cultures result in superficial responses to significant human dilemmas. As Paulo Freire has said, "No one can be authentically human while he prevents others from being so" (1970: 73).

Psychology in many aspects became alive for students through the combination of working with people from other cultures and reflecting on the applicability of theoretical concepts. Service-learning was an important addition to this course. The class journal and group discussions provided ongoing discourse throughout the semester. A combination of stories, interviews, and interactive exercises promoted understanding and sensitivity in students prior to their work with the refugees. There was some resistance to setting aside time for the service project; some students withdrew from the class, but those who stayed felt it provided a powerful learning experience. Integrating community service is a significant time investment for the instructor, but I am convinced it is worth the effort. Adding a service-learning component also requires an instructor to be receptive to feedback from students and to be willing to learn about effective models from other service-learning and community programs.

Ideally, in the future, there would be a prerequisite course on cross-cultural issues. The students were appalled at how little they knew about the world around them. If the students could have had an initial experience using the class journal to challenge and learn from each other, the second semester of class journaling would possibly have registered even more depth. Implementing a computer program for journaling would be an additional improvement. Students could log on at their convenience, and their anonymity would be assured. In conclusion, some of the students' own words sum up the experience for them:

> Wow! I actually think it would be beneficial to me to be in a cross-cultural psych class for the whole year! I have been so ignorant toward different cultures before this class, and there seems to be just too many things to learn about in a short period of time.

> By now, we have shared our thoughts and feelings, both in class and here

on paper. I thank you all for writing your true feelings and sharing your most intimate ideas. We have had some good debates and interesting philosophies.

Even though I'm a semester away from graduation, I'm still so incredibly ignorant! For me, the best possible education is through experience. I now have something more valuable than a ring or diploma to take away.

We each got a voice and a chance to "think out loud" on paper (journal). Today, my ideas have been changed drastically and forever.

Most pleasing is the focus on the future from the student point of view. For example:

I must say that working with this family who came as refugees is one of the best experiences I've ever had in my life.

I have taken special interest in this topic, and I am actually doing an independent research project next semester on . . . how the media helps shape public opinion.

I've been looking into volunteer work across seas for the summer.

It is well and good to learn, expand, and talk, but what will each of us do after we leave . . . about the issues we discuss? Action speaks.

References

Freire, P. (1970). *Pedagogy of the Oppressed.* New York: Continuum.

GreyWolf, I., J. Lintleman, and J. Postema. (1995). "Catching Students in a Web of Teaching." *Teaching at Concordia* 18: 39-48.

Kirkness, V.J., and R. Barnhardt. (1991). "First Nations and Higher Education: The Four R's — Respect, Relevance, Reciprocity, Responsibility." *Journal of American-Indian Education* 30(3): 1-15.

Muller, L. (1993). "Collaborative 'Life Stories' and Anonymous Team Journals: Fostering Dialogue and Decentering Authority in the Classroom." *American Quarterly* 45: 598-609.

Pederson, P. (1988). *A Handbook for Developing Multicultural Awareness.* Alexandria, VA: American Association for Counseling & Development.

Pepper, F.C., and S.L. Henry. (1986). "Social and Cultural Effects on Indian Learning Style: Classroom Implications." *Canadian Journal of Native Education* 13: 54-61.

Sawyer, D. (1991). "Native Learning Styles: Shorthand for Instructional Adaptations?" *Canadian Journal of Native Education* 18: 99-104.

Segall, M.H., P.R. Dasen, J.W. Berry, and Y.H. Poortinga. (1990). *Human Behavior in Global Perspective.* Needham Heights, MA: Allyn & Bacon.

Reflections on an Established Service-Learning Program: The Developmental Disabilities Immersion Program at UCLA

by Arvan L. Fluharty and Parvin Kassaie

The Developmental Disabilities Immersion Program (DDIP) at the University of California, Los Angeles is a two-quarter, full-time, upper-division program that combines traditional classroom teaching with community service and research. The program focuses on the study of developmental disabilities by having students work with children and adults with disabilities while simultaneously conducting related research under the direction of faculty sponsors.

DDIP was founded on the principles of three pedagogies: service-learning (Bringle and Hatcher 1996), experiential education (Giles and Freed 1990), and subject immersion. The goals of the program are to:

• Teach academic areas related to developmental disabilities. The subject matter offers unique insights into the human situation and can be approached from a variety of academic perspectives: humanities, social work, other social sciences, or biology. However, the umbrella of psychology encompasses the views of both social and physical sciences and speaks the language of both. Academic courses in psychology provide the theoretical context for service and research in DDIP where psychological constructs can be applied and observed directly in the service of people with developmental disabilities.

• Develop both qualitative and quantitative observational and research skills and use these in planning individual treatment programs, preparing research proposals, and presenting results.

• Enhance critical-thinking skills leading to the application of psychological and educational training to individual situations as they occur in practice.

• Encourage the development of civic values and responsibilities through participation in service activities. At the same time, the field experience tests the student's commitment to career involvement with people with developmental disabilities.

• Prepare students for graduate or professional school.

• Develop in students a collegial attitude toward faculty, community practitioners, and fellow students thereby enhancing the quality of their subsequent academic experiences.

Among the many structured and unstructured experiential education opportunities offered at UCLA, DDIP is unique in the degree of integration it achieves between service and learning. As the word *immersion* implies, students are expected to become totally involved in the program for two quarters. At the end, they leave with lasting impressions of their experiences, which often have career-determining implications. The longevity and success of the program are primarily due to the shared dedication of faculty, community partners, students, and staff in supporting and reinforcing its mission. As the number of service-learning courses increases on campuses nationwide, reflections on the evolution and current structure of this established program offer practical lessons for others.

History

DDIP developed in 1976 as the result of the juncture of two circumstances. A former girls school near Pomona, California, was available as a residential field site for UCLA students. At the same time, the Research Department at the nearby Pacific State Hospital was administratively transferred to UCLA. Pacific State Hospital (now Lanterman Developmental Center) was a large residential institution for people with mental retardation, which had on its grounds a modern and well-equipped Research Center. Pacific was one of the nation's leading centers for mental retardation research and had a multidisciplinary professional staff consisting of psychologists, physicians, biochemists, and neurophysiologists. However, the teaching role of this staff at UCLA was undefined. In conjunction with the UCLA field studies staff, the Pacific research team proposed a comprehensive program involving service placements in the institution, participation in ongoing research programs, and formal courses related to mental retardation.

Strong support was given by the UCLA Psychology Department and when the Pacific research team was integrated into the UCLA Mental Retardation Research Center, team members were given appointments in UCLA Medical School's Department of Psychiatry & Biobehavioral Sciences. The departments of psychiatry and psychology have provided almost all of the program faculty. In 1986, the program was extended to include students from the UC Riverside campus and faculty from its School of Education. The involvement of professional school faculty in this undergraduate program anticipated the current attempts to increase involvement of professional schools in undergraduate education. A developmental disabilities specialization was established in the Psychology Department for DDIP participants and noted on the diploma.

In its second year, the program was extended to two quarters to allow a more comprehensive involvement in fieldwork and research and to enhance the service-learning experience of the students. However, the facility near Pomona had been sold for development, and a new residential site for the program had to be found, a task that was to be repeated each year for several years. Finally, in 1987, when faculty attrition made it difficult to offer an adequate range of supplemental courses, DDIP was moved to the UCLA main campus and the residential component was abandoned. Much to the surprise of many who felt the student community component was the glue that held DDIP together, student enthusiasm for the program continued unabated. Since then, special efforts have been initiated to promote group activities and reinforce a sense of community, but some of the immersion dimension has been lost. Nonetheless, the program's special feeling has been maintained by students taking most of their courses together and by the commitment of faculty and staff to being a part of the student community and taking part in all its activities.

Service-Learning: A DDIP Perspective

Four basic components come together in DDIP: academic coursework, fieldwork and service, research, and a student community. Service-learning in DDIP best fits among the "complex" or "mixed" models outlined by Giles and Freed (1990) in their formalization of the meaning and dimensions of service. In these models, "the complexity arises from different dimensions of service and from different learning agendas" (350). There are two distinct service-learning components in DDIP: the fieldwork and the research placements, which are by design separate and independent so that the students have both a direct interaction and an observational or data-based perspective in their experiences. These components introduce the two major professional tracks available in the field of developmental disabilities.

In the direct-service component of DDIP — the fieldwork — students work in psychoeducational settings with adults and children with a range of developmental disabilities. Students are given an orientation, then carry out 12 hours of direct service per week for two quarters. They work one-on-one or in small groups, teaching a class as a whole, meeting with family members, teaching independent living skills, and conducting intake and discharge of clients in sheltered workshops. The service objective is to assist organizations that serve people with developmental disabilities. In the process, students are expected to work directly with individuals with disabilities and to have opportunities for active learning.

Students are expected to not only "serve to learn" but also "learn to serve" more effectively. The structure and focus of DDIP thus bring together experiential and service-learning pedagogies. Students are expected to put into practice theories and concepts learned in classrooms and to bring back to their courses questions raised through their field experience. Almost all of our students start off by "wanting to help those with disabilities." By the end, we hope to have challenged this commitment through experiences that either reaffirm it or redirect it for those who find the experience unfulfilling. Whatever the outcome, direct service remains the most exciting and challenging aspect of DDIP for most students.

DDIP expands the notion of service to include contributions to the field through research. Even so, the research experience is not meant to stand alone. The meaningfulness of research is predicated on firsthand knowledge gained through service. The pragmatics of the field guide the research questions and direct the inquiry.

The data-based research component is designed to involve students in an ongoing project through which they are introduced to the research process by assisting those engaged in it. Students eventually develop a small part of the overall project as a formal research proposal that they defend orally in a "site visit" format before a panel of faculty and staff. Although not discouraged, individual student projects are rare in DDIP. Typically, student pairs or teams work together on a project with an adviser. Students learn group skills and responsibilities, and on occasion, how to make maximum use of a "weak" associate. Research placements are recruited from a broad spectrum of UCLA faculty with projects related to developmental issues. A diverse range of possible research projects is available, which facilitates matching the students' backgrounds and interests with an ongoing project. Examples of the types of research conducted by students over the past few years, as reflected in their project titles, include these:

- Peer Social Competence Within Educational Placements (Baleva 1995)
- Effects of Health Education on Parents With Cognitive Limitations (Bakcht et al. 1995)
- Measuring Brain Myelin Maturation Using Mass Spectrometry (Senanayake 1995)
- Psychological Stress in Persons With Mental Retardation (Chua and Joo 1994)
- Indicators of Brain Damage in Experimental Hydrocephalus: Neuroamine Related Compounds in the Cerebrospinal Fluid (Orlino 1994)
- Parental Management of the Social Contexts of Children With Developmental Delays (Babb and Maya 1995)[1]

Although it is not an insignificant commitment for a faculty member to work with a DDIP student, most have found it rewarding and continue sponsoring students from year to year. Under the guidance of some of the best researchers in the developmental disabilities field, the undergraduates participating in the program have repeatedly conducted quality research comparable with, or better than, that of many graduate students. In several instances, DDIP projects have been presented at professional meetings and published in regular refereed journals.[2]

Associated Academic Structure

DDIP students earn up to 12 units of credit per quarter through the program. The core courses may be used toward fulfilling the developmental disabilities specialization in the psychology major.

Psychology M180 A&B, Current Issues in Developmental Disabilities. The core academic offering is a two-quarter, four-unit-per-quarter course on developmental disabilities and mental retardation. It initially covers history, definitions, and assessment issues. After a consideration of normal brain function and development, the causes of intellectual deficits, their prevention, and possible treatments are presented. This leads to an examination of special education, institutional systems, and the deinstitutionalization movement. Finally, law as related to individuals with mental disabilities is reviewed. Considerable emphasis is placed on current issues bearing on this subject area. In parallel with this and in conjunction with the Fieldwork Seminar, the depiction of mental deficit in literature, film, and popular culture is explored, and the effect on public perceptions of people with retardation is evaluated.

A variety of assessment techniques and grading systems have been explored to take the emphasis off grade competition and foster a cooperative learning model. For example, students have been given qualifying exams in areas covered by the course that they needed to pass at an 80 percent or better level to be eligible for a grade of B. Alternate forms of the exams could be taken until a passing grade was achieved. Special tutoring was provided if requested. All students were expected to meet these criteria. Higher grades could be earned on a contract basis by undertaking individual projects, with projects of increasingly greater difficulty being required for B+, A-, and A grades. Also, collaborative projects with other students have been encouraged. A relatively small class size (26 students this year) facilitates this approach to teaching and learning.

Psychology 181 A&B: Research in Contemporary Problems in Mental Retardation. This course provides a formal academic framework for the research experience. In addition to the 12 hours or more per week that students spend in their research site, they meet weekly to discuss the research process. While students are expected to have had some sort of research methods and design course relevant to their major, the nature of such training varies. Different research paradigms are considered, qualitative and quantitative methods of data collection presented, and statistical conventions are reviewed. In the first quarter, students prepare a brief proposal for their research using a standard NIH format. At the end of the quarter, students defend the proposal before a panel of faculty. In the second quarter, they expand this proposal into a formal manuscript to be submitted at the end of the program for publication in the *Pacific State Archives*, a journal of the DDIP. They also present the research orally at a symposium before faculty, staff, invited guests, and parents. Grading is based primarily on performance in the research setting and not on the nature of the research results.

Psychology 193 A&B: Fieldwork Seminar. This seminar provides a structured academic opportunity for students to share and evaluate their field experiences. A syllabus with weekly topics guides the discussions, which are informed by students' field experiences, assigned readings, materials presented in other courses, guest speakers, and films shown in class. These are used as the basis for instruction on special teaching methods, behavior management, and institutional regulations. Students maintain a journal of their experiences, which is reviewed weekly by the instructor. Grading is pass/fail and depends on the journals, recommendation of the field site supervisors, and evidence of professional responsibility in and outside of class. The goal of the academic component of the fieldwork is to allow students to reflect on their experiences and thereby extend the experiential learning aspect of the program.

DDIP Partners

Faculty

Two groups of faculty are involved in DDIP. Core faculty members provide formal academic instruction and are involved in the overall integration of the program components. They have classroom contact with all of the program students on a regular basis. The research/field faculty members are responsible for the service and research involvement of the students and have regular contact with only the smaller number of students under their supervision.

The core faculty has consisted of six to eight members of the UCLA Psychology Department and Department of Psychiatry. The majority of participating faculty members have had backgrounds in psychology, special education, other social sciences, and neurobiology. This diversity of faculty backgrounds represents a valuable dimension, and an expansion of the core group to include, for example, representatives from law and the humanities would be desirable. However, the specialization of a faculty participant is less important than an appreciation of the multidisciplinary nature of the focal area and a willingness to integrate viewpoints. Within psychology, developmental, educational, physiological, and epidemiological perspectives have been helpful in providing a well-rounded outlook on the subject. Input from anthropology, law, medicine, and sociology have also helped shape DDIP's agenda. The program is not static and continues to solicit new viewpoints and to integrate new approaches into its academic perspective. Possibly the most difficult aspect of maintaining a diverse core faculty has been the reluctance of departments to release faculty to participate in such a multidisciplinary, team-taught program.

The research and fieldwork faculty consists of care providers, teachers, and researchers willing to provide one-on-one supervision during the research and service components of DDIP. These professionals provide guidance on how the students' formal learning can be put to use. They, in turn, are assisted by DDIP students in their work. However, not all student placements have proven satisfactory, and a program of regular site evaluation has been necessary, especially when a placement is new to DDIP. This is a continuing task of the program staff, particularly the program coordinator, and it is important that their contributions be recognized in appropriate ways. Letters of thanks or commendation for personnel files or advancement packets are important. For the faculty members, formal student or peer teaching evaluations are available on request.

Community Partners

Strong community partnerships have long been a fundamental conceptual as well as operational component of DDIP. The Lanterman Developmental Center has been a UCLA partner since the inception of the program. Here, DDIP students assist in teaching individuals with profound retardation or higher-functioning clients, supervise in sheltered workshops, assist with recreational or music therapy, and perform other meaningful tasks under the supervision of the Lanterman staff. In addition, DDIP receives a small annual grant from Lanterman to provide transportation for the students to and from the Center. Other field sites, including local public and private schools, also give students a chance to gain hands-on experience working with people with developmental disabilities. Sheltered workshops, community care facilities, and programs such as the Special Olympics offer other opportunities where students can interact directly with individuals with developmental disabilities.

Development of appropriate placement sites and matching students with these sites have been important ongoing activities of the DDIP staff. Coordinating dispersed field sites raises transportation and administrative issues. Because a variety of agencies are involved, different customs and regulations must be accommodated. Orientation and site-specific training must be arranged. DDIP operates on a partnership model with both fieldwork and research sites, and the staff regularly visit sites to observe and discuss student involvement directly with the supervisors. Optimal field sites involve students as constructive contributors and not merely outside observers; conversely, students are expected to learn to fit into the ongoing social and institutional structure of their service sites. Accommodations must occasionally be made by students or the program to effectively meet the need of a placement site.

Students

One of the most significant aspects of DDIP — creation of a student community — has undergone several changes during the past 20 years. Originally, students lived together at or near Lanterman Developmental Center, about 60 miles from the UCLA campus. Along with the program coordinators, they operated a cooperative that provided much of the structure of the DDIP community. Although a sense of community has been more difficult to maintain in DDIP's present format, a variety of strategies have been explored to sustain this important element of the program. These strategies have included regular social events, camping trips, discussion groups, and a series of preprogram orientation sessions attended by all students. A room dedicated to the DDIP program where students could study, have informal discussions, obtain relevant reading materials, and hang out would be helpful, particularly on a large commuter campus such as UCLA.

Each year, up to 30 students are selected to participate in DDIP. They are recruited in the spring quarter of the preceding year through a mass mailing campaign and oral presentations to students in Psychology and other related departments. Interested students are given information about prerequisites and the structure of the program and are invited to attend an information meeting designed to answer their questions. The program's principal selling points are the opportunity it affords students to apply their education while serving a dependent population in actual work settings, and its ability to provide small classes with a high level of faculty contact. Usually, a panel of two program staff reviews applications and interviews prospective participants. Students are selected on the basis of how much they will benefit from and contribute to the program. They must show a willingness to enter into a cooperative learning paradigm and a commitment to serving the community. However, their academic record must also be such that it seems likely they will be able to meet the heavy demands of the program. The typical DDIP time line is presented in the figure on the next page.

Staff

In addition to the faculty, DDIP enjoys the benefit of a strong support staff, called "coordinators." There exists a strong, direct interaction between coordinators and students, with staff acting as student advocates rather

Typical DDIP Time Line

SPRING	Recruitment and interviews

▼
▼

SUMMER	Formal acceptance letters

▼
▼

FALL	Placements and orientation; social activities

▼
▼

WINTER	Courses and fieldwork; proposal defense

▼
▼

SPRING	Courses and fieldwork; Research Symposium

▼
▼

SUMMER	Edit and publish journal

than as agents of the faculty. For the most part, DDIP coordinators have been recruited from the ranks of former students, an arrangement that has helped pass on the subculture and traditions of the program. Staff coordinators take on the primary responsibility for recruiting potential students, coordinating applications, interviewing candidates, contacting those accepted into the program, and reiterating what will be expected of them. They work closely with students to arrange the students' schedules and to facilitate their involvement. The coordinators also recruit potential research and fieldwork sites, make arrangements for classrooms, order textbooks, and negotiate formal agreements with service sites. Matching student preferences with available sites is largely a coordinator function, with faculty intervening only if reasonably satisfactory matching cannot be achieved. Although much of the course-related staff function is handled by teaching assistants, the coordinators meet regularly with those teaching assistants to arrange assignments so that everything does not come due at once. Budget issues continue to put pressure on the availability of coordinators, but a strong staff function is considered essential. Effective staff coordination is what differentiates DDIP from other internship and service-learning programs in the university.

Program Assessment

DDIP provides a unique opportunity for the assessment of a service-learning program because it has been in existence for more than 20 years. However, developing strategies that would realistically measure the program's success from the point of view of all concerned presents some difficult challenges. For example, in measuring outcomes for the students, one must ask not only whether the stated goals were accomplished but also whether this was done with greater success than might have been achieved with a traditional curriculum. In other words, how useful was the addition of the service component in producing various academic, social, and personal outcomes? In the 1993 and 1994 course evaluations for Psychology 193 (Fieldwork Seminar), some measures that are traditionally cited as outcomes of experiential or service-learning — acquiring critical-thinking skills, applying theory to practice — ranked somewhat lower than expected. Instead, students ranked "gaining knowledge of the facts in the field" as the most useful outcome of their service experience.

Another difficult challenge in program assessment has been that standard course evaluations do not address the fundamental question of how the overall program format affected commitment to service. Almost all students leave with a strong determination to serve populations with disabilities, but most entered with that resolution. The degree to which their commitment was actually enhanced or diminished is the point of interest. Nearly half (45%) of the students responding to a follow-up study in 1979 reported a substantial or profound effect on their attitude toward community involvement. Other areas of strong impact involved the students' attitude toward the university, their attitude toward academic studies, and their relationships with faculty. Although the decision to attend graduate school was not strongly influenced, the choice of career was affected more strongly than had been anticipated, with between a third and a half reporting a significant effect. However, the greatest changes reported took place within the students themselves. Self-confidence, a sense of achievement, and personal insight were reported to have been strengthened.

We remain uncertain as to the best timing for such evaluations. Long-term follow-ups are the best measures of program success, but are confounded by a relatively poor response rate and the difficulty of maintaining contact with the majority of students (Ropers 1985).

Replicability

Currently, DDIP is as much a product of its own evolution as it is a program conceived from theoretical or paradigmatic principles. There has been concern about how well it would generalize to other disciplinary focuses or other institutions. Using DDIP as the model, the UCLA Field Studies Development Office has helped initiate a number of experiential and service-oriented programs. Where there has been strong faculty interest and departmental dedication, the model has succeeded.

Although the setting of a large research university such as UCLA is beneficial in implementing the research component and bringing together the various elements of the program, it is not absolutely necessary to the replication of the model. DDIP, or several components of it, should be replicable just as well at a small college. In fact, the environment of a small liberal arts college may be more conducive to developing a student community and a strong partnership with local agencies.

The partnership with the Lanterman Developmental Center has been invaluable for DDIP, but replication of the model does not actually require a large residential facility for students to have meaningful field experiences. The special-education programs at local schools and non-school-based facilities for people with developmental disabilities offer ample opportunities for students to participate in similar service-learning activities. Since the trend in the care of individuals with developmental disabilities is toward deinstitutionalization and in favor of integration into the community, the human resources that will be needed to implement this trend suggest that opportunities for the kind of program described here can only increase.

Notes

1. The following student papers were published in 1994 in *Pacific States Archives*, vol. 19: Chua and Joo, pp. 1-7; and Orlino, pp. 80-86.

The following were published in 1995 in *Pacific States Archives*, vol. 20: Babb and Maya, pp. 11-22; Bakcht et al., pp. 23-30; Baleva, pp. 31-41; and Senanayake, pp. 85-96.

2. These two student papers have been published in refereed journals: G.C. Galbraith and B.Q. Doan, "Brainstem Frequency-Following and Behavioral Responses During Selective Attention to Pure Tone and Missing Fundamental Stimuli," *International Journal of Psychophysiology* 19 (1995): 203-214. C.E. Olmstead, J.A. Lazarett, E.N. Orlino, A.L. Fluharty, K.F. Faull, W.J. Peacock, M.C. Wehby-Grant, R.J. Gayek, and R.S. Fisher, "Neuroamine Related Compounds in the CSF of Hydrocephalic Rabbits," *Neuroreport* 6 (1995): 1769-1772.

References

Bringle, R.G., and J.A. Hatcher. (1996). "Implementing Service Learning in Higher Education." *Journal of Higher Education* 67: 221-239.

Giles, D.E., Jr., and J.B. Freed. (1990). "The Service-Learning Dimensions of Field Study: Cornell's Human Ecology Field Study Program." In *Combining Service and Learning: A Resource Book for Community and Public Service. Vol. II*, edited by J.C. Kendall and Associates, pp. 349-360. Raleigh, NC: National Society for Experiential Education.

Ropers, R.H. (1985). "An Empirical Evaluation of the DDIP's Impact on Former Students." *Pacific States Archives* 10: 5-12

Applying Service-Learning to the Problem of Prejudice:
A Psychology and Theater Course

by Stevenson W. Carlebach and Jefferson A. Singer

The service-learning course discussed here grew out of a three-day racial awareness workshop held for faculty and staff at Connecticut College. Inspired by a hard look at the perniciousness of racism in our culture, each of us (a theater professor and psychology professor, respectively) looked for a way to engage our students in a similar exploration and struggle with the problems of racism and prejudice. Drawing upon the rich traditions of both our disciplines in examining social problems, we conceived of a course that would present both psychological theory/research and theater/film productions, techniques, and criticism relevant to issues of racial/ethnic identity and prejudice.

As we began developing the course, we became enthusiastic about the possibility of engaging our students in more experiential activities such as role playing, imagery, and theater games in order to help them learn about problems of stereotyping, status inequities, and prejudice. Finally, we realized that if students were to profit from these techniques, it would be critical for them to understand them deeply enough so that they could, in turn, coach others through a learning process similar to the one in which they had engaged. Ultimately, a service-learning component using experiential theater/psychology techniques became the central focus of the course.

The structure of the course drew on three learning modes that theater and psychology have in common — an *empirical* exploration of the motivations, attributions, and actions of humans in social interactions; an *empathic* understanding of an "other" through identification with someone different from oneself (through either therapist-client or actor-character relationships); and the use of *experiential* techniques (role playing, imagery, and movement exercises). To deepen students' theoretical and analytic understanding of prejudice, they read theoretical and empirical papers from psychology as well as both dramatic theory and plays[1] that highlighted issues of racial/ethnic identity and prejudice. Through analysis of films and television programs, they were also asked to become more critical viewers of contemporary entertainment in order to detect ways in which the media may perpetuate stereotypes and biases. In the interest of cultivating empathy, they were asked to portray characters from the plays they read, as well as to discuss their conflicts and struggles. As a way of understanding how strongly we are all affected by prevailing social views, historical racism in both fields was examined.[2] Drawing on these historical examples, we attempted to identify which of the scientific and aesthetic principles we hold dear today will eventually seem as wrong as the past practices of institutional racism in psychology and theater do to us now. Finally, in the interest of deepening empathy and also demonstrating the effectiveness of experiential activities, students engaged in a variety of these activities, including trust exercises, improvisation, adoption of stereotypic roles, and games, that depicted power relations/status among ethnic groups and in interpersonal relations.

Because these exercises were crucial to the course, it might be useful to give a brief example. Early in the semester, we had the students read excerpts from the books *Games for Actors and Non-Actors* (Routledge, 1992) and *The Rainbow of Desire: The Boal Method of Theater and Therapy* (Routledge, 1995), by the Brazilian director Augusto Boal. In these books, Boal presents a vision of theater as an active tool in personal understanding and in social change. He describes a series of techniques that challenge actors and audience to explore through improvisation social problems such as oppression and stigmatization. In our seminar, we conducted a workshop using Boal's techniques. The students broke into small groups and shaped one another's bodies, without words, into tableaus of oppression. After selecting, with consensus, a single tableau from each group, the students then came back together as a class to view one another's tableaus and to select, again with consensus, a single image of oppression that most deeply affected them as a group. The power of the silent sculpted images and the honest discussion of students' various interpretations and reasons for selecting images made a deep impact on the entire seminar. It also quickly established the effectiveness of using theater and experiential techniques for teaching and encouraging discussion about topics such as oppression and prejudice. These techniques allowed for a discussion of oppression without the struggle for victim status/hierarchy that often clouds a discussion of prejudice. Since all participants were able to portray incidents of oppression from their own lives, such an approach challenged the notion held by both majority and minority students that students from the majority culture (e.g., white and male) would be completely free of experiences of prejudice in their lives.

Parallel to this classroom activity were the students' service-learning group projects. The 15 students in the seminar were divided into four groups, each with the responsibility of applying the techniques learned in class to a group of individuals outside the class. The students met in groups regularly over the course of the semester, usually on their own and occasionally in consultation with us, to plan their workshops. They also had several meetings with representatives from the settings in which they would conduct their workshops.

The group assignment was that each group use the three tools of the course — empirical, empathic, and experiential techniques integrating theater and psychology — in the service of teaching about racial/ethnic prejudice. The service-learning goal from the students' perspective was to apply what they had studied and experienced in the course. Our goal for the community members who participated in the workshops was not only to provide them with information and ideas but also to transfer to them the techniques we were using so that they could continue the self-exploration process begun in the workshops.

The final, critical component of the students' service-learning experience was maintaining a journal electronically. Each student was assigned a weekly journal partner and served either as commentator or respondent. The commentator would place a journal entry into a shared computer file, and the partner would write a response to the comment into the same shared file. If they desired, they could also put their entries into a common file to be read by the rest of the class. As the professors, we had access to all comments and responses. Students would reverse roles the following week and then take on new partners the week after that. In the beginning, students wrote about readings or class exercises. As their service-learning projects took shape, we asked them to shift to writing about their experiences of working in their groups and working in the community. Their journal entries offered a vital opportunity for additional reflection about some of the challenging and emotionally upsetting readings, viewings, and class exercises they encountered. Later in the semester, they were able to use the journal entries to explore their group process issues in putting together their community projects, as well as to reflect on the outcomes of their service-learning efforts.

The Service-Learning Projects

Having exposed the students in the first stages of the course to a variety of ways of addressing issues of racial/ethnic identity and prejudice, we then worked with them in groups to apply these techniques outside the class. What follows is a summary of the activities and outcomes for each of the four groups.

Group 1 – Oppression Workshop at a Residential Alcohol/Drug Rehab Facility
One of the authors of this chapter (JAS) was serving as the staff psychologist at a drug and alcohol agency. It had come to his attention that at one of this agency's residential facilities, there had been increasing tension among white, African-American, and Hispanic residents. After speaking with the director of the facility and gaining his approval, we raised the possibili-

ty with the class that one of the group projects could be focused on a workshop to help ease the tensions at the facility. Two white male students and one Hispanic female student showed interest in this project and formed a group to create a workshop. The students visited the all-male facility and made contacts with the head counselor and with one of the residents who had expressed a willingness to help with the workshop. After these initial discussions, the students planned and scheduled an evening meeting with a representative group of the men.

For a first effort in bringing an innovative workshop to the facility, the students decided a small group of 12 men would be best. They asked the head counselor to select four men from each of the three ethnic groups. After a number of meetings in the course of the semester with us, the students chose to use the Boal oppression exercise that we had introduced in class early in the semester. They felt that by having the men of the different racial/ethnic backgrounds work together on a common theme, they could subtly address issues of cooperation and shared experience. The students believed that this experiential evidence of working together and mutual concern might make even more of an impact than a didactic workshop about the need for racial/ethnic harmony.

Though the students had originally (and quite correctly) planned to have multiple meetings with this group to deepen their sense of shared purpose, they ended up only able to hold a single evening's workshop. It was clear that they had underestimated the logistical obstacles to any community project and also had fallen into a bit of the "last-minute" college student syndrome. Still, we had an opportunity to observe the workshop conducted with the men, and it was an extraordinary evening. Before the workshop took place, we had all experienced trepidation about the willingness of the men to engage in theater exercises and strike silent poses with the theme of oppression. After all, many of these men had lived quite hardened lives, serving time in prison, surviving on the streets, and in some cases, belonging to violent gangs.

As it turned out, a decision to involve one of the residents in planning the workshop turned out to be a crucial factor. This man, who had served nearly half of his adult life in prison, embraced the activity and encouraged the men to give it a try. One by one, they began to speak up and introduce themselves to the students and the rest of the group. The students, a little nervous at first, began to relax and explained clearly the goal of the evening. They were asking the men's help in letting them apply some techniques they had learned in class to another group of people. By framing the workshop in this fashion, the students made it clear that they were there not to teach or to "experiment," but rather to learn from the men and enlist their help as a resource. In turn, they might be able to offer the men an unusual and meaningful way to look at a social problem (oppression).

With that introduction, the students launched into an explanation and demonstration of the Boal exercises. As the men broke up into their small groups, the transition gave a discreet opportunity for those who were uncomfortable with the workshop to slip out. Only two of the 12 men left and the remaining 10 engaged in a dramatic and inspiring way with the activity of creating the silent tableaus. After each small group had displayed its images of oppression to the larger group of 10, the full group selected an image of a mother holding both a baby and a crack pipe, a father separated with back turned to the family, and what appeared to be another child huddled in a third corner of the space. This image provoked a powerful discussion of the oppression of both poverty and addiction in the lives of many of the men in the room. Each of the 10 men spoke up and listened attentively, and with appreciation, to the opinions of the other men. The evening ended with one of the residents reciting a poem he had written in prison, and the two male students, who were members of a campus singing group, singing an a capella song in appreciation for the time the men had spent.

It was quite clear that the workshop was merely a beginning, and the men strongly urged the students to continue these kinds of activities. Plans were made to follow up with future workshops and also to train the residents in using the theater techniques themselves in their own peer groups.

Group 2 – Gender Stereotyping Workshop at a Middle School

This group consisted of three white females and one white male. It was spearheaded by one of the female students, who had a strong interest in mass media and its influence on our perceptions of gender roles and racial/ethnic stereotypes. In particular, she believed that children need to be educated early on and prepared for the traditional gender role stereotypes they will confront in the media. The group decided they would hold two hour-long workshops for children in the middle school years (eight to 10 years of age), since these children are fully immersed in cartoon, toy, and video culture. In one session of the workshop, they would focus on stereotypes embodied in commercials and toys. In the other session, they planned to show how images in popular magazines depict men and women in gender-typed roles. By calling and writing to researchers and educators in the field of mass media, they were able to obtain and examine some training manuals and materials for teaching viewer literacy to children.

After meeting with the principal of a local public school and gaining his approval, they made contact with a teacher willing to allow them two class periods to present their workshop. In the meantime, they were able to create a video clip of Saturday morning toy commercials that depicted girls in frilly dresses, filmed in a pink hue, playing with fashion dolls, followed by a clip of jean-clad boys leading their military action figures into mud-splattered battle. They also collected a sample of toys to display to the children. For the other workshop, they found magazines that pictured women at work in the kitchen and men at computers in the office. The children were to use the magazines to hunt for these images and cut them out.

Although we did not attend these workshops, the students reported that they experienced overall success, in particular with the workshop focused on television. The children seemed to grasp what a stereotype was and were able to generate many examples from their lives that contradicted the idea that girls only like dolls or that Mommies only stay at home to cook and clean. Though the children were able to see these ideas repeated again in the magazines, the adult magazines used by the students held less interest for them and sustained their attention for a shorter period of time than the discussion of television and toys. In sum, the group gained firsthand experience on how to conduct this kind of educational workshop on addressing issues of prejudice and learned much more about how to convey information to children in a developmentally appropriate manner. In the course of preparing their materials for the workshop, the group members also were able to apply to real-world examples their theoretical readings about gender stereotypes and status inequities between males and females.

Group 3 – Prejudice Awareness Exercises at a Camp for Juvenile Offenders

This group consisted of one African-American male, one Hispanic female, one African-American female, and one white female. The African-American male member was already serving as a volunteer for a residential camp that functions as an alternative to incarceration for juvenile offenders. The camp serves mostly African-American and Hispanic youth, with a smaller number of white campers. The student working there felt that his group could help the residents express their feelings toward each other more openly and productively by using some of the theater exercises taught in our seminar. The group, after meeting with the camp directors and receiving approval, met weekly with 10 to 15 residents for a total of five weeks. Drawing on the theater and psychology exercises from class, the students had the residents participate in trust exercises, movement games, a status workshop, and a variety of role plays.

Since the residents already had a strong rapport with the student volunteer, they quickly formed a warm and enthusiastic connection with the rest of the group. The weekly meetings were seen as a welcome break from the routine of the camp and as a chance to experience fellow residents in a more cooperative and positive light. As a tribute to the strong bond developed between the students and the residents, two of the residents (with the permission of the camp director) visited the course during the group's presentation to the rest of the class. The visitors discussed what they had gained from the group's workshops and demonstrated with group members some of the activities in which they had engaged.

Group 4 – Self-Esteem Workshop for Children in a Shelter for Battered Women

This project was an example of how service-learning projects some-times evolve to meet the needs of the community setting. The group (three white females and one Hispanic female) had initially hoped to conduct a workshop that would teach issues of prejudice and racism to children who were living with their mothers in a safe-refuge shelter. Most of the children at the shelter are children of color, and one of the student group members while working as a volunteer there had noticed examples of prejudice the children encountered in the greater community. Yet when the group approached the shelter director, she indicated that the children were strug-gling with enough sensitive material at the moment and might benefit more from a workshop with a less painful and more uplifting theme.

After discussion and brainstorming, the students decided to start with the fact that these children often felt disregarded, unworthy, and inferior due to their family problems and general level of poverty. These feelings had been magnified when they were forced to move to the shelter. The students felt a useful response to this general sense of inadequacy might be to run a weekly workshop with the goal of highlighting self-esteem and identifying more ways for the children to feel positive about themselves.

Each student took responsibility for a week's workshop and the group presented four workshops in all. The first focused on a simple esteem-build-ing game in which each child wrote down something he/she liked about each of the other children in the workshop. Once all these positives were written down, the children had to guess to which person they belonged. For a number of the children, it was extremely gratifying to hear a long list of what people liked about them recited out loud. The second week involved the students in a game of colored dots passed around the room. Depending on the color dot received, the child had to say something good about him/herself, something he/she loved to eat, and something he/she loved to do. In the third week, the children worked on drawing pictures that helped to illustrate a story they made up with that week's student facilitator. This exercise encouraged both their artistic skills and their sense of group unity. In the final week, the student leader told them a parable of a land of "warm and fuzzies" in which people gave love easily and unconditionally (she had learned this story from her own grade school teacher). Yet a few people began to hoard their warm and fuzzies and give them out selectively. This led to feuding and chaos in the land until people learned their lesson again — that "love should be given freely and not depend on what you can give me in return or what advantage you can gain." As the student told the story, she made a pompom-shaped creature of interwoven yarn ends. Each child then participated in making one and was able to keep it as a reminder that everyone can use a warm and fuzzy.

These workshops were a great success with the children, and the groups were overwhelmed by how quickly the children attached themselves to the students and how sad they were to see the workshops end. The shelter expressed an interest in having students return to run similar kinds of workshops in the future.

Conclusions

Before addressing some of the benefits involved in using service-learning to teach about issues of racial/ethnic identity and prejudice, we need to express a note of caution. We are aware that the kinds of projects our students conducted in the community were too brief in duration to be likely to have significant, lasting effects upon the participants. It can be potentially harmful to perform a kind of hit-and-run social service that raises the hopes of community participants but then offers no follow-up. To minimize this risk, we extended to each staff in each setting an offer to follow up our workshops with future activities if they so desired. We also made a point of explaining to participants that by allowing the student groups to practice the techniques the students had learned, they were helping us out more than we could hope to help them. From the follow-up conversations we had with setting representatives, we received uniformly positive feedback and no indications that the workshops had produced unintended negative effects. In some cases, the representatives told us that they hoped to integrate some of the students' exercises into future programming. Still, it is our recommendation that such service-learning experiences begin earlier in the semester to allow a maximum amount of involvement with the community participants. Ideally, a two-semester or year-long course would be even more appropriate to the kind of interventions our students attempted.

Despite the short-term nature of their involvement, students expressed great enthusiasm about their service-learning experiences and saw them as a platform on which to build more extensive efforts in antiprejudice and teaching-tolerance activities. In particular, the students found the service-learning component of the course personally empowering. By applying the exercises they had learned in class, they moved from passive recipients to active agents engaged in teaching and conversing with others outside the class about issues of racism, prejudice, and racial/ethnic identity. Rather than feeling overwhelmed by problems of bias, racial/ethnic conflict, and economic injustice, they participated in a process to encourage communication and change with regard to these problems. Even more, because the techniques they applied from their seminar are easily learned by others, the students also felt that they were offering tools that community members could use in future workshops conducted on their own.

In their course evaluations, the students made the point that the service-learning experience turned the research articles and theoretical arguments about prejudice and stereotyping into something more tangible and accessible in their lives. In addition, our introduction of electronic journaling offered students a shared forum for connecting their service-learning experiences to the readings and classroom discussions. In a pleasant confirmation of our hopes, the service-learning experiences did not diminish the value of readings and lectures, but instead made the students see the practicality of good theory, as Kurt Lewin emphasized. This is an important point to stress, because often individuals unfamiliar with service-learning fear that this approach is anti-intellectual or opposed to reading and writing. On the contrary, we found many students explicitly commented on how they went back to their readings after the service-learning experience in order to gain greater perspective and understanding of what they had witnessed in their workshops.

There are also some new challenges that this form of teaching introduces that are worth mentioning. As professors quite comfortable with traditional reading, lecture, and discussion classes, we found the additional logistics of introducing a service-learning component more complicated than we had anticipated. The students required more frequent meetings; we also needed on occasion to visit the settings and touch base with the setting representatives. Evaluation of the students' efforts was also more complex, incorporating both oral and written reports as well as individual students' self-evaluations of their contributions to the group. On the basis of these self-evaluations, we also realized that our students need much more education in group work and communication. We recommend strongly that seminar time early in the semester be devoted to teaching how to enhance group process.

In conclusion, this course offered our students an innovative and energizing opportunity to explore and then take action on a central concern in their lives and in general society. Consistent with the liberal arts tradition, they studied texts and discussed differing points of view in class and through writing assignments. Moving beyond this approach, they also had an opportunity to test ideas and skills they had acquired through community service experiences. Based on the students' own remarks to us, we would conclude that the course left them with a greater sense of possibility and hope about what they personally can do to improve tolerance in our society. Similarly, they described the greater self-understanding they had achieved about attitudes of bias and racism within themselves.

Although there is obviously a self-selection process that influences what kind of students would take this type of seminar in the first place, it is still worth noting that many of the seminar participants have continued involvement in service activities related to problems of racial inequality and poverty. Through contacts made in the seminar, two students went on to work as interns for Educators for Social Responsibility in New York City, performing similar antibias workshops for that organization. Other students have worked in programs to help high school students from inner-city environments prepare for college, while still another has gone on to community organizing activities in Latin America.

Although at first glance the combination of using psychology and theater to teach about prejudice may seem a little unorthodox, we hope we have demonstrated that the overlapping aspects of interpersonal exploration, empathy, and experiential techniques across the two disciplines offer some highly relevant and practical applications to real-world problems of bias and intolerance. While others engage in necessary analyses at more structural and political levels, this type of course offers the possibility of internal and interpersonal scrutiny and change. In the long run, engagement of both our political and private consciousness is necessary to close the many schisms that prejudice creates in our society.

Notes

1. Among the psychology articles they read were these: P.G. Devine, M.J. Monteith, J.R. Zuwerink, and A.J. Elliot, "Prejudice With and Without Compunction," *Journal of Personality and Social Psychology* 60 (1991): 817-830; S.T. Fiske, "Controlling Other People," *American Psychologist* 48 (1993): 621-628; and K. Lewin, "Self-Hatred Among Jews," *Contemporary Jewish Record* 4 (1941): 219-232.

Among the plays were *A Raisin in the Sun; Six Degrees of Separation; Europa, Europa;* and *The Dutchman.*

2. For example, we look at a discussion of the musical *Showboat* and what ambivalences the theater world experienced about its revival (see R. Breen, "Show Boat: The Revival, the Racism," *The Drama Review* 39 [Summer 1995]: 86-105). In psychology, we explored the different historical trends in studying prejudice that have grown out of ideological movements in the discipline (see J. Duckitt, "Psychology and Prejudice: A Historical Analysis and Integrative Framework," *American Psychologist* 47 [1992]: 1182-1193).

Annotated Bibliography of Service-Learning and Psychology

Altman, I. (1996). "Higher Education and Psychology in the Millennium." *American Psychologist* 51: 371-378.
    In this APA award address, Altman reflects on the past and present state of higher education and proposes a model for the future. He contends that socially responsive knowledge should be an integral part of the undergraduate curriculum, along with foundational knowledge and professional knowledge. Service-learning is presented as an effective pedagogy for integrating socially responsive knowledge into psychology and other disciplines.

Batchelder, T.H., and S. Root. (1994). "Effects of an Undergraduate Program to Integrate Academic Learning and Service: Cognitive, Prosocial Cognitive, and Identity Outcomes." *Journal of Adolescence* 17: 341-355.
    This research study compared service-learning students with students in a traditional class by statistically controlling for pre-test differences. The study found significant gains for the service-learning students on complex cognitive variables, including greater resolve to act in the face of acknowledged uncertainty and greater awareness of the multiple dimensions and variability involved in dealing with social problems. There was also some evidence that these cognitive changes generalized to situations not directly related to the content of the course.

Bringle, R.G., and J.F. Kremer. (1993). "An Evaluation of an Intergenerational Service-Learning Project for Undergraduates." *Educational Gerontology* 19: 407-416.
    Using analysis of covariance to control for preexisting differences, this study compared service-learners with students in a traditional class. It found that students involved in intergenerational visits with Senior Companions to homebound elderly persons and didactic instruction had more positive attitudes not only toward elderly persons in general but also toward their own aging. A telephone interview found that Senior Companions and clients had positive impressions of the college students' involvement. Programmatic recommendations are provided.

Enns, C.Z. (1993). "Integrating Separate and Connected Knowing: The Experiential Learning Model." *Teaching of Psychology* 20: 7-13.

Enns shows how Kolb's experiential learning model can provide a useful framework for integrating separate and connected knowing. She presents concrete examples demonstrating how the model facilitates a multifaceted inclusive approach to teaching psychology.

Hettich, P. (1990). "Journal Writing: Old Fare or Nouvelle Cuisine?" *Teaching of Psychology* 17: 36-39.

Journals are the most frequent method of reflection in service-learning classes. This article examines some of the purposes and procedures of using journals. Surveys of students found that they preferred journals to term papers because they stimulated critical thinking, provided feedback on learning, and were an aid to the self-directed expression of learning.

McCall, R. (1996). "The Concept and Practice of Education, Research, and Public Service in University Psychology Departments." *American Psychologist* 51: 379-388.

This article provides a critical examination of the narrow nature of academic psychology, dominated by valuing grant-supported laboratory basic research. In doing so, it explores the role that service can and should play in higher education and how service can benefit research and teaching.

McCluskey-Fawcett, K., and P. Green. (1992). "Using Community Service to Teach Developmental Psychology." *Teaching of Psychology* 19: 150-152.

The authors describe an approach for integrating community service into two large sections of developmental psychology. They list procedures for incorporating agencies, provide detailed explanations of student assignments, and explain the results of student course evaluations.

Miller, J. (1993). "Psychology in the Community." In *Praxis I: A Faculty Casebook on Community Service Learning*, edited by J. Howard, pp. 123-134. Ann Arbor, MI: OCSL Press.

Miller describes Project Outreach/Psychology 211, a large and comprehensive service-learning course at the University of Michigan that began in 1966. He outlines the evolution of the course, explains current procedures, and presents lessons learned.

———. (1994). "Linking Traditional and Service Learning Courses: Outcome Evaluations Utilizing Two Pedagogically Distinct Models." *Michigan Journal of Community Service Learning* 1: 29-36.

Miller reports results of a study comparing students in a psychology course with students who participated in the course as well as in optional community service placements linked to the course. Students who participated in community service reported improved ability to apply concepts outside of the classroom, but they did not differ from nonparticipating students in personal development, general mastery of course concepts, or final course grades.

Raupp, C.D., and D.C. Cohen. (1992). "'A Thousand Points of Light' Illuminate the Psychology Curriculum: Volunteering as a Learning Experience." *Teaching of Psychology* 19: 25-30.

Raupp and Cohen explain two models of community service developed in their psychology department: elementary school tutoring within a child psychology course and credit for individual placements in a variety of settings. They suggest ways to deal with organizational and academic issues.

Scrogin, F., and H.C. Rickard. (1987). "A Volunteer Program for Abnormal Psychology Students: Eighteen Years and Still Going Strong." *Teaching of Psychology* 14: 95-97.

Abnormal is one of the most popular courses in the psychology curriculum. In this course, students volunteer a minimum of 20 hours during a semester at in-patient mental health facilities, doing non-clinical tasks (e.g., transporting patients, socializing, recreational activities). A brief discussion is provided of alternative assignments that are made available, the importance of assistance with volunteer placements, reflection, and positive (and negative) outcomes that students experience.

Yates, M., and J. Youniss. (1996). "A Developmental Perspective on Community Service in Adolescence." *Social Development* 5: 85-111.

This article reviews 44 studies published between 1952 and 1994 that examined the benefits of community service on dimensions such as changes in sense of agency, social relatedness, and moral-political awareness.

Electronic Resources for Service-Learning

American Association for Higher Education

AAHE is a national organization of educators, administrators, students, policymakers, and leaders from profit and nonprofit organizations alike. The AAHE website offers articles and publications on research and public policy regarding service-learning and its role in higher education. It also links to other AAHE and service-learning resources.

www.aahe.org

American Association of Community Colleges

AACC is the primary advocacy organization for the nation's 1,100 two-year degree-granting institutions. Its service website contains references, workshop information, and information on AACC service projects.

www.aacc.nche.edu/spcproj/service/service.htm

Campus Compact National Center for Community Colleges

Located within the Maricopa County Community College system at Mesa Community College, CCNCCC is the national resource office for community colleges interested in community service and service-learning.

www.mc.maricopa.edu/academic/compact/

Corporation for National Service

The CNS is responsible for promoting participation in community service. Electronic resources include links to the Learn & Serve America homepage and the CNS Serve and Learn Monthly Updates. Links to AmeriCorps, Senior Corps, and other service-related organizations are also available. Perhaps, most important, it links to an extensive list of service-oriented educational resources.

www.cns.gov/

International Partnership for Service-Learning

A nonprofit organization, the International Partnership for Service-Learning is dedicated to the organization, implementation, and development of service-learning programs at the national and international levels. Articles and publications regarding student opportunities and program development are available.

www.studyabroad.com/psl/pslhome.html

National Service-Learning (K-12) Clearinghouse

The Clearinghouse is a partner in the National Service-Learning Coopera-tive. As a central repository of information about service-learning pro-grams, organizations, people, calendar events, and literature/multimedia materials, NSLC provides access to service-learning information through information specialists at a toll-free telephone number (800/808-SERVe) and via the Internet.

www.nicsl.coled.umn.edu/

University of Colorado, Service-Learning Resource Collection

This homepage at the University of Colorado contains a warehouse of information about service-learning programs at colleges and universities around the United States. Among the resources in the collection are arti-cles, bibliographies, syllabi, and program guidelines, as well as links to other service-learning sites. Information regarding current research and discussion of service-learning concepts and philosophy is also available.

csf.colorado.edu/sl/

Contributors to This Volume

Volume Editors

Robert G. Bringle (Ph.D., University of Massachusetts, Amherst) is professor of psychology and director of the Center for Public Service and Leadership at Indiana University Purdue University Indianapolis. His research interests include jealousy in close relationships, evaluation of educational programs, and motives of faculty and students in service-learning.

Donna Killian Duffy (Ph.D., Washington University) is professor of psychology and co-coordinator of the Activating Learning in the Classroom program at Middlesex Community College in Bedford and Lowell, Massachusetts. She has been involved in programs for students with learning disabilities from preschool to college and is interested in ways to integrate affective and cognitive development in academic settings.

Other Contributors

Jay W. Brandenberger (Ph.D., University of Pittsburgh) is a faculty member of the Center for Social Concerns and the Department of Psychology at the University of Notre Dame. His research examines social cognition, moral development, and pedagogical issues.

Stevenson W. Carlebach (M.F.A., Boston University) is an associate professor of theater at Connecticut College and the codirector of the Center for Community Challenges, an interdisciplinary center dedicated to building community service into the academic mission of the college. In addition to teaching acting and directing, Carlebach teaches negotiation and conflict resolution.

E. Gil Clary (Ph.D., University of Georgia) is a professor of psychology at the College of St. Catherine. In addition to his research on volunteers' motivations for engaging in volunteer activities, he is exploring some of the questions and issues facing the larger nonprofit sector. Clary is also engaged in conceptual and empirical research on long-term helpers' orientations, models, or philosophies of helping and their impact on helping interactions and outcomes.

Maurice J. Elias (Ph.D., University of Connecticut) is a professor in the Department of Psychology at Rutgers University and codeveloper of the Improving Social Awareness-Social Problem-Solving Project. He is a member of the Leadership Team of the Collaborative for the Advancement of Social Emotional Learning, based on the EQ work of Daniel Goleman. His books include *Social Problem-Solving Interventions in Schools* and *Emotionally Intelligent Parenting: Raising Your Child to Be Self-Disciplined, Responsible, and Socially Skilled*.

Janet Eyler (Ph.D., Indiana University Bloomington), an associate professor of the practice of education at Vanderbilt University, is codirector (with Dwight E. Giles, Jr.) of the Comparing Models of Service-Learning research project, sponsored by the Fund for the Improvement of Postsecondary Education (FIPSE), and the Reflection in Service-Learning project, sponsored by the Corporation for National Service. She has published articles on service-learning theory and research and is currently writing with Giles a book on service-learning research and a practitioner's guide to planning and implementing service-learning programs, both to be published by Jossey-Bass.

Arvan L. Fluharty (Ph.D., University of California, Berkeley) is a professor-in-residence in the Department of Psychiatry & Biobehavioral Sciences at the University of California, Los Angeles. He is one of the founders of the Developmental Disabilities Immersion Program (DDIP), and currently teaches Psychology 181 A&B.

Gregg Gambone (Ph.D., Rutgers University) is a lecturer in the Department of Psychology at Rutgers University. He has been involved in the education of at-risk children and has supervised more than a hundred Rutgers undergraduate service-learning students in Head Start placements in New Jersey.

Dwight E. Giles, Jr. (Ph.D., Pennsylvania State University), a professor of the practice of human and organizational development and director of internships at Peabody College, Vanderbilt University, recently has codirected (with Janet Eyler) two national service-learning research projects. He is coauthor, with Tim Stanton and Nadinne Cruz, of *Service-Learning: A Movement's Pioneers Reflect on Its Origins, Practices, and Future* (Jossey-Bass, in press). He is currently writing with Janet Eyler a book on their service-learning research findings and a guide for developing service-learning programs, both to be published by Jossey-Bass.

Iva GreyWolf (Ph.D., Utah State University), previously at Concordia College in Minnesota, is currently working as a supervisor for counselors in rural Native Alaskan villages in southeast Alaska. She continues to be involved in cross-cultural mental health issues.

David B. Johnson (M.A., Bowling Green State University) is an associate professor in the Psychology Department at Miami-Dade Community College, where, in addition to Human Relations, he teaches courses in student life skills and business administration. He currently holds the college's Dr. Stanley Sutnick Endowed Teaching Chair and was awarded the 1996 Florida Campus Compact's Teaching for Service Award.

Parvin Kassaie (Ph.D., University of Southern California) is the director of field studies development in the Office of Instructional Development at the University of California, Los Angeles. She administers the Developmental Disabilities Immersion Program (DDIP) and is responsible for Psychology 193 A&B, the Fieldwork Seminar.

Martha A. Kitzrow (Ph.D., Oregon State University) is an associate professor of counseling psychology at the University of Idaho and a licensed psychologist. In addition to her clinical interests, she specializes in counselor education and training, the psychology of helping, and the psychology of peace and conflict.

Jeremy Leeds (Ph.D., Adelphi University) is the director of counseling and guidance at Horace Mann School in Riverdale, New York. Previously, as assistant professor at New York University, he was a faculty leader and participant in numerous service and service-learning initiatives. He developed NYU's first service-learning course, as well as the freshman honors seminar The University and the Community. He is a member of the Invisible College of Campus Compact.

Georgia Nigro (Ph.D., Cornell University) is an associate professor of psychology at Bates College. She teaches courses in developmental psychology, psychology of women and gender, and research methods, and in her research investigates children's suggestibility and memory for events.

Randall E. Osborne (Ph.D., University of Texas at Austin) is an associate professor of psychology at Indiana University East. His expertise and interests include studying the interconnections between teaching, service, and professional development made possible through service-learning.

James Penticuff is an undergraduate student at Indiana University East. He has served as an undergraduate research assistant and as a student service-learning coordinator.

Susan Root (Ph.D., Michigan State University) is an associate professor of education and chair of the Department of Education at Alma College. She has published studies on service-learning and has a particular interest in the inclusion of service-learning as part of the teacher-training curriculum.

Jefferson A. Singer (Ph.D., Yale University) is an associate professor of psychology at Connecticut College. He is the author of *Message in a Bottle: Stories of Men and Addiction* and *The Remembered Self,* as well as many articles and chapters in the field of personality. He also is a clinical psychologist with a practice in Waterford, Connecticut.

Mark Snyder (Ph.D., Stanford University) is a professor of psychology at the University of Minnesota. His research interests include theoretical and empirical issues associated with the motivational foundations of individual and social behaviors. He also studies the applications of basic theory and research in personality and social psychology to addressing practical problems confronting society. Snyder is author of *Public Appearances/Private Realities: The Psychology of Self-Monitoring.*

Arthur A. Stukas (Ph.D., University of Minnesota) is currently applying social psychological theory to health issues as a postdoctoral fellow in psychiatric epidemiology at the University of Pittsburgh Medical Center. In addition to his interests in voluntarism and volunteers' motivations, he is investigating processes related to "principled stands" against racism.

Pamela M. Velo (B.S., Indiana University Purdue University Indianapolis) is an M.S. student in applied social psychology at IUPUI and director of program evaluation at Community Centers of Indianapolis. Her research interests include motivation of volunteers.

Kenneth N. Weadick is an undergraduate student at Indiana University East. He has served as an undergraduate research and teaching assistant as well as a student service-learning coordinator.

Carol M. Werner (Ph.D., Ohio State University) is a professor of psychology at the University of Utah. Her research interests include environmental psychology, recycling, persuasion and behavior change, privacy regulation in homes and communities, and the philosophy of science.

Stanton Wortham (Ph.D., University of Chicago) is an assistant professor of education at Bates College. He teaches a wide range of education courses, serving students who study education as part of their liberal arts training and students who go on to get certified. His research examines strategies for uncovering implicit messages in different domains, including classroom language and political news.

Series Editor

Edward Zlotkowski (Ph.D., Yale University) is professor of English at Bentley College. Founding director of the Bentley Service-Learning Project, he has published and spoken on a wide variety of service-learning topics. Currently, he is senior associate at the American Association for Higher Education.

About AAHE

AAHE's Vision AAHE envisions a higher education enterprise that helps all Americans achieve the deep, lifelong learning they need to grow as individuals, participate in the democratic process, and succeed in a global economy.

AAHE's Mission AAHE is the individual membership organization that promotes the changes higher education must make to ensure its effectiveness in a complex, interconnected world. The association equips individuals and institutions committed to such changes with the knowledge they need to bring them about.

About AAHE's Series on Service-Learning in the Disciplines

Consisting of 18 monographs to be released over 1997-99, the Series goes beyond simple "how to" to provide a rigorous intellectual forum. *Theoretical essays* illuminate issues of general importance to educators interested in using a service-learning pedagogy. *Pedagogical essays* discuss the design, implementation, conceptual content, outcomes, advantages, and disadvantages of specific service-learning programs, courses, and projects. All essays are authored by teacher-scholars in the discipline.

Representative of a wide range of individual interests and approaches, the Series provides substantive discussions supported by research, course models in a rich conceptual context, annotated bibliographies, and program descriptions.

See the order form for the list of disciplines covered in the Series, pricing, and ordering information.

Yes! Send me the following monographs as they are released.

Price per vol. (includes shipping*): List $28.50 ea   AAHE Member $24.50 ea
Bulk Prices (multiple copies of the *same* monograph only):
10-24 copies $22.50 ea; 25-99 copies $21.00 ea; 100+ copies $15.00 ea

	Quantity	Price	Subtotal
Complete Series (all 18 vols.)		$405	
Accounting (Jul 98)			
Biology			
Communication			
Composition (Mar 97)			
Engineering			
Environmental Studies			
History			
Management			
Medical Education			
Nursing (Mar 98)			
Peace Studies			
Philosophy			
Political Science (Aug 97)			
Psychology (Jun 98)			
Sociology			
Spanish			
Teacher Education (Dec 97)			
Women's Studies			
		Total	

Shipping*
Price includes shipping to U.S. destinations via UPS. Call AAHE's Publications Orders Desk at 202/293-6440 x11 if you need information about express and/or foreign delivery.

Payment (F.I.D. #52-0891675)
All orders must be prepaid by check, credit card, or institutional purchase order, except AAHE members may ask to be billed.

❑ Please bill me; I am an AAHE member. (Provide member # below)
❑ Enclosed is a check payable to AAHE.
❑ Enclosed is my institutional Purchase Order: #_____.
❑ Please bill my: ❑VISA ❑MasterCard

_____
Cardholder's Name (please print)

_____
Cardholder's Signature

_____
Card Number   Exp. Date

Bill This Order To (if "Ship To" address is different, please provide on an attached sheet) :

_____   _____ _____ _____ _____
Name   AAHE Member #

_____
Address

_____
City   State   Zip

_____
Phone/Email   Fax

Mail/Fax this order to: AAHE Publications Orders Desk, Box SL14, One Dupont Circle, Suite 360, Washington, DC 20036-1110; fax 202/293-0073; www.aahe.org. Visit AAHE's website to read excerpts from other volumes in the Series. Need help with your order? Call 202/293-6440 x11.